The author is a writer and teacher from Melbourne. She grew up on a small farm in the Dandenong Ranges near Melbourne. She spent several years living in Italy, the UK and California. She currently lives in Bayside, Melbourne.

Pamela Mc Casker

FALLING INTO PLACE

AUSTIN MACAULEY PUBLISHERS™

LONDON • CAMBRIDGE • NEW YORK • SHARJAH

A CIP catalogue record for this title is available from the British Library.

ISBN 9781528906609 (Paperback)
ISBN 9781528958325 (ePub e-book)

www.austinmacauley.com

First Published (2019)
Austin Macauley Publishers Ltd
25 Canada Square
Canary Wharf
London
E14 5LQ

I wish to thank Anthony Ash, Gillian Barnett, Judy Curtain, Julie Drysdale, Liz Gallois, Graham Lacey, Suzanne McCourt, Rosemary Rule, Janey Runci, Eva White, Robyn Jones and Chris Woolven for their advice and encouragement.

Chapter 1
Meeting

As she waits at the intersection of Elizabeth and Collins Streets, Claire lets three sets of traffic lights run through their cycles. To go or not to go? At last her resolve to cross the street firms up. She will 'WALK' obediently next time around.

Fear of crowds is a recent neurosis. One month ago, she left her family home in Wangaratta for good. But do we know, in advance, if any move will be 'for good' long term? Melburnians are born to move through crowds; like schools of fish, they are schooled in it. They weave neat parabolic curves. No one collides.

As a wall of humanity sweeps towards Claire, she steps out boldly enough but the kerb might as well be 30 centimetres high and Claire blindfolded for all her confidence in landing well. She fixes her gaze on the one tall man among the head-bobbing sea of pedestrians. He has substance, an odd impression, as he's hemmed in by the crowd. She cannot see him in his entirety. But her sense of his solidity persists. Moving forward, her left heel catches in the tram track groove. While wriggling to free herself, she falls.

Prostrate in Collins Street, her hero emerges from the sea of people to look down at her. She squints up at him. At least he hasn't evaporated in the way of city men. She feels a fluttery sensation. It's not her heart in over-drive, just her gored skirt, whose flirty motion makes a mockery of decency in Melbourne's infamous wind tunnels. A poor choice on such a blustery day. Her man of substance rights her hemline, frees her heel from the tramline, helps Claire up. She's Cinderella in reverse. Awkwardly caught, not joyously discovered.

"Phew!" She takes a moment to regain her balance. "Oops! That was embarrassing! Thank you," she says, "for keeping me decent."

"Keeping women decent isn't my primary aim," he smiles at her. She can't help but laugh.

"Let's go to the Hopetoun Tea Rooms. I'll show you what a rake I am," he offers.

"Okay, I'm Claire-from-the-country," she says. They shake hands solemnly.

"Clive." He offers her his elbow crook. It's as if she's holding a triangle by its hypotenuse.

They head up Collins Street towards the Block Arcade. There's a queue outside the tearooms.

"Bugger! I can't stand queuing," Clive says.

"But you must stand, queuing," Claire teases. "You can't sit cross-legged on the pavement."

"Well, that's rich coming from you, a fallen woman! If I have a nervous breakdown, it'll be on a bad queuing day. Queuing triggers a pathology in me," he says. "I keep a running total of hours spent fruitlessly waiting. Half my life's been decimated!"

"To be decimated you'd only lose one year in ten."

"Worse than I thought, then. A whacking chunk of life – just atomised." He splays his hands to indicate the empty bleakness of his life. "But stilettos! Killers!" He squats to examine them.

Does he have bad eyesight, or is he assessing my ankles? Claire wonders.

"Ever been in the orthopaedic ward of a hospital?" he asks.

"Every day this week."

"A nurse. Then throw them out."

Claire loves her shoes, but she nods. Averaged out and rounded up, he's nice, she thinks.

Once seated, they order teas, then gaze around admiring their surrounds. The café is situated in a gilded Victorian arcade, its walls festooned with jungle foliage. What a place for romance, she thinks! Claire hates this pre-feminist thought the minute it fires up but it's too late to censor it. She's thought it now.

New in town, and home alone too much, Claire no longer scorns belief in fate. She's alert to any hopeful sign. *Could Clive be her fate*, she wonders. How else to explain an encounter with an attractive man who's only slightly more neurotic than she is?

Clive tells her he's a medico at St Vincent's Hospital. It's where she's training as a nurse!

Convinced now their meeting was pre-ordained, her heart does the beat-skip thing – a predictor of cardiac problems or love. Is Cupid releasing perfumed darts?

Stop being a romantic fool! Claire berates herself. But Clive is handsome, with a firm jaw-line. A flop of golden hair falls onto his brow a la Robert Redford; his face is well fleshed out, his body too; his solidity is comforting. His ruddy just-back-from-the-country look is wholesome. He'd smell like freshly home-baked bread. Or newly minted bank notes.

"So, Claire-from-the-bush, do you smoke?"

"No." This emerges sharper than intended but he's insulted her intelligence.

"Good," he grins, as if she'd passed a test. "Your complexion's excellent. A lot of fresh fruit and vegetables have gone into it." She's feeling like the product of an organic farming venture.

"Mm," she says. "All our food was organic, fresh. I…"

"…like country girls getting fresh with me," he says.

"…juice fruit twice a day," she says. Oops! They're doing a talking together tango.

"Good for you. Ever been hospitalised?" he asks.

"Only every day!"

He laughs at that. "*Touché!*" Claire picks up the menu to fend him off. He takes her hand.

His palm makes a cushion for hers. "Elegant fingers!" he says. "I see a tall, blond stranger…"

"You don't believe in palmistry, surely?"

"As a man of science, I remain open-minded," he says.

He has a slick answer for everything. She laughs. "I stopped believing in star signs at ten."

"You sophisticate!" he laughs. "What's the star sign you don't believe in then?"

"Libra slash Virgo."

"Gotcha! A non-believer shouldn't know her sign," he wags his finger at her.

"It's compulsory. Nurses do zodiac and footy talk all day. What's yours?"

"Aries."

"Ah!" She's not about to tell him he's a sex-crazed ram. Their order arrives. They tuck in. Clive eats with frank enjoyment.

"Are you religious?" he enquires.

"Not in Melbourne. It doesn't work here."

"Or anywhere. So, have you taken to a life of depravity recently?"

"No. What about you?"

"I baulk at doing anything illegal, but I'd love to murder the dill who designed stiletto shoes."

Silence falls. Claire usually feels obliged to fill silences. Now she decides to let it run on, to feel the stretch and pull of time.

"Enjoying your course?" Clive asks, when the conversation doesn't ignite spontaneously.

"Yes."

"Hospitals are husband-hunting grounds. But you'll have a boyfriend in the bush," he says.

"Not that I know of."

"Maybe your luck's about to change." He grins.

"It could well be. I'm moving to ob-gyn tomorrow."

"A useful department for a woman, obstetrics. Planning a big family?"

"Ask me tomorrow."

"May I call you, then? You're pretty, willowy, smart. Healthy too."

"Healthy?"

"You've a good, high complexion, thick, shiny hair, strong nails. You'll die young only if you wear ludicrous shoes. I'll see to it you don't."

"No, you won't," Claire says, deciding to assert herself. "So, what do you do at St V's?"

"I'm training to be a urologist."

"Why that specialty?"

"Family reasons," he says. "I like being at the forefront of new research…"

"But you can't specialise in the whole gamut of diseases to stay safe."

"For a sweet young woman, you've a sharpish tongue, Claire. One fears some illnesses…"

"So, fear's your primary motivation?" She surprises herself by sounding quite grown-up.

Clive looks gobsmacked to have encountered such cheek in a half-baked health professional. "I'll excuse you since you're pretty. Was that a panic attack earlier?" he asks.

"No." She isn't about to own up to fear of crowds.

"Hypotensive then?" he chews his lip thoughtfully. "I'll take your pulse." He raises the sleeve of her cashmere pullover. She opens her mouth to protest but he clamps two fingers to her wrist.

Rarely does she wear her best clothes shopping. A lucky choice, she'd thought, until Clive started acting pushy.

Right now, she'll only give him a scant six out of ten for conversation – a bare pass. Back in Wang, Claire liked having a good natter with blokes. Her interest now being on the wane, all nervousness evaporates. Bolstered by indifference, she can be herself.

"So?" she asks, as Clive stares at his watch.

He ignores her, his brow contracted, highlighting furrows above his nose. At last he pronounces her alive and pulsating.

"Great. I'd have died if I was dead."

"*Were* dead." He's agile in deflecting her dig at him. "It's the subjunctive. Grammar matters."

"You're not an injecting drug user," he says, having checked her forearms on the sly. "Jolly good!"

"You utter jerk!"

"Now, Claire, please don't ruin your pretty face."

"The state of my face is not your effing business."

"Naughty, naughty! I don't like swearing in women. I saved you. I'm responsible for you."

"Are you a Buddhist or something?"

"Confucius say, 'She lives longest who lies back and submits to favourite physician,'" he says, his eyebrows roaming across his brow in a manner so lewd and self-mocking, Claire can't help laughing.

"You're awful, Clive," she says, but her shoulders are shaking.

"Good lungs for laughing! Forthright laughter good for heart and entire thoracic cavity."

They are feeling mellow when their second teas arrive.

Clive raises his cup. "To our friendship and our joint good health!" he toasts.

"To our good joint-health!" she amends, causing him to fossick in his briefcase for a bottle of glucosamine.

"Mama believes in it," he shrugs. "I don't, but *quelle* coincidence, hey!"

They clack china cups. They don't make beautiful music. Neither worries about ill omens.

Too bad if they clunk instead of clinking. They believe in science and hard work, not portents.

"Here's getting to know you, Claire. What lovely celadon green eyes you have."

Chapter 2
Dressing

At last Claire's Melbourne life has started. She's been invited on a date with a tallish blondish stranger. They met in Collins Street. They have a whole hospital in common whereas some humans merely share a few minor health deficits!

Claire can't help wondering if Clive might have materialised thanks to the workings of fate. But being a sensible girl, proud of her scientific mindset (albeit a novice one since it's allowed her to cling to certain aspects of her former Catholic belief system), the composition of her beliefs pie-chart looks like this: Science 65%, Catholicism 25%, Fate 10 %, although the latter is in the ascendant currently. The stock-market report of Claire's beliefs needs re-calculating daily – it varies according to the most recent Astrological Predictions in the Australian Women's Weekly or whatever celebrity swill mag she's recently found abandoned in the staffroom and how closely its predictions suit her current needs. When promised a tall, dark stranger, it's harder to abjure all her irrational beliefs.

Claire is spending D-day, her first Melbourne date-day, reviewing her wardrobe.

It's a depressing exercise made worse by the counsel of her best friends, Suz and Mary. Clothes she'd thought stylish appear dowdy when being auditioned for an imminent date. She can imagine just how lowly Clive will rate her frocks.

Examining herself critically in the mirror, she runs through her repertoire of expressions – they all seem faux – a word she's been dying to use for ages, although today she wishes she had no use for it. Sexual abandon is the expression she finds hardest to fudge as she's had no serious occasion to use it thus far.

"Trying to launch your head into orbit?" asks Mary. "Watch me!" she orders. Standing front on to the mirror, she leans her weight back on her left foot while thrusting her right pelvis forward, and hungrily ogling Claire's Che Guevara poster. Claire's chosen

Che's face to adorn her wall more for his dashing looks than for his politics.

Mary now turns her head slowly so that a cascade of hair flows enticingly (she hopes) across her shoulders.

She demonstrates a range of poses: come-hither, get lost, and those falling into an intermediate range, like boredom and surprise. Claire wonders if there oughtn't be a handbook cataloguing all the moods called-for in dating situations.

At last, having been put through her emotional paces by Mary, Claire wilts onto the bed.

"Wow, Mary," she says. "I'd no idea dating was a science. I thought it was meant to be fun!"

"It can be simple fun. It depends how keen you are for results."

"Results?"

"Successful outcomes, dill! Like getting laid. You've been a virgin way too long."

"Act decisively, girl, or you'll find your condition's terminal."

"Gosh! But won't he like me for myself? You guys do."

Claire's friends dissolve in laughter at such a ridiculous notion.

"No, he won't. Dating's like being in a play," says Suz, "you have a choice of roles: the life of the party good-time girl, the kittenish, girly girl, the swot, the sporty type, the vamp, the predator..."

"What about the nice girl who's kind?"

"Only disabled men want kind," says Mary.

"Could I be a big hair glamour puss?"

Whoops of laughter greet the latter suggestion. Suz performs a corroboree, punching the air at the idea that Claire, with her ponytail, glasses and freckles could hope to pull off such a coup. Suz is the staid Head Prefect of their coterie – a word Claire's been saving for a special occasion. She's pleased that stitched-up Suz is acting so spontaneously.

"If you can't act, just be yourself, is the consensus."

"But who am I?"

"You're a Jane Eyre, goody-goody type – so don't act the femme fatale. Be a nice girl from the country, who's clever and smart," says Suz.

"And pretty," adds Mary, who's painting her toes – even in winter, she finds an audience to repay her zeal.

"Wear that skimpy ocelot print frock but let me plait your hair. That way you'll look like a nun who borrowed a frock from a tart!" says Suz. "Ambiguity is intriguing." She pushes Claire onto the bed, grabs a hairbrush and wields it punitively, winding hanks of hair in and out until Claire knows why wound is spelled 'wound'.

Chapter 3
Arrival at Clive's

Claire wears her best frock. The ocelot spotted number. She feels paunchy wearing it.

Should she hold her stomach muscles taut all evening or should she relax and breathe?

Mary offers her a wide belt, an engineering trick that helps. She says, "You look 'fine', Claire." Suz insists that she should splurge on a cab this freezing late May evening.

Once the cab pulls into the driveway, Claire bolts; not that she's eager for her date to start, but anxious to get it over with. In the stairwell, a premonitory wind gust tears at her plait. It tears her eyes up too. Claire loves homonyms! The squall lashes next door's pittosporum, cleaning her face of make-up and revealing freckles.

"Enjoy drainage boy!" Suz calls, withdrawing from the gale before she can reply.

The first disquieting omen comes in the form of a spring that pierces the ageing cab's upholstery and Claire's upholstery as well. It forces Claire to ponder her virginity. Here the upper case is needed and a drum roll. Her VIRGINITY! She's clung to it against all demographic trends, and yet it seems shameful in an almost 20-year-old. It's 1987, after all.

"Did ya team win?" the cabbie asks.

Claire knows that a footy team is one's passport to acceptance in Melbourne even if that team is Collingwood, the most reviled in the League. The Magpies, as they're known, engender frank hostility even in liberal-minded citizens; any mention of this team calls forth invective outbursts in the meek. Melburnians need Collingwood like Catholics need hell. This team lets them vent their tribalism; it draws the venom out.

"Yep. The Magpies, she lies." She hates football.

"Great third quarter!"

Claire sinks down in her seat and prays he'll shut up. He does. Good. Maybe she can use mind control on Clove of India too.

What will he expect of her? An Aussie bloke's ideal woman is said to be 'a deaf and dumb nymphomaniac living above a pub'. Bad luck, Clive! You'll have to settle for a bookworm renting near a fish and chip shop.

Alighting, her panty hose snags. With the bodily awareness nervousness bestows, she feels each nerve-ending register the progress of the run as it snakes its leisurely way up from her knee. It builds a silken ladder to her moist and fleshy regions.

She forces her reluctant feet up the path to Clive's small terraced-house's door. It's pretty, she'll learn by daylight.

She places one foot in front of the other, wearing overly high-heeled boots; she keeps a brave smile planted firmly on her dial, while holding her tummy in, her bum out, and thinking too. What a work of art is woman!

Clive opens to her tentative ring, "Ciao, Claire," he says. He wears a barbeque apron with bosoms. He grasps her right hand and squeezes it as if testing fruit for ripeness.

His hand is warm and dry.

Bad luck, Claire thinks. She'll be the one stuck in the role of 'Nervous Nellie' playing away from home while he'll enjoy the home-ground advantage.

"Come in," he says. Clive squeezes himself against the doorjamb to allow her to slip past. The trouble is she's not slipping anywhere as his fake bosoms, along with those she's been equipped with since 11, block her way.

The two stick as fast as insects on flypaper. Clive gestures towards the back of the house with an imperious flick of his head but he himself remains in situ. Next, he wriggles as if buffing Claire with fine-calibre sandpaper. A mad idea but they almost come unstuck.

Claire tries unbuttoning her coat with her wine-bottle hand. She hooks her index finger into the first hole and liberates its toggle. Hooray! Three to go! She wriggles her shoulder, lowers her head, hoping to peel her coat-sleeve inside out and over the bottle. But until her right hand is free of Clive's persistent grip, she's bound to fail.

She has a brainwave: "For you, Clive," Claire says, handing him the wine.

Clive checks the label, "Chateau Tahbilk Shiraz, fabulous, ta," he says, grasping the bottle without taking hold of it. They stand jointly caretaking this bottle as if part of a *tableau vivant* at a wine fair. "Can you manage your coat?" he asks.

"What does it bloody well look like?"

Her words galvanise Clive. He eases them over the threshold and since his upper limbs are occupied with hers, he slams the door with a nifty kick. If he ever loses the use of his hands, he will survive!

"You take the wine. I'll manage my coat," Claire says. But Clive seems paralysed.

She mimes the peeling of her shoulder strap over her head, by raising her arms upwards. This manoeuvre forces his arms to rise in mimicry of hers as if they're maypole dancing.

"Hang on," he says, "you'll want the bed." Still gripping the bottle, he backs her into the first doorway; the room's light comes from a silk-fringed whorehouse lamp.

Backed up against the bed, Claire sees a bedside table for the wine. She makes a beeline for it, drawing Clive after her. Meanwhile, she wonders whether beelines are necessarily straight. Surely, bees ought to meander about in search of the widest range plants to pollinate? She could kick herself – and would do if only she had control of her feet – for giving brain-space to such irrelevant thoughts when she has a real problem to solve. But one's subconscious thoughts aren't always irrelevant, are they?

While Claire's high-heeled boot is left to fend for itself, it snags on the rug. Her non-bottle arm wheels about, keeping her upright, while her bottle arm conscientiously holds the bottle up for Clive's perusal.

She overbalances onto the bed, detaching the bottle from Clive's grip; she barely avoids smashing it on the bed-head and launching the evening in a shower of glass.

Clive, fearing to let the wine out of his sight for an instant, follows her. They lie bosom to bosom. Claire's blush mechanism being temporarily disordered, she giggles helplessly.

Clive lies there like a stunned slug. "I'd hoped to get you into bed eventually," he says, licking his lips. "But I wanted you for dessert, not entrée." His voice emerges as thick as molasses. "Are you ready to eat?"

"No. I need cooking first," she laughs. "And I'd like to get to know you."

He looks at her as if memorising her face for an exam. "Good," he says, "there's not much to know about me. So, we'll take the short cut." He drops the wine onto the floor. He unwinds Claire's bag strap and starts in on her coat. He manages its buttons but needs to roll her from side to side to free her arms from the sleeves.

She imagines the surgeon he is: slow and painstaking. She lies there deader than a fish on a slab, fearing he'll whip off to the kitchen for shears, but he remains patient and methodical, viewing setbacks as challenges, treating her arms as if double jointed.

Once the coat is off, he sees her boots. "Good Lord!" he says. "More idiotic footwear."

"It's thanks to my shoes we met!" she says, shocked by his petty self-righteousness.

"Be careful or you'll end up a fallen woman. You've been warned," he says, as if issuing her with a summons.

"Okay. So, I'm utterly frivolous," Claire says, in a bid to disarm him with her candour.

But the twin thumps of her stilettos hitting the floor alert her to his stratagem.

Chapter 4
After the Fall

Claire's date with Clive unfolds as pure slapstick. They couldn't have performed better with practice. She lands like a porpoise on a silk duvet so shiny she'd have skidded off had he not fallen on her like a sack of spuds. You'd think Claire had ordered a tonne of ballast, and Clive was filling out the order precisely.

Horizontal, his fleshy parts overlap hers. She's like a sausage roll filling in a double crust.

He starts undressing her. She shoves him off the bed.

He hits the floor with a thud. Lies there unmoving. Claire does the mirror thing – no moisture forms. She slaps his face. She feels like she's patting a lump of clay into shape.

She phones for an ambulance. "Number 128A Drummond Street, Carlton," she says.

When Clive opens his eyes, it's clear he's been feinting. He orders her to call back, cancel the ambulance. When she hesitates, asks whether he might have sustained internal injuries, he sits up and cancels it himself, scorning her use of the term 'sustained'. "You sound just like a nurse in a TV series," he says as if nursing, the defining fact of her life, were somehow laughable. She asks how she's supposed to sound.

He doesn't reply but gets stuck into her, blaming her for their misunderstanding. It's all her fault, he tells her, his voice lower now, for coming to dinner dressed like a lustful animal.

When she protests that this is her only proper 'dating' frock and that Clive has no right to blame a frock 'retroactively' for his bad behaviour, he guffaws.

"Proper! Ha-a!"

When he recovers himself, he bestows upon her his sincerest expression. "Dear Claire," he says beseechingly, "sorry. It's just…I thought we'd skip the time-consuming bits."

"You think affection is time-consuming?" she asks.

"Yes, and overrated. Same etymology as affected! Etymology has nothing to do with ants, by the way."

"I know that, you patronising shit!" Claire says, "I collect words."

"Ha-ha!" He cackles evilly. "You funny thing! I like you already."

"You were about to more-than-like me, Clive."

"Yes, he admits, I would have liked you and licked you but only with your frock's consent." His eyes roll suggestively.

"What about feelings!" Claire protests. Her body shakes in full agreement with her words; meanwhile, the part of Claire that can stand outside herself looking in knows she's acting more indignant than she feels.

"Feelings," he mimics, "I had feelings all right. I felt like sex." He helps her up onto the bed and climbs up beside her. He pats her rhythmically, distractedly, as if she were a pet dog.

"Now you rest, Claire."

Claire lies there as unyielding as a plank under the duvet. He parcels her up in it. Kneads her back through the feather-down, until her shivering lessens. She starts enjoying the male smell of him – all damp tweed and tobacco, though he doesn't smoke. "I guess I should have said 'no' more emphatically," she admits, meanwhile making sure her muscles remain taut. "I'd hoped for a good natter."

"You came here for a natter? Then try talk-back radio." But he gathers Claire into his arms like a fond old uncle. He folds the duvet around her. She feels like she's swaddled in bubble wrap for posting home. She shivers still. Clive massages her shoulders, cradles her tenderly.

"I had big hopes for tonight," Claire says. "Silly me!" She smites her forehead histrionically, realising that, although the hist word is one on her list for using quickly, thinking it doesn't count. "I thought we might have fun and laugh and like each other," she says, "and then maybe…"

"Stay!" he pleads. "My behaviour was unforgivable. Sorry."

Claire sits up, enjoying his remorse. Has the balance of power shifted her way? Her breathing settles.

"Listen, Claire. 'Tiamo' in Lygon Street does a mean pasta take-away. Do stay for a quick bite to eat. And while I'm gone, please fix your eyes, Hon. You look like a raccoon." He gives her a quick kiss on the forehead, removes his apron and heads out.

While he's away, Claire wanders around looking for the bathroom. She finds 19 C horse portraits, a knobbly wool couch, a banana tree sculpture from Bali and vertical blinds. *What would Suzy make of all this tat*, she wonders. If Claire mentioned the blinds, Suz would tell her to get the hell out – that he was a chainsaw murderer in a surgeon's disguise.

The weirdest object is a photographic print; it looks like an x-ray of the male urogenital system; it's beautiful enough to pass as art. It's a gorgeous tropical rainforest plant, tinted in soft greens and cerises. Maybe it's a teaser for his dates. Euw! A urologist's Rorschach test?

The phone trills.

"Aleksandr?"

"Wrong number," she says.

"You friend?"

"My friends think so."

"Of Clive?"

"Ah, Clive busy." Broken English catching, she thinks.

"Say to him Ray and Charles Eames cheap Monday. View tomorrow. Footstool." The man disconnects.

In the bathroom, Claire washes her face and dries it with a scratchy towel. Okay, we got off on the wrong foot, she tells her mirror image. But since I must eat somewhere, I shall stay.

The wire reinforced shower-screen and pink and grey sixties mosaic tiles are ugly in a good way. Clive's home has a gritty integrity. Clive is not confused but merely confusing. He's an anarchist scorning bourgeois taste. Claire pees relieved.

Chapter 5
Meeting Alex

Clive returns with just one portion of take-away. Claire hopes it's for her. She's starving.

Heightened emotions burn through calories. Alas, Clive divvies up their meagre allowance.

On entering the lounge-room, he has two bowls balanced on his forearm, napkins tucked into his under-arm, while a salt and peppershaker is secured beneath his chin. His head is free for thinking, and his feet for walking.

They chitchat while drinking ruby-coloured Shiraz. They're onto their second bottle.

Claire's not sure how this has come about as she's barely moistened her lips. Clive must have been putting it away stealthy as a cat approaching an unguarded fish on a counter-top.

The wine bottles had emerged from a stash in a lean-to beyond the kitchen. Despite the extreme cold, the fire remains un-lit and little warmth emerges from the Rinnai gas heater. But it's not too bad, Claire supposes, the wine has geed their circulation up. Scented candles add a festive note.

Clive sees Claire rubbing her arms. "Hang-on, Hon, I'll get you a wrap," he says.

"Is your heater broken?" she asks.

He shrugs. "Probably. I'm hardly ever home. I don't feel the cold." He gets up and returns with a blanket and drapes it over her shoulders. "I've some ideas for pollution-free heating, if necessary, Claire," he raises his eyebrows at her interrogatively.

"Keep them to yourself, Clive," she says tetchily. "Is that a patchouli candle?" Claire asks.

"Yes, but you're a younger woman. Surely you don't remember the sixties?"

"I'm nearly twenty."

"That's old enough," he says.

"For what?"

"For anything!" he does his lewd eye-roaming thing again.

"But you're 28. Now that's really old."

"That's exactly how it ought to be. The man a little older."

"Why?"

"Women have sharper instincts. Men need the extra experience age gives us."

A clever comment, she thinks. Even the most unwavering feminist couldn't argue with that. "My mum wore kaftans in summer," she admits. "There's photos of her holding me when I was a baby."

"My mama had a curly perm with a hint of afro. Afterwards, she cut her head out of all family snaps dating back to that era. She's never followed fashion since that day. She deludes herself that fashion follows her," says Clive.

"Gosh! To be so sure of yourself!"

"Mama doesn't harbour self-doubt." Clive raises his glass, demanding Claire's acquiescence.

She mirrors his gesture. "To Claire," he says. "To the two of us getting to know each better after ice-cream."

"No," says Claire. "To getting to know each other. Slowly." They clink glasses.

Clive begins speechifying, "Freud, Roman hands, countrymen, lend me your ears."

"Here you are." Claire rids herself of the orecchietti she hasn't been enjoying, transferring them to his bowl. She feels her date is starting finally.

Clive uses the ears to circle in sauce the nipples of his bosom apron, whose condition by now is dire – he's had it on most of the evening. Then he discovers that, pierced, the ears make beaut whistles. His behaviour is juvenile even by Claire's young brothers' standards. Is this really a date in sophisticated Melbourne? They won't be discussing Proust anytime soon, she decides.

The front door opens with a crash. Loud footsteps sound in the hall. Claire waits for Clive to react but he remains calm.

An exotic-looking man stands in the lounge doorway. He's taller than Clive, and slender, with the attenuated look of subjects of El Greco. He must be the flatmate, she presumes. His hair is drawn into a ponytail; he has the intensity of a character actor – poles apart from Clive's leading man good looks.

Claire grabs the ear that Clive's been daubing his bosoms with – she won't have a stranger witnessing their juvenile behaviour. Gosh! How quickly 'they' have turned into a 'we'.

The man is unfazed by their disarray. He has an air of other-worldliness about him as if he were an alien visiting earth. It's as if everything amuses him, and nothing surprises him.

"Hello, Claire. You're Clive's Madonna of the MMTB safety zone?"

She nods, blushing.

"Your stilettos are famous. Clive reckons you're six-foot four in heels."

"No way!"

He looks down at her bare toes. She feels quite naked, though it's only her toes on show.

"He's had it off with your shoes already. Hm! It's a pleasure to meet you, Claire."

"Shouldn't you introduce us formally?" Claire asks Clive.

"Sorry. This is my twin brother, Alex, Claire. He owns this dump. He's not a bad bloke, actually."

"Nice to meet you, Claire." Alex reaches across the coffee table for her hand. Because it's hiding pasta, she gives it to him clenched.

His huge hand swallows hers; he raises both their arms and shakes them in the air. *"Arriba La Libertad!* What's this?" he asks, prising her fingers apart.

"It's only an ear," she says, blushing.

"We never lend our ears. Ah," he says, examining the contents of her hand. "I knew a food collagist once. She saved bad food. This is collage-quality."

"It wasn't bad. But I'm no gourmand. Just a nurse," Claire stammers. Something about Alex makes her feel she should apologise for herself.

Clive stands, removes his apron again. "Delicious!" he enthuses. "Alex, will you please look after Claire while I go for ice-cream?" He pats himself about his person, meanwhile chanting spectacles, testicles, receptacles and keys. "Any flavour you favour, my dear?"

"No. Anything will do," Claire says. "Let me come with you." Claire's loath to remain alone with Clive's unnerving brother.

"No way. We'd never pull your boots back on," he says.

"Oh!" Claire says, as her date exits.

"Well done, Claire. You're the first girl I've met who isn't a total fusspot." Alex examines her palm. "Hm. You've a long lifeline but your heart-line's unresolved."

"I don't believe in astrology or fortune-telling mumbo-jumbo." Claire wonders why she's sounding so tetchy.

"Ah! I see a tall dark man with a pigtail entering your life."

"Clive's not dark."

"Then he can't be the one. This man will force you to renounce astrology forever."

"But I disbelieve in it already."

"Good! You've made it easy for the bloke. The impression he gives is louche, I'm afraid."

"Mm. Not yet having added 'louche' to her word list," Claire responds neutrally. Alex is the last person to whom she'd show her linguistic shortcomings. "Oh. Alex, there was a call for you."

"Oh?"

"Something about Ray Charles and a footstool with a view."

"Have you been drinking, Claire?"

"No. That was mostly Clive," she indicates the wreck of empties and curls of plastic among wine rings on the coffee table. "Or perhaps the bottles emptied themselves…"

"Bottles have a way of doing that around Clive."

Chapter 6
Meltdown

Clive can't stand queuing. Queuing's about fairness, and fairness is a crock along with equality, fraternity and the other one. He moves through his isometric exercises. He wants svelte, not sweaty. Buff, not bulgy.

He's in Fitzroy, buying ice cream, hoping to impress a sheila. At 28 he should have grafted on a wife for the essentials: shopping, housekeeping, intimacy. He'll choose a wife stress-free after his finals. Meanwhile, he window-shops, builds up a database of desired qualities like in a police photo-fit.

His brother had arrived home while he and Claire were on their first course – but before intercourse. A virgin. He'll need a decent ice cream to get anywhere with her.

He'd totally nailed the accidental-on-purpose fall onto the bed. Convinced Claire it was her fault. Removed her boots. Made all the textbook moves. But she'd rejected him. A spirited woman. She'd almost left. It took much grovelling to persuade her to stay.

Once urology's in the bag, he'll stagnate. He can't remain single forever, not in a universe subject to gravity, a force 'extant between all bodies possessing mass'. From what he's seen so far, Claire's mass has aggregated in all the right places.

Gravity, if he remembers high school physics aright, works in inverse proportion to the square of the distance between two bodies. If their degree of separation doubles, their gravitational attraction quarters. Yet here he is in Fitzroy, thinking fondly of Claire from four kays away! How good would he feel beside her? WOW! KAPOW!!!

Last year he'd taken up yoga. He'd rolled around in unnatural postures. But it was hard doing nothing in such a spine-wrenching way; it annoyed him more than queuing had.

Measurement is 'anathema to the yoga experience' said the yoga teacher whom he'd dated, hoping she'd help him fast-track nirvana.

He's often criticised for being a quantifying man! Sure, he's obsessive the way he calculates the ratio between monthly earnings in $Ks and his patient morbidity rates: his bottom-line versus his patients' flat-lines. Means bugger-all of course. No nexus exists between salary and surgical ability.

Still, whatever's countable counts. In May, he lost an elderly client. Sad! Messed up his average!

Clive focuses mindfully upon his fellow-queuers. They sport nine o'clock Homer Simpson shadows, grubby sweat-shirts bearing inane adages. Their grotesque jogging shoes have more individuality than they. 'Tubby hubbies in trackies' – their bloated visages announce. They form a distinct social class: the sixth estate. Like Clive, they're counting the cost of Charmaine's ice cream against the fleeting harmony it will foster at home.

Heartless bugger that Clive usually is, tonight he feels for all wage-slaves in bondage to households of squalling babes when 'babes' means something else to him. The irony of language!

He gets their clothes. Let singles snigger up their premium leather jacket sleeves! But fleecy cottons – washing-machine ready are practical for baby puke. He has an urge to hug the guy behind him, say, "Mate, I feel your pain," but he'll be thought queer. Not that there's anything…

Clive can hardly wait to be the progenitor of a large litter. What fun he'll have teaching them to swim, ride, shoot hoops. But establishing a solid family unit needs research. Finding the right partner is paramount; he has a list to tick off, all names alphabetised. Claire has somehow subverted his system: he thought he'd done the Cs.

"Help ya?"

"Ice-cream please!" Clive's voice emerges croakily.

"Yep?"

"That curvy little parfait number that comes in pistachio."

"All gone," ice-cream man says, like he's feeding a baby with a spoon. No curvy parfaits left.

"A tub of pistachio then."

"No, there's fruity, creamy or astringent. What's the missus want? Ah! No missus? No worries, you'll meet someone." Ice-cream man winks, he's onto Clive.

"Yorta see my sister; she's a doll," ice-cream man whispers, leaning in.

Is this a Greek bearing gifts, he wonders. Greek Aussies carry the wisdom of the ages in their back pockets! "No. No sister, thanks, just tell me what I want," Clive says.

"Stick with the classics. Vanilla, for instance. Decorate it with sprinkles for a second date."

"Don't need a friggin' second date."

"I'll need second wife soon, calls some dill in the queue." Clive flips him the finger.

"One vanilla tub, then? Sprinkles?"

"No. I bet you have two curvy flutes in the fridge outback."

"Too toe fin knee toe!"

An Eyetie! Aha! So, it's Italians rationing the good sorts here. He takes out $100. "Name your price."

"Nothing doing. Curvy's gone."

Clive grabs the vanilla tub, the sprinkles. He leaves his note on the counter. That'll make his point. He exits, fuming. Bloody market forces! Every six seconds a pretty girl falls off the shelf, her DNA floats off to fill the public gene pool. She's lost to him, doomed to waste her eggs in a suburban blasted heath, so said 'The Age'. Girls disappear faster than ice-cream melts.

He stumbles on the pavement; can't right himself. Ends up in the gutter. Where else!

Best jeans torn. Maybe looking punk will prove he's cool in grungy old Fitzroy.

Eventually Clive gropes his way upright. Pedestrians give him a wide berth. Think he's a druggie loser. And he is a loser. Even Charmaine's lot knows that the missus wants strawberry swirl.

Does he even want a missus? Yes! Married, he'd have someone in charge of ice-cream flavours…

He lets the Saturday night revellers flow around him; he's a rock plonked down in the river of life. Those living life whiz by him; they get on with it. Clive? He's paralysed. When it's safe to move, he staggers to the Porsche 911. Its loan agreement's in his wallet. Earlier, he'd figured out that finally he owns the exhaust in its entirety. It seems he's stuck down at the arse-end of both medical specialty and car ownership.

He folds himself into the car. *What's with the watery eyes*, he wonders. *Just sad. Sad. Sad.*

When his tears dry up, he engages first. Merges with the traffic. Dawdles homewards.

Love's not about being struck in the solar plexus, winded by a powerful force, he decides. It's more like sinking into a mineral bath at the spa in Hepburn Springs. It does you good to be immersed in something bigger. He'll BE in love as the self-help books urge. Wallow in it. All he needs is a suitable object of desire. Whom? Claire might do. Mentally, he tries her on for size. Chants: "I love Claire. I love Claire." He repeats this mantra 50 times.

Did he turn into Johnston Street on auto-pilot? Who knows? He's in it now. Crucial traffic lights all blink amber tonight, raising stress levels in drivers who are start-stopping all over the shop. Not Clive. He's cool. His yoga lessons are paying off belatedly. It's odd though. Clogged arterials are rare of a Saturday night when bourgeois Melbourne dinner parties.

Are the fates helping him focus on his resolution?

Despite the cold, the ice cream melts. Another shove from fate! His baby feelings for Claire mustn't be allowed to liquefy. At the next amber light, he sounds a fusillade on the horn. Claire is enough, and enough is enough as surely as a rose is a rose.

He opens the window. Inhales. Bugger the smoggy air; bugger his exhalations rising like mist before his face. He'll surrender his singularity to the marriage police, settle down. You earn a lot, you spend a lot. And when a man can't spend what he earns, he takes a nurse who takes a child, then, heigh-ho the merry-o the doctor's out of hell.

Claire will raise Clive's happiness quotient immeasurably.

A beep sounds. He's about to give his antagonist the finger, and shout "Shut the flip up, ass-hole!" but instead he forces himself to wave in a family-friendly way.

'Victoria: On the Move!' says the number plate ahead. He hits the accelerator; he calls out,

"Upwards and onwards!" He positions himself for overtaking but moves back into the slow lane. I queue. IQ!

Dada will like her far too much; thus, giving him the edge in matters oedipal. He vents his spirits with a triumphal riff on the horn.

Chapter 7
Dishes with Alex

Claire is at Alex's place in Carlton. So it's not Clive's after all. How many other unsubstantiated claims has she swallowed? He's told her he could 'quite possibly' love her up to 98%.

As in 'up to 97% of dentists recommend Breathfresh'. *Has he ever worked in advertising*, she wonders.

She's doing what even the most enlightened females know to be their lot – the dishes. Who can resist their tidal pull? Left to crust up overnight, they need serious elbow grease. Women would rather suffer earlier than late.

Claire is miserable beyond cheering. Maybe the dishes will excoriate her. She'll wallow down around the painful end of her emotional spectrum, letting humiliation run through her like an enema.

Clive's a serial philanderer apparently. Wow! Alex hadn't wanted to tell her. She'd pried it out of him.

She plunges her hands into the suds; soggy pasta bits float in the murk. The water makes her fingers swell. The sight of them disgusts her, but she leaves them in the slops to pucker up.

There'll be no dirty plates for Clive to throw at the wall; she'll leave with her dignity intact, meanwhile Clive, astounded at her grace, will miss her. A bit. She'll abandon her belief in the 'happily ever after' myth. Her parents' happiness has unfortunately left her without a protective layer of cynicism.

For months, she's felt as ripe for love as a squishy peach grown by her dad on their Wangaratta farm. She'd dared hope Clive might be the recipient of her cargo of unallocated feeling! Boy, what an idiot! She stomps around in her high-heeled boots her duffle coat on, so she can leave the minute Clive gets back. Alex looks on his mouth agape. "He's crap at bringing home the ice-cream," she says. "I'd eat it tub and all. Why does anger make you hungry, Alex, while sorrow takes your appetite away?"

"Don't know, Claire. Leave him the dishes," says Alex. He reaches over to turn off the tap.

Alex reminds her of Heathcliff, her fantasy man throughout her formative years. How can wild, dry Heathcliff be the brother of cheesy Robert Redford? "Tell me, Alex," Claire asks, "are his evenings of love-making pre-scripted?"

"More or less." Alex starts scraping plates while she stacks them in the sink. "You're a surprise. You're not even blonde."

"Thanks!"

He turns her to face him. "That's a compliment! Clive goes for the dumb blonde disaster, usually." He puts his arm around her shoulders, and they stand looking at their reflection in the kitchen window.

Alex seems to see something through the glass that's lurking in the darkness. "Good looking couple," he says, referring to the two of them. "If he hurts you, I'll exact revenge."

"How?"

"Exactly! Wreck his Porsche."

"Porsche? Gosh! Why own a posh car, not a house?"

Alex shrugs. "Pessimists, like me, scrape together the necessities. Optimists assume someone will take them in. They buy whatever says 'rich and cool'. Such faith in the benignity of life."

"Ben…what? With you I'd have to carry my word book everywhere," says Claire.

"I'd marry both you and your book."

Claire searches his face for irony. "Don't tease me. Alex, do his girls get a lift home?"

"I'll drive you home, Claire."

Claire's resolve melts. She weeps, her tears mingling with wash-up water. It's greyish with floaty green bits. Must be the sauce. It's beautiful, like an art installation. Claire sees beauty in the middle of humiliation. Has she inherited her pioneering ancestors' grit? Those brave souls slashed and burned like crazy so a spoiled girl like her could grow up in an orchard, and drop her Catholicism on a whim. Claire's tears fall with a plop and a recoil splash. Her shoulders shake.

Alex drops his cloth. Holds out his arms to her. She nestles into his neck hollow. What a man!

Panther lithe, more solid than a grizzly bear. He presses her head into his smelly overall. Ripe but nice.

The front door bangs. Claire jumps guiltily, tries wriggling out of Alex's embrace. His grip upon her intensifies.

Clive enters. Claire's struck anew by his film star looks.

"Are you having a loan of my future wife, Alex? Unhand her, brute."

"Claire needed comforting," Alex keeps his arms around Claire.

"What is it, Angel? Didn't we fall 98% in love?"

"Up to 98%, you said," says Claire. "That means zero, probably."

"You utter cynic! Didn't I formalise our plight? Plight you my troth?"

"No."

"Well, I'm plighting it now!"

Alex's arms fall away. His eyes narrow. "Be serious, Clive," he says, sounding like a midday soapie star.

"Claire is the answer to my life's conundrum, Alex. She's my what next?"

How can I be the solution to someone else's problem? Claire wonders, seconds before she's caught up in the moment. This must be a *folie a deux,* she thinks. She'd studied French at school.

Clive dumps the ice cream, picks up his car keys. Wrestling the keys from their ring, he drops down onto the linoleum, takes her hand and slips on the metal key ring. "I'll eat my own cooking in the garage with the car running unless you promise to be mine."

"Your...what?" Claire asks, wanting to seem obtuse.

"My, um, partner, wife," he finishes in a whisper, as if the word once spoken aloud might hex him. He inserts her thumb through the key ring. "Please." He looks so abject saying this that Claire starts giggling.

Despair and happiness are nearer neighbours on her emotional spectrum than she'd realised. She holds her hand out. I'll have the Porsche key.

"Have the Porsche," Clive says, rising to his feet and hugging her.

"Some girls might hold you to it."

"I had a nervous breakdown queuing, Claire. The thought of you was all that kept me going."

"Nonsense!"

"Well, I had an epiphany at the very least! I saw my future without you in it. It was ugly. Are you going to congratulate us, Alex?" He turns, but Alex has scarpered.

Chapter 8
Tango

Claire's alone in Clive's bed – where is *he?* She rests awkwardly on one elbow, and scribbles in her diary; she persists although it cramps her arm!

Last night after becoming engaged, they did dishes so he could bed her guilt-free. That bothered her – that a man in love could behave so temperately; that his frantic urge to bed her could be postponed for housekeeping. "Let's do it," he said referring to the dishes. Fair enough, she'd thought. Who wants a mess to face in the morning?

Clive had reinstated the dishcloth dropped by Alex, who disappeared after the proposal. He'd started slopping it over the soapy dishes. But she's a conscientious nurse. Is this infringement of hygiene standards sufficient to trigger their first argument? Probably. But she hadn't ripped into the delicate tissue of newfound love for the sake of a few billion salmonella bacteria. Their love should keep them safe from ills and chills.

They'd got stuck in, waging war on all germs a-breeding in the slops. They'd formed a neat ensemble. As kitchen sink productions go, theirs was classy. The Ken and Barbie of housework.

They moved as one. She'd happily spend her life tied to a sink with Clive keeping her company. Normally, she hated dishes. Did this mean love was a form of psychosis?

Then the hot water ran out.

"Let's eat the ice-cream while we're waiting," she'd suggested.

"It's refreezing."

"But Clive! That's no good. It crystallises into icy shards. It harbours bacteria."

"Ooh! Harbours, dearie me! Who swallowed her nursing textbook? I've a better idea," said Clive. "Let's tango."

"On an empty stomach?" She was dismayed. "Are we going to subsist on love alone?" she'd asked.

"You're always hungry," said Clive, as if she'd been banqueting for hours instead of surviving on two orecchietti. "I hope you won't prove too expensive a wife to feed." He'd sounded like a grazier restocking his pastures with cattle that did their own foraging, but he'd smiled.

She'd bitten her lip, refrained from nagging Clive about her hunger. "But dance without music?"

"Stick by me girl and you'll never want for tunes." He'd assumed the stance of a dancing teacher. She'd stepped up ready. He'd taken her in a boat-prow hold, arms pointed stiffly in the direction they were to head. He'd let go of her for a minute to pluck a dirty plastic flower from a vase on the window ledge; he'd stuck it between her teeth. Claire felt a gag reflex rising but she'd kept it down. He'd started in on a homemade song that went: *da dum dada dum dada dum dum*. Its lyrics went like this: *"All lovers should learn how to tango. It's better than eating a mango. Groove to each move. Because we're in love. Here at last it's a blast when we tango! Ole!"*

Wow! Her beloved was capable of off-the-cuff witty spoofs. He sang he was inventive, impetuous, and hers!

They headed for the backdoor, high-stepping with the histrionic deliberation couples adopt when tangoing, a way of making love while staying mainly vertical. Clive's fluency brushed off on her.

Once the boat prow of their arms collided with the door, they made a slick reversal involving a 180-degree realignment of limbs, then they'd stuck their noses in the air and headed for the sink.

On reaching the climax – the bit where Clive was meant to deliver her backward bending form to an imaginary point an inch from the floor and after a moment of suspense to raise her up again, they'd fallen in a muddle of limbs and gales of laughter.

"Oh, Clive," she'd gasped, since he was pressing on her rib-cage, "I really do…love you."

"Ditto *mon ange!*" he'd replied, in Franglais.

Gosh! He even spoke the language of love surgically! she thought.

Their romantic interlude was done, the dishes weren't. They scrambled upright and rolled up their sleeves. The dishes seemed neither a chore nor a bore with her beloved helping.

He took each plate before it reached the draining board. Anticipated her every move. They were as one. Soapsuds drifted prettily, leaving only the faintest of smear trails for *son amour* to polish off with his Port Douglas tea towel. They were moving as if born to wash dishes forever.

No collisions marred their performance. Only love, a powerful instinct, could transform this boring chore.

Already this morning, with early light seeping like buttermilk through muslin, life seems more prosaic!

Claire didn't go home last night. Clive was insistent that they start their lives together as they meant to go on. She'd have been happier taking it slowly but when Clive annexes you, then he must have you _now_! She feels a frisson of excitement to find herself so essential to this Clive guy, who, when all is added up and averaged out, seems admirable.

Why wouldn't he let her go home? She's wondering about this now it's morning and her intoxication has worn off and he's not in bed with her. Did he fear his resolve might weaken if allowed wriggle-room? Is she part of a commitment phobic's 12-step plan, his hostage, his pledge to remain engaged, become a family man? But does she want to be the solution to someone else's problems before she's catalogued her own?

Last night Clive had had a note delivered to Suzy letting her know that Claire was fine, and that she'd see her in the morning. Is he buying her?

Chapter 9
Trying to Sleep

In love for the first time, Claire feels like Cinderella plucked from a life of drudgery by her prince. She pities her girlfriends, who mere hours ago were mocking her unworldliness.

After the love-making scene – to which the reader wasn't invited – they turn off the bedside lamp for sleep. At least, Clive is well and truly ready for sleep; it's just one more bedtime for him.

For Claire, it's different; her life has reached its water-shed. *But why call it a water-shed*, she wonders. Drab imagery. The water part is fine because water is to earth what air is to life.

But what's the shed bit about? A water-shed would shed. Perhaps it's to remind us we can't hang onto joy nor store a reservoir of goodies in cupped hands. Happiness will leak out over time.

She steels herself to relax (an oxymoronic ambition if ever there was one) under the red counterpane, but with Clive a dead-weight pinning her to the bed, she can't let go.

There's something quaint about her fiancé. Last night, just before 'shut-eye', Clive turned to her with serious intent. Naturally, she was expecting some noble dictum, a summary of their life together so far, but instead he'd given her a lesson in the uses of 'will' and 'shall'.

Didactic, but he's preparing her to 'fit into his family' – too old a family to fit in with hers.

Claire knows she should sleep tonight. Tomorrow is her moving day. A day already bound to be stress-filled. But instead she has decided to celebrate her life's change of genre; she'll farewell drab kitchen-sink realism, welcome her rom-com days. She'll watch and wait and think and breathe for both of them.

First-time sex shouldn't be celebrated by doing what you do every night of your life – falling asleep. No! She'll claim her womanhood by keeping vigil. She'll feel crap tomorrow but at least she'll have squeezed pungent eucalyptus oil from the gum tree of life.

She'll run the movie of their love-making through her mind, replaying it over and over, until it's a worldwide event, worthy of being relayed on a looped tape forever on TV, like the moon-landing!

She'll milk it for all it's worth, evaluate each gesture, enumerate each endearment, each caress. She cannot rate her own performance. And to be fair, Clive's is unrateable by her – she can only say that he seemed diligent.

So here they are, curled up like twin crescent moons, quiescent as imagoes awaiting their transformation into something altogether other. The pair of yoked bullocks on 'Farty' Artie's farm next door to her family farm springs to mind but she repels the image.

She resolves to make a break for independence once Clive's breathing has steadied into its regular whoosh and snort: the soundtrack to a marriage, she supposes.

At last his breathing settles. She wriggles her shoulder out from under her lover's chin.

She shoves off the heavy arm that pins her down. She rolls onto her side. Gasps. How long has she waited to breathe normally, deeply, naturally. Phew! It is obscene the relief she feels flying solo again. She wedges the spare pillow under her left knee. At last she's resting on a level plane and not clinging to a crater, about to plummet into a black hole.

Claire falls asleep eventually. She awakes to find she's clinging to the piping around the mattress-edge. Having always slept alone, she is unused to the minute adjustments a heavy proximate body forces one to make. Is she a mattress-pea princess?

She lies and stares at the ceiling. Despite the heavy curtaining, it's already dawn and as her eyes adjust, she can make out the decorative rose on the ceiling. Luckily, the upended coffin in the corner becomes a wardrobe or she'd have taken it as an omen and skedaddled.

In the milky film of morning light, there's nothing to exercise her superstitious side. But what of Clive? Claire's probing fingers find no evidence of life.

Chapter 10
Morning After

A note on Clive's pillow informs Claire that Clive's at the hospital. Shouldn't he have told her she'd find herself abandoned as soon as she'd thrown in her lot with him?

Claire had slept after all. Her romantic idea of a vigil had failed through sheer exhaustion.

This morning, she can hardly believe in last evening. She's alone again. Were Clive's feelings for her a mere low-grade affection? She feels she's been married and divorced in one evening.

His note says: 'HOSPITAL'.

She's awakened to someone else's décor. It's all Mexican whorehouse-style ox-blood reds and silk fringed lamps. She'll have to din it into her head that his belongings are now hers, whether she likes his stuff or not.

Her life started at 10 pm last night. It was a sharp-edged transformation. No wriggle-room, he declared. Claire feels as if her life's Dark Ages have travelled express to the Enlightenment, ignoring all epochs in between.

Claire's hardly exhilarated. She has a panicky fluttering in her stomach, as if she's losing her grip on the crumbling cliff of life and is about to slide into a void. Have all twenty doors of possibility that had been standing ajar slammed shut? Have her life's choices been whittled down to one? Is love a loss of opportunity?

A knock sounds at the door.

"Yes?"

"It's Alex. Are you decent?"

"Yes."

The door opens. His grinning visage adorns the slit between the jamb and the door, making his face seem longer than ever. He opens the door, gives a mock-courtly bow and says: "Greetings, Sister-in-Law. Your fiancé has charged me with the honour of organising breakfast for you."

Oh, so Clive *had* remembered the semi-homeless waif abandoned in his bed. "Thanks Alex," Claire says, "but I went foraging during the night; already I know there's nothing in the fridge."

"How about bacon and eggs from the corner shop?"

"Great! I'm famished," Claire admits. "All I had last night was ears."

"One cannot love on ears alone; one needs heads, elbows, fingers, brains…pasta tubes or pipes; an excellent invention the water pipe; viz the Romans, their aqueducts. I love pipes, I'm a plumber."

"Weren't there always pipes?"

"No. Like the wheel, they had to be invented."

"So how did prehistoric men water their lawns?"

"Now you're teasing me."

"Maybe. I feel like all Clive's duped and desperate women, Alex. He decided a proposal was the only way of…you know," she says blushing. She feels a wave of self-pity rising from whatever low swampy pit such feelings come. She presses her lips into a straight line, cracks hardy. But her inconvenient shoulders start to shake. Claire hopes Alex will think she's laughing.

He hurries over. Sits on the bed. He envelopes her in arms so long they look like nana forgot to stop knitting his birthday jumper. She breathes him in along with gulps of air that fuel her sobs. His smell is fresh and very male. He unearths a hanky from his jeans pocket; he lifts Claire's chin to dab at her eyes. She pushes all thoughts of microbes clean from her mind and submits. He's like a painter preparing a canvas for a seminal art work. Thinking this, Claire starts to laugh but her gulping giggles and the intensified shaking of her shoulders convince him of her distress.

He hugs her to him tighter still. "Listen, Claire," he says, "I gave you the wrong impression last night about Clive's philandering."

"Alex," she says. "Already I know that as witty and charming, as he is, Clive will be hard work as a fiancé, if that is what he is. I half expect to find myself back home tonight. He'll blame all this", Claire indicates the disarray of the bedclothes, "on strong drink." "And do you know what, Alex? I wouldn't mind too much. This was an adventure, but can it be real?"

"Claire, I don't know what to say…I'm sure he loves you."

"Thanks Alex, you're a kind, sweet man."

"Stop telling me I'm kind, Claire," he says sounding pissed. "Okay, some breakfast?"

"Yes, please! I was so hungry in the night, I sneaked to the kitchen and polished off some milk that was on the point of going off. Clive thinks I'm a doll that doesn't need to eat."

"Clive doesn't get eating; his nourishment comes from fluids."

"Yes, he even brought a night-cap to bed with him."

"When he's married, he'll eat more, drink far less, I hope."

"We tangoed! I didn't think I could dance but…"

"He wafted you about the room?"

"Not wafted, it was more like a fascist's stomp."

"Good simile."

"I love English. I'm a philologist," Claire admits, bashfully, then wishes she hadn't skited. "Don't tell Clive."

"Your secret's safe with me. I am one too."

"One two what?"

"Another philologist, dummy. I love Shakespeare."

"Me too!"

"Do marry Clive. We'll make totally compatible in-laws. We'll talk at Xmas and birthday parties." Alex strokes his chin thoughtfully. "He needs you, Claire. He's lonely."

"Lonely. But he's popular at work. I asked around. I reckon he exaggerates; thinks it's cool to seem vulnerable. *I'm* the lonely one," says Claire. "I mean, fancy accepting a proposal from the first man…"

"Well, get un-lonely. Don't marry just to cure your loneliness."

"But Clive is a catch; he's handsome, fun." Claire's trying to convince herself. Her words thrum in her head. She's wobbling all over the joint, a spinning top on the wane. But…No.

"You're right. Make me a strong coffee, Alex. I'll bail right now and no harm done."

"What's the hurry? Claire. Hang around. Keep me company today."

"Oh, gosh! That foreign man who called. He said he had…a footstool or something."

"Ah! Sergei. Come to his shop with me – it's amazing."

"But there's Suz, my flatmate, waiting."

"She nice?" he asks. Claire nods. "We'll take her too. But don't move in yet. You'll get stuck."

"By moving in, I'll get to know him faster."

Alex sighs. "Is that a book you're leaning on?"

"My journal," Claire says proudly.

"You take your journal on dates?"

"Don't tell."

"My lips are sealed. But promise me you'll go to the country before you break it off. Observing the St Johns in their native habitat will give you something to write about."

Chapter 11
Breakfast

Claire is spending the first day of the rest of her life with the wrong twin.

Alex cooks breakfast: one of those immense fry-ups country folk enjoy.

"I'm watching my figure," Claire tells him. She's unsurprised when he offers to watch it for her. The St John boys chime in with cute quips faster than bell-ringers on speed.

They eat in the kitchen. Claire is dressed in Clive's jeans with the legs rolled up and the waist belted. The kitchen looks cleaner today. If nothing eventuates from her night of love, she'll be leaving one small corner of the world cleaner than she found it.

The marbled Laminex table with zinc edging is quaintly retro. The Kelly's in Wang is merely old. Alex's chairs have grimy foam-padded plastic seats – practical and comfortable, a quality she values since experiencing Melbourne's love affair with unstable Frenchified bentwood chairs.

There are five differently patterned surfaces, including sunburst wallpaper, gold starred venetians, speckled Laminex counter tops, swirly lino, and some faddist has attempted to stencil a starburst pattern on the walls. In one corner of the room, the ever-expanding universe retreats.

Aren't we humans quaint? The way we decorate our caves, make them uniquely ours, Claire thinks, knowing the insight's not original enough to share with her lover's clever brother.

Alex chatters through breakfast. He's as keen to know about her life on the farm as Clive had been incurious last night. Claire answers as honestly as the occasion merits; with new friends, she romanticises family life somewhat.

"Happy childhood! Loving parents!" she says. "Not ideal for a moderately educated girl like me."

"Why?" he asks.

"Because genes and upbringing make me broody."

"A lot to be born?"

"Ha-ha! Our parents' heroic fecundity plus Catholicism are to blame for our big family. Mum would have had it easier with fewer of us."

"But she'd never wish you away," says Alex, empathising.

"I'm not too sure about that."

"Bloody Catholic clergy. Unless their flock risk their health and wealth, they get no oats." He glares at her indignantly.

"Don't blame me, Alex. I'm not the Pope. Besides, I was awake half the night," Claire says, then blushes.

"Ha. Didn't realise my brother was so amaaazing," he says, sounding wounded.

"Calm down, Alex. I'm exhausted and I dread facing Suz." Alex looks at her with concern. He goes quiet. Claire uses the break in Alex's harangue for a sip of coffee. She pokes at the egg yolks with her toast-soldier. Nice and runny, whites firm, the bacon crisp, not burnt. Despite this awkward conversation, she can't help feeling happy suddenly.

"What do you farm?" Alex asks.

"Everything. We subsist, making butter, keeping bees. Recently, Dad started making wine. Mum tells him it's 'beaut' and forces herself to drink a glass each week. Dad says, 'Drink up, we can afford a glass each night,' but Mum winks and says in a parody of her Irish forbears: 'It's not a wine for the wasting of – it's only for special occasions.' Dad squeezes her bum to say thank you.

"There's olive groves, immature. Apples and pears in commercial quantities. Apricots are turned into delicious jams. Mum makes ricotta; her cheddar's awful. We've chooks, and Dad shoots rabbits for stews. Pigs. We're not allowed to name them in case…There's water cress by the spring."

"Boy, What an industrious lot. My olds eat bunnies, but Dada loves his roast beef. We're in debt. Your family life seems idyllic."

"You Sins are rich, aren't you?"

"The portraits in the hall are disappearing. Ma conjured up certificates of provenance so paintings can go off to auction rooms when things are desperate. Bet your olds don't have faux ancestors."

"Faux. Write it in my book, please," Claire indicates the tabbed notebook on the table.

"Consider it yours," he scrawls the word in his vertical tented hand.

"Mum's style is hippie retro; she's papered the walls with hessian sacks. Surprisingly good. Last year Dad tried organic farming. He only produced some scrofulous veggies."

"Scrofulous?" Alex says.

"Yes. Do you want that one?"

"I've got it already."

"Smart Alec!"

"Smart Alex!"

Claire places her toasty soldier carefully on the plate and attacks him with her fist.

"Dear Claire, there's no one I'd rather be killed by. You're so half-hearted." He sniggers mercilessly. "Now drink your juice, boot up and let's go get your things."

But her boots won't go on over Clive's jeans. He pushes, Claire pulls. The boots buckle at the ankle. They fall back on the bed! Is Claire forever doomed to fall when she's around these twins?

Alex goes off for socks and thongs. "Wear these!" he orders.

"Only a drongo would wear thongs and socks. I'll put my frock on."

"Ridiculous. You'll die of cold in that flimsy seduction frock."

"It's not a seduction frock. The crucifix was meant to tone it down."

"Then it didn't work, did it? Your legs looked very long last night."

"My mum made that frock," Claire says, hands on her hips like an angry child.

Alex gives Claire a solemn look. "She ran out of fabric. Should have used her wheat bag wallpaper!"

"You didn't have to look."

"Couldn't help myself. Come on, we're squabbling like brother and sister. Let's hit the road before we have a proper fight."

Chapter 12
Clifton Hill Walk

They climb into the ute and head for Clifton Hill. "What's Suzy like?" Alex asks.

"She has character."

"We all do," says Alex, rather pedantically, Claire thinks.

"She has strength of character, I mean. She automatically knows what's right."

"Not open-minded enough, then. Serious people hold issues up to the light, look for flaws, weigh up arguments before making decisions; there's always new information to consider."

"Suzy doesn't need to change her mind. She leaps to the right conclusion instinctively."

"She's a blooming wonder, then. But how do you know it's the right conclusion since you're implying you're not as clever as she?"

She's been checkmated, Claire realises. With Alex around, she'd live in constant fear of seeming foolish. "Suz can be impatient with lesser mortals," she says aloud. "And she doesn't suffer fools. Like you, Alex."

"Am I a fool?" he asks and grins when she groans and grasps her forehead. "But I *am* suffering you gladly," he says not taking his eyes off the road but giving her a quick tap on the knee.

Claire gives him a gentle back-hander to match his back-handed compliment.

"Ouch!" he complains.

She wants to tell him that it was meant affectionately but she stays silent. She mustn't tell him how to take her – what'd be the point? She sighs. "Suz hates emotional, illogical people like me, and she's even more waspish than you are, Alex."

"Good, I'm glad you take me seriously. I'd hate to be thought bland!" His good humour returns.

"With those she doesn't know Suz can seem arrogant," Claire explains, "but she's shy, you realise when you know her. Her IQ's off the charts."

"Impossible. If it's been measured."

Claire ignores this jibe. "Her family's rich. She went to PLC. She's travelled everywhere but never skites. She knows hers is just dumb luck. She's as small and dainty as I am tall and clumpy."

"Clive says you're elegant and willowy."

Claire blushes and turns away to indulge herself in the merest of smug private smiles for the benefit of the unfolding streetscape of stately Fitzroy North. Alex offers no opinion upon Clive's compliment, but he hasn't implied that it's ridiculous. This pleases Claire to a stupendous extent.

"Suzy's blonde," Claire continues, "with short naturally curly hair that frames her face and makes her look angelic. Her blue eyes see into the core of you; she always gives you a straight answer and she's loyal."

"How will she react to your desertion?"

Claire wishes Alex hadn't used the 'd' word. She ponders the possible origins of 'desertion'.

It'd probably feel like being in an emotional desert, she supposes, empty and solitary. She sighs.

"I reckon Suz will see it as a boon," Claire announces boldly, "she'll think I'm moving on with life instead of deserting her." While saying this, Claire knows she's whistling in the dark.

"Clive mightn't want you seeing much of Suz."

"Why not?"

"He'll want you dancing attention upon him; obsessive and adoring."

They pull up near the girls' flat on The Esplanade. This posh-sounding address disappoints.

The park, a ribbon of native grasses with occasional elms, hardly aspires to the botanical. Any hint of water views is belied by a dirty trickle of Merri Creek way down in a gully that ferries industrial pollution from the northern suburbs to the Yarra River.

"Okay, Claire."

"Come and meet Suz," she pleads, wanting him for the distraction he'll provide.

"No. Screw your courage to the sticking point."

"I'm not Lady Macbeth about to murder anyone."

"Mm," says Alex sceptically.

Claire curls herself into the neatest shape she can manage on the farm utility's bench seat and has a good cry. Odd. She's not usually a sook, and she'd never play upon Alex's feelings. But she feels as guilty as Eve in the Garden of Eden.

She'd seen what she wanted and had taken it!

"I'm ashamed, Alex. Let's go back, get my frock and boots. Clive will just have to wait for me."

"Clive, wait? Ha!" Alex reaches across the bench seat and pats her shoulder. "You're not totally callous, Claire. That's good. When Aunt Aude died, Ma said: 'Fred's coping so well – getting on with life.' But Aude would have wanted Fred to miss her for a bit. It's tearing you up deciding whom to hurt, Suz or Clive. But however you play it, you will make *someone* sad. Forget all that win-win situation bull!"

"You're brutal in your honesty, Alex!" Claire holds her head in her hands as if keeping a sunflower upright past its time. "I need a walk. Come?"

"Sure," he says. "I'll shut-up. Let you think."

They head off along the track through bush beside the creek. Since moving to Melbourne, it's been a favourite stroll for Claire. The path veers downhill. It's tricky in thongs and socks.

Claire's usual confident swagger's gone AWOL; she'd have liked Alex to see it, she's proud of her walk. One's gait is an odd thing to be proud of, she realises. Still, this awkward amble's therapeutic so far. Concentrating on keeping her toes squeezed tight is helping her fend off discomfiting thoughts.

"Alex," Claire says, when used to her new gait, "what does 'all's fair in love and war' mean?"

He sighs, "Can't we have an amble through the bush without things getting heavy? I guess," he says, after a pause, "if war is mud and blood and trenches, so is love. When the chips are down, we put our own survival first. Love is an all-out battle for domination."

"What a pity your parents' marriage is bad," she says.

"Not at all. Warring bonds them. If you think love's all scented candles, then cancel your Women's Weekly subscription."

"My parents are partners, not competitors."

"Ha!" barks Alex.

"Clive will pay my share of the rent for three months. Is that fair?"

Alex gives her a disgusted look.

Claire is busy glaring back at him when she stumbles on a rock. She'd have come a cropper but for Alex's reflexes.

"How idiotic, to wear thongs bushwalking," he says, helping her upright.

"You...!" she says, not at first realising he's teasing her. Lucky it's not Alex she's attracted to, she thinks. They'd have an awful, bellicose marriage. But she catches his eye, and he's smiling.

It's hard to know how to take him sometimes. Luckily, she doesn't have to take him. She shuts up, watches her feet and listens to the birds. They're having a mid-morning conference. Or are they mocking the two of them? Did the early flowering wattles attract them here? Ribbons of light filter through the gum trees' meagre foliage. Life's beautiful. And sad.

"You girls from happy homes unsettle the rest of us with your easy optimism... or you would if we believed in you," Alex remarks, out of the blue.

"Excuse me for my happy childhood. And, sorry you can't believe in me. But it's not like I'm God and it's up to you to decide whether I exist or not."

They go on in silence after that. It isn't a companionable silence, more a resentful one.

Claire is so over Alex. She feels his judgment weighing on her shoulders like a backpack. She grips her thongs between her toes. She'll soon be as capable with her lower limbs as her husband-to-be, closing doors and drawers in the funny way he does. This thought gives her the giggles.

Alex flicks a puzzled glance her way. But there's no chance she'll share this thought, or let him save her from another fall.

Back at the car she gives Alex a see-you-later-if-I-live-through-this-ordeal wave and heads towards the flat.

Chapter 13
Telling Suz

The flat in Clifton Hill is of unexciting cream-brick with grey cinder-block inserts. Very sixties! It's hardly a notable architectural style, but Suz and Claire love it dearly – it's their first home. Oh, the parties they will have, the heroic Spaghetti Bolognaises they will cook just as soon as they have a quorum of friends to party with!

The flat's cream interior provides a blank canvas on which to exercise their decorating muscles. Its northerly windows give onto an Edwardian red-brick house with an old-fashioned garden, replete with peach, apple, and loquat trees.

Claire climbs slowly, postponing her knock upon the door. She inches upstairs like a crab, squinching her toes together to persuade Alex's thongs to stay on her feet over hiking socks.

Claire's a bolter. In her usual hurry, she takes the stairs two at a time. Now, her awkward gait gives her time to marvel at the sly low person she has become. Is she really about to throw away two years of friendship on a one-night stand?

Yes, she tells herself. Mother Nature decrees it should be so. A woman in love isn't in charge of her life. She has surrendered to destiny and hormones! The latter have sussed out a sperm-donor tailor-made for fathering Claire's future family. To fight it would be pointless.

Claire's overwhelmed by the idea of love. Clive is her future. Her 'destiny is unfolding as it should', to quote her mum's hippie precept.

Does she love Clive, she wonders. Does she even like him? Maybe not. At the very least she admires his academic achievements and his stupendous reserves of confidence. Is he charismatic? Of course! Does he make Claire herself more confident? Yes!

It would be stupendous ingratitude to thumb her nose at fate. Lovers belong to a distinct social class – one older than those described by Karl Marx. Lovers are life's emotional nobles. They're bound to accept this happy turn of fortune's wheel. Love has elevated them.

Nonetheless, it's random and unfair. But is it Claire's fault that the world's constructed thus?

She's been plucked from drear spinsterhood by a prince. She: love goddess. Suzy: handmaiden. But has she earned her cornucopia of luck?

At the door, she presses the bell; to have used the key would seem like breaking in. Suz opens the door, smiling. "Thank God, Claire. I was worried."

"May I come in?" Claire asks.

"Silly question." Suz gives Claire an affectionate punch on the arm.

Once inside, Claire takes Suz's arm and steers her to the couch, their only seating and placed on the diagonal so they both have an optimal view of the 24-inch TV over in the corner. She thanks God for their sparse furnishings. Claire won't have to watch the pained/brave expression on Suz's face. Imagining it is bad enough.

"Shall I get us a cuppa? Then you must tell all."

"No, thanks." Claire will rip off the Band-Aid of treachery fast; be cruel to be kind. In hurting her friend slightly, she'll be making herself and Clive exceedingly happy. And two smiles trump one frown…

Claire knows there's no Great Accountant in the sky reasoning this way. Some things are just plain wrong. She's blithely abandoning Suz after a mildly successful one-night-stand.

Leaving a true friend for a brand new one. Has Claire been hankering so cravenly for male approval that she'll move in with any vaguely handsome man whom she quite likes? Oughtn't she love him passionately? She'd been sloshed enough from hunger and bad wine to think she did last night. But now…

"Suz, I've got good news," she says. Why, do lies come out rhyming? "Great news!" Claire's voice cracks and echoes in her head. "I think…I've fallen…Iminlove."

"Love?"

"Love," Claire snaps.

"Are you sure?" Suz, won't let anything go until she's wrestled all implications out of it.

"Sure, I'm sure!"

"Sure? Not the urologist?"

"The urologist. Who else?" Claire wonders why they're echoing each other's words.

"I'm moving in with him."

"But not today!"

"I'm afraid so."

We all ought to hear warning bells whenever the weasel words 'afraid so' are uttered.

These words mean: I know I'm about to do something unforgivable but I'll do it anyway.

"Shouldn't you see him until you're sure?"

"I've seen him. All of him. He insists we start our new lives as of now." Claire wonders at 'as of now'. She's never used such constipated phraseology before. It's like starting a letter, 'being in receipt of yours etc.'. If she lets this scene run on, she'll hate herself even more.

Claire very nearly says: "I must be *there* for him," a phrase she'd sworn never to utter, even on pain of death. She stops herself. Standing on the brink of this verbal sinkhole is proof that moral decay is underway, if not total linguistic disintegration. Worse still, she fears uttering verbal epithets more than hurting Suz.

"Never mind, Claire. It's all good," says Suz. In allowing this abominable cliché past her vigilant goalie, it's clear how hurt Suz feels. Suz tries keeping her hands clasped in her lap but she cannot still them. They twine around each other like pet snakes. Poor Suz, usually a paragon of stoicism and poise!

It's nice of her to assume that Claire is worrying more about Suz than about the chore of telling her. "I wish happy things weren't so sad," Claire says, hugging Suz. She buries her face in her friend's shoulder, which gesture twists her neck a bit. She can smell Suz's lavender bath salts. "And don't worry about money," says Claire. "Clive will pay my share of the rent until you find someone."

Suz draws her lips in, calculating. "So, he's lay-bying you!"

Thank God, the waspish Suz is back! Claire thinks.

"Okay, Claire. Nothing to be said. Let's get you packed."

Claire feels perversely disappointed that Suz hasn't fought harder for their friendship. Was that what she'd wanted to happen? To be dissuaded from her recklessness?

A knock at the door startles them.

Suz fluffs up her hair and opens the door to Alex. "Hi, you must be Clive," she says, sounding desperately upbeat.

"I'm his brother, Alex."

Seeing Alex through her friend's eyes, Claire notices for the first time how exotic and handsome he is.

"Helping with the move?"

"If that's okay."

"Sure. And golly, what super news!"

Alex examines Suz's face for signs of irony. He can't decide. He smiles at her.

"Well, let's get on with it," Claire says, not liking the way Suz and Alex are making cow-eyes at each other. They'd be hopeless together. Alex is too...

Chapter 14
Packing

Suz helps Claire pack her things. They work in silence. Suz doesn't chatter. Conversationally, she's a sniper. She takes the high ground, says what's what and then withdraws. To Suzy the background buzz of small talk is worse than elevator music. Thanks to her influence, Claire has modified her tendency to chatter nervously.

They fold the contents of Claire's wardrobe. She mainly wears jeans, T-shirts and roll-necked pullovers and vests with the occasional tartan skirt – a retro choice – when out of uniform. If you're reading this, don't feel superior. Everyone's clothes screamed eighties in the 80s. Is it a crime to have been born in 1968, the year kaftans invaded the west?

What might have been a tender leave-taking scene is made awkward by Alex, who's trying to help but is frustrating their efforts by getting his untidy limbs in the way. It is as if he's there to impede the moving process and not to hasten it. "Go and have a smoko, Claire suggests," hoping he'll take the hint and wait on the balcony.

"What makes you think I smoke, Claire? Are tradies supposed to be unhealthy yobbos?"

"No," she assures him, puzzled by his venom. He sure is moodier than Clive, she thinks.

"Perhaps you could make us a cup of tea then," Suz suggests. "You'll find everything approximately where you'd expect to find it."

"But I have no expectations of your kitchen, except that it'll be cleaner than mine," he says, and stays put. Myriad expressions cross his face as he struggles to make himself insignificant.

At six-foot four, he's not to blame for his extraordinary spatial needs, though his emotional intensity is all down to him. It seems he's taken it upon himself to display the feelings Suz and Claire are hiding.

"You wanted me here and now you can't wait to get rid of me," he sounds aggrieved. "You'll need me soon enough for the cases."

Why does Claire feel that Alex, unlike all the men she's ever known, is fascinated by the awkwardness of this leave-taking scene and is reluctant to miss out on its smallest nuance?

Eventually, they close the cases on Claire's things. Her bursting wardrobe's been collapsed down into two bag lady bundles that might've been vacuum suctioned. She feels her life's been summarised, and divided by four.

Suz and she face each other, both wishing they hadn't been thrust into the role of actors forced to make their farewells on a stage, for that's how Alex's presence makes them feel.

He's absorbed in their kitchen sink drama. An indie film director, he moves about the set, looking for novel camera angles to exploit.

"I'd no idea you felt ready to get married," says Suz, a trifle peevishly. "I thought you wanted to live a bit before you settled down."

"That was before I met Clive." Claire glances over at Alex, hoping for his approbation, but his eyes slide away. "It's not the idea of marriage…it's meeting the right person. You don't know…until you know," she says lamely. "I hate leaving, Suz, you know I love you to death, it's just that…"

"…You love someone else more."

Suz's words hit Claire like a well-aimed blow. "I love you both…You can't quantify love precisely."

"So, live with me and gradually fall in love with Clive!"

Claire can't believe that Suz is pleading. All that magnificent dignity of hers! Gone!

She rubs Suz's arm as if to swab her skin before an inoculation against treachery. "I have to go, Suz, he wants me badly. And now!" she insists. *But does he really?* Claire wonders.

"You're worried that he won't want you in a month!"

Claire's not sure whether this comment is born of caution or cruelty.

"Moving in with him is the only way to find out."

"He's your little experiment? He'll help you grow up? Don't worry, Claro, I understand."

Why do Aussies do this? Give you a diminutive that adds a syllable to your name? Claire wonders. And why the hell is she wondering this now?

"I get it. You want to love him at close quarters while you love me distantly. You'll keep me here, with your room fully paid up, so you've something to fall back on when things don't work out."

"No, I'm sure things will work out. I...love him."

"Love is love," says Suz. Platitudes are contagious, apparently.

"One day soon you'll be lucky enough to feel the way I do," Claire says, her lines emerging with less sincerity, now she feels the ordeal will soon be over.

"You mean, one day soon I'll be silly enough to do something as risky as you?"

While this is going on, Alex stands stock-still. Uluru trying to shrink to pebble size?

No! He's more like a caged lion, that can't fight or flee and doesn't want to. He fidgets with his ponytail; he draws it so tight, he puts his hairline under stress. This is a macro level tic.

His eyes flicker from Suz to Claire and back again as if they were actresses vying for a Logie TV award, he the judge.

Now he starts pacing, apparently suffering the separation stress that Claire would have been feeling had she been a half-decent person. It's as though he has a greater stake in the outcome than either flatmate.

The poky lounge room doesn't help. Nor does the siting of their only decent piece, a Japanese hibachi from the Asian Bazaar in Queen's Parade. It holds the prized Monstera Deliciosa plant that's flourished in the northerly sun until it rivals next door's Moreton Bay Fig. This obstacle forces Alex to change direction every three and a half paces, at which time he performs a ludicrous skip-step manoeuvre. He resembles a rake being scraped across a stage at the whim of a giant in the wings.

"Stand still, Alex," Claire orders him. Oddly, he obeys.

"Bye the way, Suz, you keep the hibachi. You've always loved it so."

"I doubt you'd get it downstairs in one piece," says Suz, making it clear that this concession won't be mistaken for generosity.

She and Suz hug. Claire notices that Suz, her tiny friend, already has a small roll of flesh above her bra-line at the back – the one men never see because their gaze is focused upon women's fronts. It makes her want to weep. She sheds a tear or two, then mops her eyes with her sleeve, though only Alex sees.

"Well, take care," Claire says, aware of the subtext of her words: you'd better take care of yourself because I won't be around if you get into strife. "It's been great, honestly."

Suz critiques this inanity by refusing to make eye contact and allowing her head to bob mechanically at the far wall as if she were a toy nodding dog at the back of a car.

Claire screws her key from its chain and leaves it on the phone table with a guilty little wave. Alex gestures benignly in her wake like an obsequious waiter.

They'd have got well out of earshot if not for the sock/thong footwear quirk. Why the hell hadn't she changed shoes when she could? Before they clear the stairwell, Suzy leans over the landing and calls out: "Don't forget those pottery wine glasses, Claire."

"Oh, surely you can use them, Suz." Ouch! More rhyming!

"They're not me," she says, implying that these ugly drinking vessels are instead very 'Claire'. In fact, they were a moving-away-from-Wangaratta gift. She'd thought them quaint at first. What genius came up with the idea of burying a ruby, semi-translucent beverage within a vessel that disguises all that's beautiful about it?

"You'll use them, Claire; they're very you."

Ouch, even sweet Suz has an edge to her personality! They leave the cases downstairs and climb back up again.

While Claire wraps the glasses – she's stretching the meaning of the word glass to breaking point – Alex exploits the hiatus in the proceedings to wonder aloud whether he and Suz shouldn't get together some time. And Suz responds, too enthusiastically for Claire's liking, exclaiming at what a 'super' idea this is. In saying 'yes', her voice rises girlishly.

Missing is her caustic tone of earlier as she makes arrangements to 'see' Alex.

Claire feels cross at how Alex has hijacked this scene – the tender parting of two long-term friends – and turned it into a Lonely Hearts' Club meeting. Is she being a bitch? Claire wonders. But what annoys her above all is: why do we say 'see', when we mean hear, touch, taste, smell?

Chapter 15
Chest of Drawers, Prahran

Alex helps Claire free up a drawer for her smalls. His room is brim-filled with books, drum kits, guitars, an unmade bed. Concert posters proclaim musical tastes: Jackson Browne, Van Morrison, Dylan, Leonard Cohen, Jethro Tull, Crowded House and Claire's own beloved Joni Mitchell.

There's a Che Guevara poster. Che's face reminds Claire of someone. As Alex flicks the bedspread across so she can perch on the bed, she glimpses his face juxtaposed with the poster.

She can see Alex in Che, though the latter has more facial hair.

What a tumult of clues for Claire, the archaeologist of souls. Unlikely to be invited in here often, she's like a thirsty prospector drinking it all in. Her understanding of whom her new brother-in-law might be is firming up, but she knows artefacts can mislead. They proclaim: this is my persona, but we're persons actually.

Alex sighs. "I can't get your drawers into my drawers."

"I'll leave a case packed in the wardrobe," Claire decides.

"And scrabble about at 5.00 am? No way."

"I'll manage."

"Gees, Claire, I can picture your pioneering ancestors inventing things with nails and string. Makeshift's not good enough for my new sister. Let's check out the furniture marts in Chapel Street. Come!"

They set off in the ute.

Life is weird. In one weekend, Claire's gone from trams and cabs, via a part-interest in a Porsche key, back to a battered ute as usual. It's rags to riches to rags. No humble Ford to soften the extremes.

They park at the grimy end of Chapel Street. Alex opens her door. Where's his disapproval of her over Suzy gone? They drift leisurely down the shopping strip.

"If you travel its length from South to North, you'll have gone from down-and-outer digs and pawn-brokers to power broker territory in under an hour; from serf to slave-driver in just the one revolution," Alex informs her.

At the lights in Malvern Road a turning vehicle shaves close to her. Alex grabs her arm and pulls her close. "Use your loaf," he calls after the car. "Careful, Claire. Melbourne isn't Wang."

He offers her his elbow-crook. Once across the street, each assumes the other responsible for uncoupling their caboose. He doesn't. She can't because he's saved her life. They chug along awkwardly but more-or-less in step – all that one can expect of any human coupling. Claire is preternaturally aware of the neural activity going on usually unnoticed within; the busyness of nerve endings when focused upon is phenomenal. A lot is happening where bodies meet: shoulder, elbow, hip.

She's often walked like this with Suz when shopping, heads together, sharing confidences, but today her bodily awareness is electric. She fakes a greater interest in the window displays than in their sizzling proximity. Is he feeling what she feels? It should be obscene in in-laws.

She feels warmth where her duffle coat meets his oilskin boundary rider's coat. Alex's clothing is an affectation in the city, but she's in a forgiving mood.

Many second-hand shops have congregated on this strip. Claire has a theory about 'retro'.

Some love or hate it with a passion. She's mildly enthusiastic about 20% of it. Not everything has merit just because it's old. Still, it's fun to trawl the antique markets, seeking bargains.

"Look Alex," she says, "Mary is into corn-cob kitsch. She'd go crazy with her bankcard here."

"And Suz loves ruby glass. Me, I prefer Kartell novelty furniture. Would that tubular console work for make-up?"

"Maybe," Alex says, "but Kartell cylindrical cabinets will be valuable one day – get one anyway."

"But it's $40. Clive mightn't think it suits his décor."

"Décor! Clive has stuff, not décor. I'll buy it for you. A moving-in gift."

"Thank you, Alex."

They go in, pay, arrange delivery.

They drift past clothing outlets with racks of trackie daks and parkas spilling onto the street.

Pine furniture emporia sell lacquered beds for those just starting out in life. It's the desperate end of consumerism. Having found oneself a roof, and covering for one's nakedness, what's left apart from food? Plenty. Claire's visited top-end shops in Chapel Street, whose jeans sport designer rips and gouges. At this end, clothes thin and tear along stress lines.

She wanders along deep in thought; is it better to have so much that it costs to look faux poor or merely to have too little from the get-go? She sighs nostalgically for school uniform days. No time wasted on unimportant choices. Self-expression! What a con!

She turns and misses Alex. He's disappeared! She trains her eyes on the straggly groups, but she sees no incongruous farmer's coat. Soon he appears from inside a furniture auction house.

"Claro Love, I'm here." He beckons her towards the arcade. She blushes; only her dearest friends call her Claro. Alex's use of 'love' unnerves her. It's meant avuncularly, but…

Unsettled, she takes his hand as a lost child might. "I missed you, Alex. Oops, I missed seeing where you'd got to." Gee, I'm not allowed to miss him, she thinks, dropping his hand like a hot brick. She'd only lost sight of him 60 seconds ago. "I'm blathering, Alex. Sorry."

"Don't be sorry."

"Sorry…"

"I hate people who are always sorry."

"You hate me?"

"No, on the contrary…I…"

Life has moments when life's clutch engages of its own accord as if for a sudden gear change.

It's as if life's steady impetus is set to stall unless its progress gets a cranking up. It's like coming upon a seesaw holding identical twins. You can't tear your eyes away until you know what happens next. Here's your chance to alter things, to give your life and fate, a good hard shove towards the daring. But the notion that the slightest pressure from one's index finger can either ruin one's life or tip the balance to the true is probably illusory. If fate is pre-programmed into our lives, shouldn't it also be programmed to telegraph its outcomes in a timely way to us protagonists?

Is this her seesaw moment, Claire wonders. Damn! Where's her Juliet balcony?

She's playing for time, too cowardly to move. She wants Alex to say, 'on the contrary', and then go on to spell out what she hopes they're both thinking. Meanwhile, she's allowed to stand there nodding passively; her gender encourages cowardice, but Alex must be manly, take control. She acknowledges it's unfair but she's been through a lot recently. Is it her fault, if, upon reaching life's tipping point, she can't exploit the moment, but clings to old allegiances instead of embracing something, someone else?

All she can say in her defence is this: how can what is be wrong? What is just is.

Alex shoots her a despairing look before turning away. She can see by the sad slump of his back that he's only pretending to browse the arcade's treasures; pretending absorption in bric-à-brac's tawdry charms. He's feeling as torn as she.

She follows him deep into the arcade; she decides she might as well go along with the rough draft of her life's script for now.

Alex shepherds her through aisles jam-packed with starter furniture. Out back there is an office occupied by a man whose belly would overhang its belt had he not been fully reclining his oak tip-tilted office chair. The cigarette hanging from the corner of his mouth impedes his speech as much as the ash trail on his shirt concerns him – hardly at all.

"G'day, mate. How's it hangin'?" asks Alex.

"Come si, Komsomol."

They laugh uproariously. She doesn't get the joke.

"Sergei, meet my new friend, Claire."

"Oh, gosh, the phone call. The blind singer and his, um, stool," she says, blushing.

Instead of chastising her, the pair hoots with laughter. "You had a lot on your mind last night, Claire," says Alex.

"So, things hangin' good with you?" Serge says, inclining his head Claire's way.

"Sorry to disappoint you, Serge. Claire is my brother's fiancée."

Must I be your brother's fiancée forever? Claire wonders. *What if it's a mistake?*

"Too bad luck. My love life rubbish also. Natalya with bonzer bazookas want to be friend."

Alex shakes his head sadly.

"A Macintosh is coming, just by way," says Serge.

"Real deal?"

"You never pick difference."

Claire wonders whether Alex collects old raincoats. She's a stranger in her own land while Alex moves easily between worlds. "My chest?" she asks, to get things moving.

"No problem with your chest. Aleksandr, you marry this girl. She is gold. Too good for Clive."

"She's taken," says Alex testily. "Listen, we need a chest of drawers for Claire's drawers."

Serge removes his feet from the desk and throws his cigarette stub into the bin. He stands and a tidal wave of displaced flesh ripples southwards. "Not much in. Just cheap pine crap."

"Find something under twenty bucks. Untreated. I'll finish it."

Serge leads them to a workshop.

"That one, do you?" Alex asks Claire. "Ten bucks, Serge?" he asks, when she nods.

"Fifteen." Sergei sighs.

Claire fumbles in her purse.

"No this is on me love, you buy us a cappuccino. Now let's see that stool."

Chapter 16
Facial

Claire's moved her undies to the chest of drawers. She and Clive are having their first evening together alone. Together or alone? Only a pedant would ask.

She's eager to start living her new life but unsure how to fulfil her part of the bargain.

If Clive pays for the roof over her head, she'll be cook and cleaner. She doesn't have a big culinary repertoire. Can't even get them fish and chips tonight. All her savings went into the knee-high boots – well, not into them literally – but they were leather, bought to impress. "An investment in your future," Mary said.

Apparently, the boots did the trick. She's established a beachhead in Clive's life. There's 17 dollars to last until Thursday. She's not one to let her funds run low. If Clive knew, he'd think her profligate. She'll walk to St V's all week to save on fares.

Italian boots! Ridiculous! Claire berates herself; she usually spins her salary into fine strong filaments. Makes it last. The boots were her downfall. In the dark of Clive's bedroom, no one would've guessed they were leather, let alone Italian. Would Clive want a pair of boots moving in with him or a warm thrifty sexy woman who can cook…a bit?

Claire empties out the fridge, stocktaking. There are eggs, cheese, bacon and bread from breakfast. Unfinished Asian food is in plastic containers: old takeaways looking so set and lacquered, they remind her of the plaster of Paris dishes at the entrance to Asian restaurants.

She junks them without the benefit of a sniff test. They'll have a cheese omelette tonight.

Tomorrow she'll buy an AWW cookbook for all the dinner parties they'll have.

Later, Claire learns Clive hasn't any friends, just people he knows from work; people he drinks with at Xmas parties; women he dates Saturdays. His Melbourne life is bleaker than hers, but she doesn't know this yet.

Claire irons her uniform for work. She squeezes her belongings into Clive's wardrobe, folds her civvies in the chest of drawers, so he won't feel crowded.

Is she being overly polite? Maybe. But she wants this...whatever it is to work. Clive almost matches her mental template of the man she wants to love. She reminds herself they have medicine in common.

She's shoehorning herself, effortfully, into his life. There's no Claire-shaped space for her to inhabit yet. Alex has helped more than any brother would. She sighs. She'll find good crockery, organise a romantic nosh-up *mit* candle.

In the bathroom, she shelves her cosmetics. The eyes looking back at her are raccoon eyes!

Her normally translucent skin looks pasty.

Self-maintenance is over-due. A good soak in the rust-stained bath will be relaxing, and then she'll have time to pamper herself before Clive's due home.

She washes and conditions her hair to tame the frizz and applies an egg-white facial from the Australian Women's Weekly, filched from the staffroom bin just last week. She never buys magazines down the celebrity swill end of journalism.

An article opened her eyes to unpalatable facts about womanhood. Good looks don't last, it said. Sure, she knew that already, subliminally. The entire advertising industry is based on this assumption. Without a regimen of defoliation, steam, anti-rides ointment, moisturiser, women become aesthetically offensive.

Her gorgeous fading mother should have alerted her to the unuttered truth of femaledom.

Even the best favoured won't be adored once the apples fade from their cheeks. They may be liked and respected but rarely loved. Her mum ought to have left her a note upon turning 13 saying: U2 LB UGLY 2.

She'd have ignored the warning back then but a tiny seed might have germinated, saving her from vanity. But who'd want to be loved by someone so superficial anyway? Aren't plain men loved?

Uncle Tom, a jovial ex-VFL player is paunchy with age, all jowls and broken capillaries, yet Aunty Jane loves him as much as ever.

Today she's ready to heed the spectre of old-womanhood hidden within her. Is she fearful of losing her fiancé before their engagement's one-day old? Yes. He's chosen her for her face and not her finer traits. Is he worth pleasing? Maybe. If she wants a normal life with babies in the mix, she may have to keep her side of the bargain.

Her facial accomplished, she lies under Clive's famous red quilt using her upturned palms as claws to keep her mucky face from spoiling the bedding. She wills herself expressionless to preserve her egg-white glaze. It's hard to be desperate and bland!

The front door opens and Clive calls: "Honey, it's me. Just dropping off my work things, I'll nick down to the Royal to pick up some booze. Beer? Wine? Spirits?"

Yesh! Please don't open the bedroom door, she prays, wishing she still believed in prayer. "Miine," she calls through horizontal lips.

"I'll get us a video too while I'm out and a Tex Mex. You like the extra hot?"

"Mm," she says. It comes out as a growl. The door slams shut. At least he won't see her looking like a pav but he doesn't say: "I love you, Claire," the way men do in movies.

She pushes off the quilt, whisks off the cucumber eye patches and eats the evidence, runs to the bathroom and scrubs at her face. The egg has dried hard. There's a spray-on cream in the fridge. It may act as a solvent. She spreads it on her face just as Clive returns with provisions.

"God Lord! Is this a vision I see before me? A fruit-free pavlova?"

"Ease onn dease ee."

"Do you always rhyme in white-face? It's sweet."

Claire cries.

"Oh, *mon ange,* you poor little thing. Are you pie-eyed over me?" He holds her at arms-length to save his jacket.

"Caa tallg."

"Well, if you could talk, what would you say?"

"Oii faffe will raaack."

"Sorry, I can't talk pavlova," says Clive. "Here's a post-it. A pen."

I TALK! FACE CRACK! Claire writes.

"I thought I'd bought a flawless beauty. I'll have to activate your warranty toot sweet!"

"NO FUNNY 2 TRU."

"Darling, I love you whatever your flavour."

"WIP FACE QIK!"

"You mean quickly. I abhor the Americanisation of the language."

64

"I hate you, you pretentious jerk!" she says.

"Oops, now you have cracked it." Clive finds a roll of kitchen paper. Tenderly, he lifts her chin towards the light from the naked light bulb illuminating the kitchen. He removes most of the cream. "Now off to the bathroom, Madam Butterfly. Use my shaving cream. Leave it on for one minute. Then steam off the residue. You'll be lovely in the morning."

"You want me lovely. Shiiit!"

"Don't swear. An' it's lovely you'll be, me dairlin'."

Chapter 17
Post Facial

Claire has been applying unguents to impress her fiancé with her natural beauty when he comes home early? Damn!

Her egg white and whipped cream facial reminds him of 1, his mother's doughy face, and 2, a pav. He banishes her to the bathroom to clean up before presenting herself fresh-faced in the kitchen all the better to re-enact their tender homecoming scene.

Claire doesn't believe in any of that kitchen goddess nonsense, but she slinks – at least she hopes she's slinking; if she doesn't slink tonight, she never will – into the kitchen, wearing a loose-knit chemise that's tightly belted at the waist plus her Italian boots. Having allowed her hair to fall loose and fluffy to her shoulders, she feels desirable. Clive's not in the kitchen. Nor is he in the lounge-room where there's no wine, nor candles, nor potpourri.

Disappointed, she struts to the dining room to find him on a recliner nursing a Scotch – nursing it literally – it's being grasped by the pointy bit of his chin that's resting on his collarbone while he turns through *The Age*. He's dextrous in swapping one body part for another.

Claire imagines him suturing a client with his knee-crook. The warped domesticity of this scene evokes a car-wreck, or whack in the face with a bunch of scotch thistles. But she's relentless.

She sneaks up on him and wraps her arms around her man.

"What the f…!"

"How was your day, Hon?" Claire asks, determined to get her lines said before her sacking.

Clive retrieves his glass from under his chin, takes a deep draught and snorts. "A day's a day. It went, thank Christ!"

"Sorry, Clive, I don't know how I should be in a marriage."

"Oh, Claire. Lose your script. And tomorrow turn yourself into toad in the hole. We'll have the laughs and dinner too."

"Clive, I want to be a proper wife."

"Who wants a *proper* wife?" he says, pinching her bottom. "You're only on probation," he says, wagging his finger at her.

When she fails to laugh, he relents. "Surely you Catholic girls know how a marriage goes."

"A marriage doesn't 'go' like a car on automatic. It needs coaxing." Claire knows she's sounding hysterical here. Thank God Alex is out tonight and not witnessing this, she thinks.

"In my experience, you marry, then get on with it."

"What's your experience?"

"Watched the poor suckers from med school who married early."

"'Poor suckers'?"

"The couples who don't fuss over everything get by," he says.

"I don't want to get by. I want love romance. Ecstasy!"

"Good Lord! Ecstasy? That's asking a lot. Take my olds – no ecstasy but they're happy antagonists.

"They quarrel. But they own property in common; they've something worth fighting about; they hold different views on integrity, fairness and politics. But they jog along together well enough. Sex is the key. Whenever they hate each other with a passion, they tear at each other's clothes."

"You know about your parents' love life?"

"They're in a draughty old tower room, and we kids would hear shouting and throwing of silver-backed hairbrushes, then after a while the chairs on the Titanic moved about.

"'Harkest thou, Clive, two separate entities are about to merge,' Alex would say. Things would go quiet for a bit, then the tower room would rock like a yacht in a hurricane. Risky doing it up there like bull elephants mating. Alex and I used to lie below, stifling laughter and praying the ceiling wouldn't fall in. We bet our pocket money on the energy and duration of the encounter. Stormy nights were best. Maybe danger added something."

"Why were they shifting furniture?"

"Twin beds. Ma wanted us to believe their sex life was over. Their beds had mini handcuffs to bind the legs together when needed. Dada made them, said they were to catch tiny thieves."

"Good story. Am I supposed to fight with you?"

"No, Claire, my parents' case is probably unique. But marriage should come naturally."

"Like language acquisition, loving should be effortless." He snakes his arm around her waist.

"Just like hugging is."

"Needing someone to love is universal," he goes on. "I've been so lonely lately."

Claire is shocked by Clive's honesty. It's at odds with how she'd seen him. Alpha male. Proud. Unfailingly capable. How many Australian blokes let their neediness show?

"I love your honesty," she says. Any doubts about marrying a desperate man she isn't going to dwell upon.

"You're perfect, Claire."

"Shouldn't we just live together for a while?"

"No, Claire. Last night I knew it was time to give in, settle down."

Is marriage giving in? Claire wonders. It sounds as if you're accepting failure. "Why me?" she asks, disingenuously. What a fraud I am, she thinks, to beg for a compliment.

"You got me there," is Clive's immediate reply. Claire's shocked, but after this stumble, he finds his lines. "You're the one; I like you. Enormously. I saved your life. We talked, bonked."

"I hate puerile cartoon words like bonk; it sounds like cheap bedsprings pinging. It's not a word for something meaningful."

"Whoo!" Now Clive holds his ears, wiggles his fingers at her and pokes out his tongue. "Meaningful?"

"Yes! Sex is more than bedsprings bouncing up and down. Women are more than cars that handle well…"

"Ooh, you terrifying feminist, you!" He laughs delightedly and pinches her cheek.

"Shack-up sounds like we're sheltering in a hut until the weather turns," she cries.

He stares at her, puzzled.

"Sorry," she says. "I'm pathetic."

"No, you're perfect! So are we. We two snuggling in our cosy cave. Better than establishing a joint domicile."

"You didn't ask me how it went with Suz," she says, aggrieved.

He shrugs. "No need. You went. Suz didn't went."

"You heartless bugger!" she pummels him with her fists.

He folds his arms against his face as if cowering from her. "Okay, what more do I need to know on this subject?"

"My life isn't a subject. You could have pretended to care."

"You want me insincere? God forgive me for not lying."

"Okay, since you're desperate to know, Suz didn't die of heartbreak. She's dating Alex."

"Great! Where is he?"

"Out. Clive, can we eat before I die of malnutrition?"

"Of course, honey," he says, and kisses her hand.

"I'll make that omelette."

The telephone trills.

"Holy shit! Hardly poured my first Scotch before Mater's on the blower. She can sense my desperation for a drink way down in Warrnambool." He reaches down and rips the cord from its socket. "That'll fix her. She triggers pre-emptive guilt in me!"

Claire wonders what pre-emptive guilt is. She replaces the jack in its socket. Immediately, the phone rings. "Answer it, Claire, tell Ma to go away and die."

Claire lifts the handset. "Helloo?"

"Are you Claive's new cleaning lady?"

"I'm Claire, a friend."

"Ay haven't heard of you beef whore."

"Aym a niyew friend," Claire says, yielding to Ma's posh accent. "Here's Claive."

Clive takes the handset. "Bonsoir, Maman!" he says.

From what Claire can hear, the olds are entertaining. Clive waves her over so she can share the handset. A Scrabble tournament is underway. The guests are getting supper for their hosts. How odd! Claire thinks.

"Mama asks if they should cheat a little – since they're playing for real money and they've a stinker of a butcher's bill and Gwen and Len are rich as Croesus. A win with 'synchronicity' could keep them in food for a week," he tells her his hand covering the mouthpiece.

"But you won't have enough tiles," says Clive, even before mentioning that cheating's not on.

Apparently, his mama will nick the extra tiles from the pile. Once she's enjoying her cream cake, Gwen won't notice. They'll exploit Len's three-word score 'city'.

Clive's hackles rise. "Treat your friends well or you'll lose them, you decadent squattocrats."

Chapter 18
Cooking

"How come you forgot the food but not the grog?" asks Claire.

Clive gives her a mock-rueful look. "I went to the bottle shop first. Nothing left for food."

His face droops in a parody of remorse. But his eyes twinkle. "Bankcard's maxed out – the Porsche." He shrugs sheepishly.

Claire searches the cupboards once more as if her diligence may yet unearth something but as she'd feared, finds nothing but the breakfast eggs, an antique Rosella sauce bottle and parmesan. "Okay," she says. "We'll have omelette. What do you eat normally?"

"I eat normally, normally," he says. "Take-aways. Tinned spaghetti in tomato sauce."

"No fruit or veggies?" Claire asks, scandalised.

"There's strawberry ice-cream from the shop," he jokes. He opens the can; its contents emerge with a satisfying whoosh as it plops into the saucepan. He begins heating it but forgets to turn the gas down; it roils along briskly.

"You could grate the cheese, Claire. Grater's in here," he indicates the drawer with his foot.

"Parmesan's in the fridge." He sets about organising the cutlery drawer while Claire saws at a hard wedge of cheese. Clive pulls out a retro chrome and plastic chair and rests his feet on the chair opposite. He holds his head.

"You okay?" she asks.

"Big day at work. I usually don't sleep with my women, not sleep, sleep," he smiles goofily.

"You're the one that didn't get away. Don't worry, I'll get used to you." He stares into the distance as if he's glimpsed an unwelcome vision of his future.

"Listen Clive, we can live together, see how it goes," says Claire. "Drunken promises don't…"

"No. You can't get out of it that easily, Claire. We're *promessi sposi.*"

"I didn't know you spoke Italian."

"We've lots to learn about each other. We'll be okay," he says flatly.

Does Clive always keep the easier tasks for himself, she wonders. He's not 'entertaining' now, she thinks. Was he ever entertaining? She sniggers at her own silliness. Maybe it will be like this between them for all eternity. She, grating frantically, he, fiddling with cutlery.

Clive makes eternity seem long. He doesn't talk while cooking. She mentions this.

"What's to say? We know each other intimately," he protests.

"We had sex. That's not 'knowing'. When Suz and I entertain, we also entertain our friends with stories, set them at ease," Claire says. Clive studies her face as if he's trying to read her, a deeply wrinkled 'v' above his nose. He doesn't get it, she thinks. Why would he bother putting anyone at ease?

She feels dispirited. He's merely a self-centred shit for whom she feels a peculiar attraction. She'll get over him. Best not tell her parents yet. "That Kristen, who called earlier," she says, referring to a woman who'd come to visit Clive, "were you dating long?"

"A fortnight. She wanted to be a doctor's wife. Desperately. But blokes want to win women over. I liked it that you rejected me. But some girls don't bother. That's worse than being rejected."

"I feel like I'm a commodity. As if you bought me with the shopping!"

"No!" He reaches out to pat her on the bottom. "I forgot the shopping. But you! You're a staple like wheat."

"I'd rather be a luxury, like chocolate," says Claire, sighing.

"What do you want from me, Claire? Should I interview you? How much do you enjoy cooking on a one to ten scale?" He adopts a mocking falsetto voice. "Who's your favourite pop group?"

"Van Morrison! And I'd like some more wine," she says, sounding angrier than she feels.

"I'd hate to be married to a lush," he says, but he takes her glass and pours a generous slosh, without spilling a drop and it's his third tipple at the very least. "To new-fledged lovers!"

They clink glasses while Claire concentrates on spilling neither tears nor shiraz.

Clive swirls the shiraz. "Aerate before tasting," he says, oblivious of her distress. He gulps greedily. "Ah!" he says, pretending to read the blurb on the bottle. "It's from the Clare

Valley; it has a generous body, and a smoky aroma that stays with you all night long…"

"Ha-ha!" she acknowledges his attempt at humour.

"Listen, I'm not good at talking, Claire. I'm shy," he admits, pouring more wine. She studies him puzzled. "My only steady girlfriend, Fliss, was in primary school with me."

"What happened?"

"She came to Melbourne. Couldn't settle." He shrugs.

"Thank you. That makes you real, Clive, vulnerable."

"What's good about vulnerable? Boys are 'Strong like King Kong'." He thumps his chest.

When Claire doesn't respond, he groans. "My life is about being in control," he rubs his face.

When he looks up, his eyes are shining with tears.

Clive's earlier buoyancy has gone. Is he sincere? He can act. She decides to believe him for now. She wants this to work out. Going back to Suz already feels like a retreat. "Thanks for being honest, Clive," she says.

"I guess," he shrugs, as if the compliment doesn't please him. "My brother Alex is my rival; he has no real qualifications. But he gives me one hell of an inferiority complex," he says.

"Oh, gees!" he says. In losing concentration, he's burned the tinned spaghetti. *Could anything make the prospect of dinner worse?* Claire wonders.

"Don't worry, I'll steep it in olive oil." He does so and gives it a whirl in a blender.

Pronounces the brown gloop as good as new.

"Won't it still taste burnt?" Claire asks.

"Burnt is one of six basic flavours we humans recognise," he says.

"Yeah, so we can avoid it, surely?" She throws him a derisive look, it's the best she can manage, her annoyance being so lukewarm. Superlative disdain is for literary lovers whose grand passion has dwindled away. Two nobodies hankering after recreational sex can hardly expect to feel such heightened angst. They're not Anna Karenina and Vronsky, are they?

Chapter 19
Living with Clive

Last month Claire moved in with a man with a view to marriage. His name is Clive.

Clive St John Smith, although she didn't know his full name when upon impulse she agreed to their arrangement – a pity he hadn't been called something unattractive like 'Puspimple'.

As her first proposal, it was exciting. A month in it feels like Clive has swallowed her whole, an amoeba reproducing in reverse.

Claire's family in Wang has not been told. She'd promised to finish her course before settling down. She dreads hearing the fake lift in her voice as she convinces her family how gre-at it all is. Claire's not as besotted as a young woman newly in love should be. The logical part of her brain tells her to scarper, but her sex hormones emit contrary signals.

The trouble is her will's been sapped. She's stuck with Clive for now. Love isn't the heady dizzying state she'd expected. Their union relieves her loneliness somewhat. It's like she's a non-driver who's driven a lorry up a narrow lane and can't back out 'til doomsday.

She'd fancied she was stepping boldly into her future, when, in reality, she was backing away from independence, burying herself in a family-shaped hole.

At 19 her life had stretched out before her. She'd had chances choices talents to explore.

Does she fear failing at freedom? Is that why she hitched herself to the first half-decent man she encountered? His gallant rescue of her in Collins Street had allowed her to wonder if fate had played a part in their meeting.

Clive has a secret power: he comes bracketed with a ready-made family unit that includes a kind brother and quirky olds. So, Claire, relieved to be retiring from all that demoralising clubbing and pubbing that her friends are resigned to, had stood by paralysed as the rabbit trap of matrimony's metal teeth closed on her ankle.

It's gratifying to be needed by someone. But the responsibility of having to save Clive is weighing on her. All that tosh about her curing his 'loneliness' was a ploy to mask his real demon: alcohol. Claire had always fantasised about saving lives like the intrepid Nightingale had done. Meanwhile, Clive simply needed her as his unpaid carer. It seems the two are made for each other.

The trouble is: Clive is at his most beguiling and when drinking and playing hail-fellow-well-met with friends. On Saturdays, he's funny, clever and relaxed. In company, Claire can detect no ugly drunken side to him. Alone, he becomes morose, withdrawn, angry. That he's able to deal honestly with Claire she puts down to the fact he reckons she's no quitter.

Claire understands his disinclination to stop drinking. He's an amusing drunk. When in party mode, folks are drawn to him. She understands her role in his life: it's to encourage him to drink a bit less and see he gets home safely when he's legless. He worries that in giving up or in drinking moderately, people will like him only moderately!

Surely, people have recovered from worse than drinking, Claire thinks. Sometimes she dreams she's looking in on someone else's little life, wondering: why does that silly girl imagine her meagre supply of love can save her man? Her dream-self calls out, warning her to run, but frozen in place, she's overwhelmed by an avalanche.

Claire wants Clive's parents to like her; as a new couple, they have few to share their joy.

They're rarely playful at home alone. There's too much loud TV of a night, too many Taco Bill containers flow from the bin. Claire has given up on trying to persuade Clive to take food seriously. Cook. She's lowered her standards to fit in with his. There's too little talking, too little laughter, and bouts of love-making are rationed on work nights. Meanwhile, the drinking of Scotch goes on and on.

Claire mourns the happy coupledom she should have had; there's no teasing, tickling, being playful. Their progress is seemly, like the passage of a royal carriage when they should be hip-hopping with abandon in the City Square. If not now, when will they be joyous?

Mama summons them to Arcadia. She's vexed that her favourite son is marrying outside their set. Claire had regarded Clive's mama as the unshakeable stone in her sandal. Now she wonders if Mama's disapproval is all that holds them together.

Claire does love Clive. She's not cleaving to him merely to spite his mama. She likes sleeping with him now that she's used to him; he smells manly and he's unfaithful only with Jim Beam; he's a conscientious medico, a practised flirt, the situation's novel. She enjoys saving up for bits and pieces that say something about the people she and Clive aspire to be.

She catches nursing colleagues' envious glances. "If she can snaffle a surgeon, why can't we?"

"It's a fluke," they whisper.

"She's not even the prettiest," Nola says.

Mary sticks by Claire loyally. "A clever guy like Clive chose Claire as much for her kindness and sunny nature as for her looks. Men don't have to be shallow."

Suz hasn't recovered from their break-up. She can't utter Clive's name, which limits conversation. Her epithet, 'that man who's paying me to keep your room empty', implies he's crassly buying Claire from Suz and keeping her old room as a bolthole because neither believes they'll last. Claire thinks this assessment rather mean.

Alex is rarely out of Suzy's conversation.

"Last night Alex and I went to dinner," she'll say. "Chinese. Three chef's hats!"

But you're not materialistic, Suz, Claire thinks. "The Flower Drum?" she asks. "What do you two talk about?" Claire asks.

"Shakespeare. Everything. He's a genius!"

"Shakespeare?"

"Alex." She sighs deeply at Claire's inanity. "And next weekend we're off to Port Fairy."

"Meeting the parents?" Claire asks, knowing Alex hasn't mentioned Suz to his parents yet.

These two are always going out. Claire can't ask Suz whether they're also staying in.

Tacitly, Suzy marks off the boundaries of their intimacy.

Chapter 20
Meeting the Olds

They turn off the highway at Colac. Clive is taking the long way around to give Claire a feel for the countryside. It's pretty. Gentle rises fold into one another like egg whites coaxed into a soufflé mix. Drama may be lacking but even tiny slopes yield enticing views of the district.

Despite this, she suspects that *over there* will look the same as *right here* does. She remains expectant, moving through the landscape, daring it to surprise.

Actually, it's not so very different from Wangaratta if you remove the splendour of the Victorian Alps (*Although why would anyone do that?* Claire wonders). The Victorian Alps are mainly discerned as a eucalyptus haze from Wangaratta. Down here the undulating paddocks' gentle rises rest against a backdrop of white wintry sky. It's as if two two-dimensional planes met at the horizon, where they'd been sewn together at a right angle, like scenery in black and white movies, with clumps of mid-range verticals: stands of gums and scrub. The vegetation flanking the creek banks looks to have been daubed in at a later stage.

Australia must have been a shock for the squatters with their Anglophile sensibilities, she thinks. But they couldn't have helped loving this corner of Victoria. Passing through this pretty landscape Claire finds it rather complacent. Clive stays silent, hoping to entice gasps of admiration from her. He gets tired of waiting, turns to her and asks: "Well? Do you like it?"

"Yes, it's very…scenic. Nice." She doesn't want him to get too conceited.

"Nice." Clive's disappointed. "It may not be the Victorian Alps, but I love it," he says.

"Of course, you do," she replies, rubbing his arm comfortingly.

"Here it is."

"What?"

"The hamlet of Smithfield. There's not a lot of it, so don't blink. It's got a church, the pub, the Mechanics Institute, a general store, a garage, a small hardware, and an artist has set up shop in the old bakery. Mama hates anything that brings tourists in. Oh, and there's a primary school and a Greek fish and chip shop, with real booths."

"Your mother would hate a chippy, wouldn't she?"

"Not at all. Con is happy to deliver to Arcadia on Bonnie's days off. Saves the two of them setting fire to the place while heating up their baked beans."

"Oh, I was expecting roast beef down here."

"Not if Bonnie's away. Look: here's the sign, population 151. But the Evans are expecting."

"Why so precise?"

"If you have a baby in the middle of the night, you'd better be out there with a can of paint by morning. It's a two-teacher primary school," he says. "They need every kid they can get on their register to keep the second teacher. There's a rumour that kids who leave school never really 'leave', if you know what I mean."

Claire thinks she knows, but she can't shake the sinister image of a necklace of tiny skulls threaded on strings and decorating a blackboard.

A hundred metres further on, they take a right turn through a rusted wrought iron gateway and clank over a cattle grid leading to an avenue of tall poplars and stately banks of cedars sheltering Clive's family home, which is known around here as the 'mock gothic pile'. From here it reminds her of the Great Hall of Montsalvat in Eltham, where Clive had taken her for a drive one Sunday.

Clive stops the car and lowers the car roof, so they can make their entrance in high style.

"But my hair!" she protests.

"No point in having a convertible if you don't convert."

The drive terminates in a *porte cochere.* She asks Clive how it's spelt. The drive's turning circle has an arrow indicating one should keep right.

They pull up short of the porte-whatever – it isn't raining – not yet and here, out in the open, the Sin Sens (his olds) will get an eyeful of Clive's gorgeous new…fi…car.

Claire hopes it's her they're looking at as they start raving: "How utterly gorgeous! What curves! You get what you pay for in this life," says Clive's mama. "So sleek! Top notch. A conveyance worthy of my son. And such a sleek chassis! What's its cc?"

"Is she paid for yet?" This is Clive's papa and he is grinning pointedly at Claire, saying this.

He's kidding, but she doesn't know whether to glare or smile.

"Daarling, you've come a long way from your Volkswagen days," says his mama. "Let's hope this one serves you as well. What's her name?"

"Moneypenny!"

"What did you pay for the 007 plates?" Clive's papa asks.

"Enough," he says. "She's pretty, and she's built to last," says Clive, putting his arm around Claire. "Mama, Dada, this is Claire, my new fiancée, who runs beautifully."

Claire doesn't like word 'new', but at least he is claiming ownership of her. She clambers out of the car eager to greet the Sins and to be first to offer them her hand like the queen does.

But Clive remains transfixed; he seems to have become involved with his conveyance at a profound level.

"Some chassis the lass has, even better than the car's!" exclaims Hal. "Good long legs so I assume she's a fast woman."

Claire doesn't begrudge Clive's papa his innuendo, seeing he's approving of her.

"Da, show some respect for Claire," Clive says in a facetious tone. He runs his fingers across the wood-grain dashboard but his shoulders are shaking with laughter.

Dada moves awkwardly down the terrace steps to the car. Claire diagnoses a skeletal problem of some sort. "I'm Hal," he says. "Delighted to meet you, Claire dear. Welcome to the family. Pardon my sense of humour; it's a little outré." His eyes smile, saying this.

"Of course. May I call you Hal?" Already Claire likes him. She shakes the tiny paw he offers her; he raises her hand to his lips in a courtly way. He's a tortoise emerging from his shell. Sweet and benign.

Mama is built like a front-end loader; she's dolled up like Queen Elizabeth in a ram's horn hairdo that's lacquered heavily.

Claire's judging her unkindly but the Sins are having too much fun with her.

Cynthia wears a paisley-printed one-size-fits-all jersey frock. She favours Claire with a smile that seems about to turn into a burp, but once it resolves itself, she receives a brisk handshake, and a howdy-do. Then she turns and spreads herself over her firstborn – he's still immobilised in his car – like margarine on toast. She pries his hand from the gear stick before giving him a kiss that lands wetly on the lips!

Chapter 21
Settling In

Claire has met her fiancée's parents, who are more excited about Clive's Porsche 911 than her, and the way Hal runs his hands caressingly over the car's flanks, she's glad.

She's Clive's '*new*' fiancée. One of a long line. Were her predecessors tried and found *wanting*? Or, did they flee, *wanting* different in-laws? Claire supposes it's fair that the olds withhold enthusiasm if she's just another fiancée. Even she can hardly believe in the engagement.

Cynthia calls Bertie, the outdoorsman. Bertie has been working on a nearby holly hedge all along, judging by heaped prunings lying on the terrace; he's so thin and dark, he blends with the shrubbery. Bertie acknowledges Clive with a curt nod, picks up their bags from the car's luggage rack and takes them inside.

"You have separate bedrooms," Mama says, her mouth set in a straight line. Claire tenses up, fearing this will enrage Clive, a worshipper at the altar of 'free love'. She steadies herself for stormy weather. Clive's emotional barometer has recently concertinaed his fair and fine settings thereby enlarging his scope for bracing moods.

But Clive still plays adoring swain to his rather coquettish mama. "Three hours in a sardine can but worthwhile to see your profile," he says, holding Cynthia's chin aloft and turning it so he can examine her face from every angle, except full-on, from whence she looks like a pug dog with an overbite. "You're still the beauty in the Florentine cameo," he says.

Is this the oedipal relationship Alex has hinted at? Claire wonders.

"Hush, Clive. If you wanted to see my ageing visage, you'd visit oftener."

"Mama! It's hard establishing oneself in a profession."

"I saw the hoops your father had to jump through to succeed in town. But he had a name down here already. We fixed you, Hal, didn't we?" She smiles fondly at her man.

"You sure finished my career off!" says Hal. He can fight his own battles, Claire decides.

Hal was a scientist with an engineering company, Clive explains. The olds met at a house party down here. Mama was from Camperdown originally. One thing led to another.

"Dada was hired by Ma's family firm. He still wonders if he got the best of it, don't you, Da?"

"Cynthia was part of a package deal," Hal says, placing his arm around his wife's shoulders.

"I've yet to exhaust all her charms!" he says, diplomatic in the extreme.

"Ma, we're sharing a room like we do at home," Clive announces, late in replying to his mother's announcement. It's like he's in a movie whose sound track has gone out of sync.

But once he's extracted himself from the Porsche's fuselage he stops grumbling. It seems his protest was a reflex; he carries the file of medical papers up the steps, apparently resigned to the arrangements.

Mama and Dada follow climbing slowly. At the top Cynthia pushes her glasses onto the bridge of her nose and examines Claire. She is looking for suspension failures. Subtly, Claire wriggles her bra straps higher so they pull their weight. She draws her shoulders back, tucks her bottom in, tries smiling like a film star who's sure she's universally admired.

Cynthia smiles sceptically. She's onto Claire. "You're tall, but you don't inhabit your body," is her diagnosis. She studies Claire as if her eagle eyes might render her a heap of carrion.

Claire wills herself taller, stronger, prouder.

Cynthia raising her hand to shield her eyes, looks away across the expanse of paddocks. "I hear you're from a mixed farmlet, dear. We're graziers. At least we were. Our southern boundary lies along that creek," she tells Claire, pointing; the other boundary's out of sight. *She's saying something, but what?* Claire wonders. That the ownership of vast acreages is a matter for pride? That money is the measure of a man?

"Mama, you haven't yet welcomed Claire."

"Friends of Clive are always welcome," she enunciates, careful not to seem too welcoming.

"How are you Laydee Saint John Smith?"

"How am I? It's nice to be asked, sincerely, for a change. 'Howdy do' down here means, don't tell the truth even at death's door. But since you asked me, I've dicky hips, swollen ankles, arthritic knees, palsy, dropsy."

"Dropsy platey," says Hal, and they all laugh.

"We're the Sn Jns. Call me Cynthia, I can't abide Cyn."

"Sin's unforgiveable," says Clive, bursting to laugh aloud.

"Then the bedroom situation will suit you. Claire's near us. You're in the annexe to Bonnie's room. You'll be attending the Uniting Church tomorrow, shriven?"

"Uniting, not united," says Clive, winning him a wry smile from Hal. "Shrivelled not shriven."

"Claire is Catholic. All's up for grabs. I may convert," he stirs.

"Ooo!" Cynthia looks dismayed.

"Mama, can we go in? We're starving," Clive says.

"Arriving at 1.30 pm, I thought you'd have eaten."

"We don't eat the rubber sandwiches at servos. Surely, you've bread and ham."

"I'm sure you'll find something edible." Cyn wheels her arm expansively as if they had the whole property from which to go a-foraging.

"Thanks," says Clive. "Now the bedroom sit…"

"There's no situation. Not since your Cuban fiancée hooted all night long…"

Clive looks down at his loafers but he goes quiet. Claire's sad to see him so humbled.

Clive's father is looking off into the distance, stocktaking. He's an extinct bird – an affable dodo perhaps, though the way his neck emerges questing from its collar, he seems like a tortoise testing the ambient emotional temperature before laying his neck on the line.

They head toward to the oak and metal door. It takes some effort opening it. They file through. Clive, keen to see where Claire's been tucked away, dumps his baggage on the flagstone floor and follows them through a grand hall bigger than Claire's entire home. It funnels guests from out to in and separates entertaining rooms from workrooms, Claire supposes.

Its array of ancestors' portraits, poorly lit by low-wattage wall sconces, proclaims that here is a family that can afford to import crates of old portraits. The panelling shouts substance; twin stairways curve right and left, duplicating the building's impressive features, as if waste didn't matter. The left side's been roped off. A dome allows light to filter through. It's odd finding classical features in a building looking like neo-gothic Montsalvat. It's a bit of this slapped up against a bit of that, according to which architectural style was in the ascendant when additions were done, Claire guesses. The dome is held up by colonnades that support a mezzanine gallery upstairs.

They shuffle to up Claire's room via the right staircase.

"I hope we'll get to know you, Claire," says Mama, "although one weekend's all we usually get with Clive's girls, before poof," she mimes a dandelion's filaments being blown away.

At this botanical image, a sneeze almost undoes Claire. Does Mama emit toxins?

"Mama, I'm serious about Claire," says Clive, catching up with Cyn on the landing. He hooks his arm through her elbow crook. "Do treat Claire well. I'm no longer single."

Claire's heart swells.

"Oh, it's all relative, we're all relatives, said Oppenheimer or was it whatsisname?" Cynthia asks her husband.

"Einstein, you mean," Hal says, and they both laugh as if pre-scripted wrangling were a crucial part of their daily ritual. Dicky hip or not, Dada's determined to make the most of moments of family conviviality.

Reaching the top, Cyn says, "What about wee Fiona from the Border Country?"

"Claire's from our border country, Wangaratta, Mama."

"But from a mixed farm! Fiona was of solid Scottish stock."

"Like lamb soup," says Clive.

Claire hears a gargling sound. She hopes Hal doesn't choke on his laughter.

Chapter 22
Cold Collations

They eat in the conservatory, whose dusty glazing obscures the view. The room resembles a Salvos Store; it's furnished with chintz sofas, wicker, an Australian Blackwood sideboard, grandfather clocks, and enough walking frames to furnish a nursing home.

There's an open fireplace; it's well alight and crackling. Claire is drawn to it; she wishes she had the cheek to warm her bum – both bum cheeks, actually. She smiles at how shocked Clive's mama would be. Greedily, she eyes off a nearby armchair but forces herself to wait until invited to sit.

Garden views are obscured by dirty windows. A Virginia creeper has grafted itself onto the outer wall. Claire feels imprisoned in a novelty snow dome that's being crushed by a futuristic plant oozing malice. Some shoots have entered via a cracked window that's been inexpertly taped up. Apparently, a decision's been made to leave it be. *Does this room possess its own microclimate*, she wonders. Some leaves are clinging on well into June.

There's nothing to indicate there are extensive pastures outside. Some imbecile has let bamboo run wild. It has colonised whatever garden once existed beyond the glazing. Claire shakes her head in disbelief.

She goes to the window-wall. As expected, farm views are obscured. She understands the Sins' reluctance to bring the outdoors inside. Farmers love/ hate their land. It's a sinkhole in which funds glug away. The hardiest crop their asset grows is weeds. And disappointment.

But this much overgrowth reveals a pathological hopelessness. With a Whipper Snipper, she could save this gothic ruin, endear herself to Clive's parents, who'd then allow her to sleep with her beloved. She so dreads sleeping alone in this spooky spidery dump. But, no, she tells herself: behave, Claire. Don't interfere.

The salad's lettuce leaves are limp, the quartered thick-skinned tomatoes are accompanied by ham that's grey at the edges, pink in the middle. Could she carve out a slice comprising just the pink bits?

No. Best tell them she's vegan. She should be anyway. Logically, it's the only ethical way to go with population pressures on finite pastures. She's vowed to become vegan the minute her bacon sandwich cravings fade.

Claire passes the plate to Clive saying, "It's all yours, darling, remember, we said we would become vegan from the end of the financial year."

"We did?" He shoots her a puzzled look.

"Yes," she says, sticking her tongue firmly in her right cheek so the olds can't see, and hoping Clive will take the hint.

He sighs. "Good, at least as a vegan, you'll be cheap to feed." He fills his plate with seething micro-life. "You wouldn't believe my fiancée's appetite, Mama."

The conversation turns to Clive's exams; a sensitive subject as he failed one recently but hadn't told Claire. She expects he'll be discomfited at this public exposure. He's not.

"Didn't want to worry you with hospital stuff, darling," he explains, with a blithe wave of his arm.

"What about the ten K you owe us?" Hal asks.

"Can't bleed a stone, Da," says Clive. "If I were you, I'd fix that window for starters. Then you can stop heating the outdoors."

"We've far more extensive repairs to make, Clive," says Hal. "Lose that idiotic car. Look around you. Your inheritance going to rack and ruin," he indicates places where the grout is crumbling its way out of the bluestone walls.

Clive crosses and re-crosses his legs. He rubs his temples. "That car is everything to me," he says, anguished.

"Then it's no time to embark on a wedding," says Cynthia.

"Oh, that's okay," Claire pipes up. "Mum sews. We'll host the wedding at the farm. We have a veranda with a view of the dam and a Weber for the roast. Sulphur crested cockatoos…" her sentence tails off. Even to Claire's mind, the image isn't appealing.

The expression on Mama's face is thunderous. "Not even when hell freezes over will I let an amateur to sew me a Butterick frock for my son's wedding celebration with tomato sauce, flies around a barbeque, stagnant water and bird poop to contend with!"

"Perhaps it wouldn't work," Claire admits, her eyes lowered, studying her sneakers. "I haven't mentioned the engagement to my family yet. They'll be thrilled, once they know…" Oops!

She's said too much.

Cyn and Hal give each other significant glances saying: what sort of girl who's snaffled the scion of an important family wouldn't boast about her coup? Even Clive looks hurt that Claire hasn't told her parents of her marital success.

She'd promised her parents she'd qualify before marrying, she says, but she succeeds in sounding shifty. "I phoned," she adds, "but my youngest brother took the call. Maybe he forgot…"

This is a white lie. Claire's five-year-old brother would forget anything told him that hadn't to do with insects, or toys. Her fib soothes Clive's hurt feelings hardly at all. Claire feels bad. She would rather imagine the invisible God she no longer quite believes in cross with her for lying than see her boyfriend hurt.

"Your parents don't know?" Clive is aghast. "So that's why they've never phoned to con…"

"I guess…"

"A damned good guess, seeing you kept it from them. Ashamed of me?"

"I need a trousseau first," Claire retreats to the bride-to-be's catch-all excuse. A blatant lie.

Clive glares darkly, but Cyn, getting the importance of trousseaux to gels, nods vigorously.

"I'm 19, Clive," Claire pleads, wishing Cynthia and Hal weren't providing such a keen audience for their 'chat'. Two pairs of eyes flicker between the affianced most eagerly.

"You're too young," says Mama. Her smile is now so wide that all 32 teeth are getting an outing. Now that Cynthia has efficiently rid the family of Claire, the latter is extra keen to wed their heir.

"We're engaged, Mama," says Clive. "Get used to it."

Happier, now that the veneer of family civility has been chipped away, Cynthia unclenches her jaw and relaxes into the sofa. Her tongue roams across her teeth as if a lateral movement over her personal Stonehenge mirrored the swathe her son may yet cut among ranks of debutantes.

She recovers sufficiently to start spooning up yesterday's potato salad from the silver salver. It's only mildly oxidised, thanks to the density of the mayonnaise in which it's doused.

Meanwhile, she clanks her spoon loudly against the dish.

Why must she draw attention to herself? Claire wonders. Even silent, her seething nerve endings could power an electrical storm.

Cynthia hands Claire a poison chalice in the form of a limp salad. Under the lettuce, a reservoir of greyish liquid forms a lake.

Chapter 23
Conversation in Conservatory

They're still in the conservatory. Finding common ground conversationally is like playing hopscotch leg-less. Ought they stick with Liberal Country Party matters, try duck shooting, point to point or will animal husbandry do the trick?

"About church tomorrow…" Mama recapitulates.

Clive, chastened over his loan repayments, says, "Okay, Ma. But Claire's Catholic."

"Don't worry, I'm just about over my Catholicism," Claire says.

"When will you have completely recovered?" asks Clive.

"Soon. Alex is curing me."

"He's bullying you, I suppose?"

"No. He says sensible things about religion being the opiate of the people."

"He shouldn't be influencing you," says Clive, frowning.

"He talks, I decide," Claire says. "But, honestly, Clive? Do you want me Catholic?"

"Yes. I quite like the idea of huge Catholic families. A broody wife. The whole disaster."

"Really?" she whispers. "You said you were an atheist."

"I'm a fairly half-hearted one, but now I've found you, I'm rather keen on the idea of family and piety. Having a wife who's a believer was part of your charm."

"But I wasn't a believer. I wish I'd known exactly what you wanted in a wife." Claire's shoulders heave. Clive hops out of the beanbag in a single leap, hurries to her, pats her shoulder. "Sorry, Hon. We fell too hard to check our spousal wish-lists and must-haves."

"I feel as ambiguous about kids as I do about religion," Claire says, tearily. "I'd have said so, if I'd known it mattered. There's never time for us to talk. If there had been I'd have told you church-going was a habit in Wang. An outing. There were so many of us. We'd squash into the back of the old truck, not legal, really, but in Wang…"

Cyn and Hal shoot anguished looks at each other.

Claire is laying the yokel thing on thick. Despite her tears she's enjoying her power to make Cynthia's lip curl. "We got away with murder…Knowing the cops so well…" Her sentence peters out.

Cynthia's eyes seek Hal's, but he's dabbing at his whisky-spattered tie with a hanky.

"We went to mass for the ritual of it. For friendship. Melbourne is different."

"God's not omnipresent in Melbourne?" says Mama, pleased with herself.

"I haven't come across Him yet," Claire says.

"Cynthia's Uniting now," says Hal. "Remember how I'd drive her to Warrney Continuing Pressies so she could ogle those bag-piping men in skirts? We've a Uniting Church in Smithfield these days. They all hug during services; there's a goodly roster of godly gals for floral arrangements. Scones. Tea. The minister has a speech impediment. When all's been said and nothing understood, Cynthia meditates. It's cheaper than her Community Classes. There are few really avid Methodistical types to catch fervour from. Me? I like the way they belt out hymns. 'Immortal, invisible…'" he warbles.

He's shushed by a look from Cynthia.

"The intention counts with the Almighty, not the execution."

"But you don't believe in Him," says Cynthia.

"Precisely. I sing, to annoy Him."

Claire's barracking for the dipso dodo. Logic's not his strongest point but he's the best ally she'll find down here. "Stand up to the old b…" is Claire's silent message to Hal.

"Cynthia's piety used to cost us a fortune in petrol," Hal says.

I'll bet, Claire thinks. All that driving across blasted heaths at midnight with one's coven searching for the eye of toad and the requisite essence of newt's bum would impoverish anyone.

Claire knows it's childish to let mild dislike of Mama triumph, but she's indulging herself.

"Be boring if we were all Pressies," says Hal, rising gingerly from his armchair and shuffling to the sideboard for another splash of Scotch to decorate his tie.

He has a tremor. Claire worries along with him to the sideboard and all the way back to his chair until he settles into it; she's concerned for this dear old man's dignity, although it's too late for his tartan tie and the Viyella shirt with the elbow-patched cardigan.

Safe again, he takes up the pipe he's been filling and refilling while they chatted. It's still unlit. Perhaps the ritual tamping and filling is pleasure enough.

"Well," says Clive. "What next?"

"Alex is coming with Susan."

"Suz!" Claire feels put out. She'll be outshone by her petite and elegant former friend.

"Been seeing her for a month, the old dog!" says Hal.

Seeing her! Suz is a size 4. He'll have seen her all right, thinks Claire. And felt and smelt.

The idea of her friend's happiness leaves her feeling depleted. It's proof she's a bad person.

At least Suz will quash all conversations hinging on animal husbandry, she thinks. *She won't care whose bull is in, on, over, or covering some bloated cow that's been put up to it, under it.*

"Susan is a Forsyth from Berwick abhorrently. Old family," says Cyn, pleased.

Claire feels incandescent with rage. No. She doesn't – it's a cliché, and Claire has sworn to eschew all clichés on pain of death. But, if forced to listen to any more drivel, she'll shrivel.

"Death's as old as it gets in my family before it starts to stink," she says, shocking everyone including herself.

Silence lands like a silken parachute over them.

Emboldened by her success in shocking them, she continues. "Mum and Dad had a pa and ma who had one of each ad infinitum; they've traced their line back to whatever swamp they crawled out of!" Shit, she thinks, why mention the swamp just when I was going so well?

Cynthia gives Claire the silent treatment though tendon activity in the region of her neck reveals some amusement at Claire's swampy provenance. Eventually, there's a loud guffaw from Hal. "Well said, Claire. Too much loose unscientific talk goes through to the keeper around here. None of us arrived without a progenitor or two. Cynthia's saviour excepted."

Claire intercepts a placatory glance Clive makes towards Cyn. It says, *yes, Claire is rough around the edges but give her a chance, Ma. Together we'll smoothe her out.*

"So, what set everything going?" Cynthia asks.

"It's all about space/time continua," says Hal vaguely. All nod sagely.

"No one ever explained this to me adequately, or am I stupid?" Ma's face is empurpled now.

For once Claire feels sorry for Cynthia. "I know what you mean," she says. Naturally, Cyn assumes she's agreeing with the proposition she's stupid! And for Claire to deny she meant what Cyn thinks she meant would be to admit she'd have been justified in doing so or why be thinking along such subversive lines in the first place? Claire feels a headache coming on.

Hal, oblivious of any silent communication says, "Good on Alex. A bit of fluff! Just as we were wondering…"

"No, Hal, we don't wonder about things like that…"

"Like what?" asks Clive mock-innocently.

"You know, dear. And don't call visiting girls 'fluff', Hal," she says.

"Alex won't be down for an hour or so. What shall we do this afternoon?" asks Clive.

"Claire might enjoy a run along the coast," says Hal. "Not that you'd be doing the running, my dear, the car would," he smiles at Claire, goofily. "We'll show you the beauty spots. Have scones and clotted cream at the Dunes Tea-House." Hal seems nicer by the minute.

"Okay," says Clive, "Get your coat, Mama. A bit of what you like won't hurt. Do the books later," Clive pleads. Clearly, he loves his mother despite their public wrangling.

"Too busy."

"Ma, I brought Claire here so you could get to know her."

"'Start', you said. Well, I've started. Overall, she's rather …nice." Cynthia sounds unhappy at this verdict. "She's natural…" Her words are drowned out by hailstones pinging off the roof.

Chapter 24
Alex Arrives

They're about to play Monopoly. It's fitting as the Sins monopolise a swath of land in the Western District. There's a battering at the front door.

It's Alex and Suz, arrived before Claire can make amends for her snippy start with Cyn.

Maybe the new arrivals will help disperse the static in the air.

Clive introduces Suz. Alex stands proprietorial and proud. Suz charms everyone by doing nothing in particular well. Soon they're all smiling and laughing. Claire has tried analysing Suz's social charisma; it's not effortful. It consists of no showy gestures nor flamboyant catch phrases. There's nothing to emulate. Suz becomes the still quiet centre of any room; she's like an insect emitting calming frequencies to neutralise all in its vicinity, Claire thinks, making a rough stab at an analogy.

****

"Be yourself," Clive had said as they'd approached The Lodge.

"I don't have a fully settled me to be," Claire had replied.

"Well, just act like you do with me," he'd said.

"Should I cuddle them?"

"No! Be natural, you dill."

Claire held her head in her hands. "It's easy to say, 'be natural'."

"What's the big deal?" Clive had taken his hand off the steering wheel and rubbed her back.

"What if they don't like me?"

"*They* don't even like each other much."

Claire turned to stare at Clive, the scrunch lines above her forehead are deep. "Really?"

"Really," said Clive.

"But families are meant…"

Clive raised his eyebrows. "Families aren't all boringly bourgeois like yours."

"Mine aren't even bourgeois. Just peasant hippies. *Declassee!*"

They drove in silence for a bit. "I won't…change," said Claire. There's a 'challenge me if you dare' tone to her words. Her ears seemed to have undergone a pressure change; she'd felt her voice echoing in her head.

"If you won't change there *is* a real you," said Clive. "Just be it."

"Yes," said Claire, remembering a high school text. "'It's better to be authentic than liked'."

"'It is better to be feared than loved'," Clive had quoted back at her.

Gosh! Claire had thought, *Is this a sign of erudition in my man!* "But Machiavelli was telling princes how to cling to power; he wasn't telling Cinderella how to wow her in-laws," she'd said.

"I'll wipe off your smuts before we arrive, Cinders."

"Thanks, Clive. You're quite kind."

"Quite?"

"Alex is the k…"

"Bloody Alex," Clive had removed his arm from her back and accelerated around a bend.

****

Thanks to Suz, the mood in the room warms up. It's all about the Importance of Being the Real Suz, Claire guesses. Bertie is gonged in from his outdoor work to make a cup of tea.

"Bonnie the maid is away. No one else is qualified to boil water," Clive whispers in Claire's ear.

"Guess what, Mater, Clive says. Suz is Claire's best friend. How great is that?"

Mama's eyebrows, arching, indicate that she could list several things, but she holds her tongue.

"It's no coincidence, I suppose," she says purse-lipped.

"No," Claire says. "Alex met Suz when we were out together in the ute."

"You and Alex used to go out together, did you?" Cynthia asks, screwing her eyes up and squinting at Claire.

"Not out in the dating sense. We were out driving; though if you include my chest, we went out twice that day." Oops! Claire could slap herself.

"You've a bad chest?"

"No, I didn't have one…" Oops, wrong way, go back, Claire thinks. Seeing pitfalls looming, she looks to Clive for help. But he won't meet her gaze. With a front row seat at Claire's abyss, he's relishing the mirth this misunderstanding will generate.

"No," says Alex, hopping in to help. "It's not that Claire's chest was bad aesthetically. Not that I was looking at her chest. I'm no judge of female attributes. But it wasn't big enough."

"Why are we discussing the dimensions of Clive's fiancée's bosom?"

"Mama. Claire's chest is perfect – not her bosom. But at least she has one now…"

"Has she had enhancement surgery?" asks Mama.

"No, Claire's bosom was always fine…I mean I guess it was…I didn't always know her.

"And even if I had I wouldn't have…judged. She needed a chest for items women…need…"

The too cool Alex is in meltdown but he's hanging on, his gaze fixed on a distant point, as if he were committed to following a rainbow to its end, however rough the intervening terrain.

"I needed a chest of drawers, for undies," Claire says. "There was no room for me in Clive's chest – he wears boxers. They require more space than jocks." Claire moves her hands in and out to denote the size differential between boxers and jocks; it looks like she's playing accordion at an ethnic festival.

"Why doesn't everyone wear jocks?"

"Jockettes have deleterious effects on male fertility," says Clive.

"Clive! If you must have a fiancée, do organise space for her. So, when did you meet Suz?" Cynthia asks Alex.

"The day I drove Claire to Suz's place to get her things."

"Why take Claire if you were getting Suz's things?"

"I was getting Claire's things."

"What was Suzy doing with Claire's things?"

"They'd been sharing a flat." Alex's voice emerges as if through a knife sharpener.

"Oh. Why didn't you say so?" says Cynthia.

Alex opens his arms as if crucifixion was imminent and desirable, then he lets them fall.

"So, that's how you met Suz? Nothing to do with chests?"

"Nothing, Ma. I took Claire to Prahran because Clive was on call."

"Hope you're not sneaking off with Claire when Clive's out?"

"No, Cynthia," Claire says. "Alex and I weren't sneaking around. We went out that day quite publicly because…" Claire gives a freakish cackle. But doubled over, it looks like she's crying.

Alex shakes his head. "Clive couldn't move her…"

"Emotionally?" Cynthia asks. "Well, now, she's deeply moved. Buck up, dear," she says.

"Claire needed me to get her things from Suz's place, of course," Alex protests.

"There's no 'of course' in any of this," says Cynthia, quirking up the corner of her mouth.

"You see," says Alex, now in public-speaking mode. "Imagine it's the morning after Claire and Clive's great love has been declared. He cave man. He wants her now. But Clive is working, besides he'd never use his Porsche as a removal van. Anyhow, that day Claire needed my help to walk since she was wearing thongs and socks…"

"Why?"

"Well, it's winter if you hadn't noticed."

"Wearing thongs in winter!"

"Had to. She couldn't get her boots on over Clive's jeans."

"Why wear Clive's jeans in the first place?"

"She'd been wearing a skimpy frock the previous night with wild animal skins on it."

Thanks, Alex, for that unnecessary detail! Claire thinks.

"Was it a dress-up party?"

"No! All I'm saying is she'd have died of cold without jeans. I went along to hold her arm, keep her upright…"

"Was the gel inebriated, then?"

"No! But she might have fallen out of my thongs on that windy track because I've got big feet," Alex says, his voice becoming more emphatic with each word. At last he leans back in his beanbag looking like a marathoner who's finished badly.

"I know, dear."

"If I hadn't driven Claire, I wouldn't have met Suz," he says tiredly.

Suz beams hugely.

Mama struggles out of her chair, goes up to Suz. Takes both hands in hers. Smiles winningly. "Alex seems happy," Cynthia says, "despite all this nonsense about chests."

"Hear, hear," says Hal, red-faced and wiping his eyes.

Chapter 25
Snakes and Ladders

The Monopoly board can't be found. Hal suggests they play Twister, despite his hip. *Is he a randy old goat, notwithstanding his gentlemanly demeanour?* Claire wonders. He seems keen to compete with his sons in some oedipal by-play. An image of all six writhing like pythons flashes into Claire's mind. It's not pretty.

Clive will play. *Does he have a thing for Suz?* Claire wonders. Once this thought enters her brain, she cannot let it go, although there's no evidence for it to fatten upon. Is she marrying an untrustworthy man? A viper of jealousy bores into her gut.

"I'm with Cynthia," she says, "Twister's for kids." Her words earn Claire a nod of approval from Cyn, who announces she has an errand to run. In no time she's heard speaking with animation on the telephone.

"Be a sport, Claire," says Clive. "It's the only 'fun' we're having this weekend." He's referring to Mama's bedroom arrangements – they're in Cyn's 'isolation wards'. Anyone ascending the creaky stairs from the gallery level in the dark would crack a borer infested stair tread and fall to the bottom of the social ladder.

Alex and Suzy, in keeping with their Most-Highly-Approved-Couple status, have been allocated a king-sized bed in old stables recently converted to self-catering flats; flats that are *Charming and Exclusive,* so the sign at the gate says. So far passing trade hasn't braked even momentarily. Cynthia seems pleased that all nouveaux automatically know they'd be outclassed.

Eventually, it's the ice-cold flagstones that swing the deal for *Snakes and Ladders*. A grin bisects Cynthia's face. "I love this game. Primeval," she says, licking her lips. "An all-out contest between good and evil."

"It's an Indian game originally," Hal informs Claire. "'Good' deeds are rewarded, the 'evil' punished. Be good in this life, get an easier ride next time around if you care to believe so."

"What qualities are considered 'evil'?" Claire asks.

"Anger, lust, drunkenness, debt, pride, greed, killing and lying are vices," says Hal, ticking them off on his fingers.

"No hope for me. I've practised them all," says Clive.

"Not killing?" Claire's aghast.

"Only by accident, in theatre," Clive says, shrugging. "Someone must die for progress."

He's just teasing, Claire decides. "And the virtues?"

"The three As. Asceticism. Asceticism. Asceticism."

"No Presbyterian forgiveness?" she ventures.

"Never was. Pressies are assigned pass/ fail marks at birth," Hal shrugs disconsolately. "The Elect of God," he says his mouth turning down at the corners. "No points for behaving well, so they don't; nor should we the non-elect – wouldn't help us anyway. Be as good or as wicked as you wish," he says. "Won't make a scrap of difference." Hal gives them all a sardonic stare.

"A gross generalisation!" says Cynthia, coming in on the end of this. She has an uncanny ability to come up with the right cliché.

"So, there's no incentive to do good?" Claire asks.

"No," says Cyn. "Good people feel virtuous. But it doesn't get them through the Pearly Gates."

She grins triumphantly.

"Let's get this kiddies' game show on the road," says Hal.

"If it's all about chance," says Cyn, "why do I win oftener than not?"

Hal acknowledges this truth regretfully. "Cynthia possesses all virtues going by the wins book we keep."

"What's a wins book?" Claire asks.

"Don't ask, Claire," says Clive, rolling his eyes. "You'll only encourage them." He finds a12x12 board in the armoire, sets it on a spindly games-table whose top hinges out. They gather around. Clive and Claire sit on an old couch, Hal and Cynthia take wicker armchairs, Alex and Suz share the beanbag.

Claire notices, while trying not to, the easy way Alex and Suzy settle on the bag. She rests an elbow on his knee – they seem too comfortable for a new couple.

Claire's token falls on more long ladders than short snakes. Clive's don't. He's a bad sport, getting red in the face and banging the cup on the table.

"That's an empire flip top table you're laying into," says Cynthia. "Goes back to Napoleon."

"Bloody despot's wonky table's skewing my throws," Clive grumbles.

Alex snorts. "That table is worth five Porsche repayments," he says.

Clive sits up and regards the table with respect. "Monthly repayments?" he asks. He gives the dice a wild shake but throws a 'one'. "Bloody Napoleon!"

Claire observes Cynthia closely. Whenever her token lands on a snake, she slides it across the line. When caught cheating, it's due to the warped board that's been made in Upper Chad. She seizes the cup in both hands and shakes it, a look of ferocity on her moon face.

Claire plays to lose, nervous of the actual cost of snatching a win from such poor losers as this lot. Ultimately, it seems Hal's dead ancestors are barracking for him. A shaft of eerie afternoon light floods the conservatory as clouds part to admit the sun's last rays; they proclaim Hal's triumph; it's written into the 'wins book' in Hal's scratchy hand.

There's a knocking on the front door. Cynthia struggles from her chair and, turning more agilely than a woman with her catalogue of complaints ought, she applies her finger to Hal's shoulder, jabbing him back into his chair. "This is *me*," she says, and scurries out, bumping the tokens clean off the table as she goes.

"Now she'll fudge the outcome," he says, gloomily. "The cunning ways Cyn cheats you'd never believe. Unless I'm watching with an eagle eye, she moves my chess pieces around of a night. It's Rafferty's Rules."

"She cheats in front of you?" Claire asks.

"Whenever I go to the loo or to replenish my glass," says Hal, "whichever eases my most urgent need, Cynthia swaps things about cunningly." An undertone of awe in is heard in Hal's voice. "She convinces me I've made the stupid move she has me making. I've sent away for a land camera, Claire. From now on I'm documenting the state of the board. That'll fix her."

Claire wonders at Clive's progenitors; both look decidedly dotty.

Chapter 26
Fliss Arrives

Cynthia enters the conservatory beaming. "Guess what?"

"Guess what what?" asks Clive.

"A little visitor happened by," says Cynthia.

"A short-ass?"

"Don't be rude, Clive. A visitor who's petite but substantial."

"Really?" Clive drawls like a rich twit in a BBC series. "Why announce him fulsomely?"

"He's a she. Quite someone in these parts. She's making us high tea as we speak," says Cyn.

"I only want Bonnie at teatime." Clive makes a slashing gesture to silence Ma.

"We'd be lost without your little friend," says Cynthia.

"Uh-oh!" says Clive. He gives Claire a brief assessing glance; it carries a wealth of meaning.

He's saying: oops, I should have told you, earlier, Hon.

"Felicity awaits in the kitchen, with a wee small favour."

"Let her ask her wee favour publicly," says Clive.

"Fliss just now happened by with her organic eggs. They're super fresh, laid by her free-range hens; now she happens to be turning them into sandwiches with her home-baked sour dough bread warm from the oven. Let's not lay waste their freshness with jaw jaw!"

Why is Cyn repeating 'just now' 'laid', and 'happens' over and over? Claire wonders. *Is she faking spontaneity?*

"Hallelujah!" says Hal. "I could murder a sanger."

Me too, thinks Claire.

"All right, then. Tonight's the LCP's Bachelors' and Spinsters' Ball. Fliss happens to have mislaid her partner."

"He went free-ranging onto greener pastures, then?" asks Clive.

There's too much delaying mislaying and free-ranging, Claire decides. She's sitting calmly, keeping her emotions in check for fear they'll free-range from hysteria to jealousy and back.

"Fliss was your first fiancée, Clive," his mother reminds him.

Claire, having her first adult onset asthma attack, struggles to breathe, awaiting Clive's denial. But he squeezes her hand. Looks deep into her eyes. "Sorry, Hon."

"How many fiancées altogether?" she asks.

"Oh. I..." He waves his hands about as if dispersing smoke.

Cyn barges on while Claire sits like an unlovable lump. Ugly, un-petite, yet insubstantial.

"I said to her, 'Fliss, now I've met Claire, I know she'll let Clive partner you at the B&S.'"

"You said what?"

Mama prepares her final address to the jury. "Fliss is our community's mainstay."

"Ha!" Clive says, caressing Claire's hair. She doesn't lean in to acknowledge his touch. She sits straight backed, eyes forward.

"Fliss has become pals with dear Tammy F." Ma looks at Claire, taps her nose meaningfully.

Claire examines her blue runners, says nothing.

"For poor Fliss to miss the ball when everyone's in attendance...Do postpone your engagement for the one evening," Cynthia implores.

"What? Call a truce to catch up with old girlfriends, Ma? No."

Claire's heart, diaphragm and chest expand at Clive's protestation of loyalty under duress.

"You persuaded Fliss' hens to lay so late in the day, it's a bleeding miracle. Kept us on light rations, so we'd swallow anything you cook up. All to test the strength of my feelings for Claire. Well, I love her." He draws Claire close and kisses her temple tenderly. "Tell Fliss, no."

Claire wonders if Clive's keenness to thwart Cynthia has intensified his love for her.

Clive makes a stabbing gesture with his finger. "You persuaded Fliss to make us tea on the promise of a date with me. I do not equal a curried egg sandwich!"

Alex gives an involuntary yelp of mirth too soon cut off by a coughing fit.

"Stop planning others' lives. You take the cake, Ma."

Cynthia beams. "It's Bonnie's boiled fruitcake with extra cognac to celebrate your engagement with the eggs."

"I'm not affianced to Fliss' curried eggs!" says Clive.

"Don't be facetious, dear," says Cyn.

Claire gets a vivid picture of eggs curried as soon as they were plucked from under hens lined up in a row ready to let loose one each. Plop, plop, plop. She gets the giggles. Claire can see Fliss plucking her own curry leaves while they played 'Snakes and Ladders'; her leaves thriving out of season as plants do in these parts. She sees Fliss forking eggs onto the sourdough loaves baked in anticipation of Cyn's recent phone call. They've been set up.

Claire covers her face with hands. To an observer she could be laughing or crying.

Cyn moves into her Academy Award winning performance. "Clive, I'd never manipulate you, dear boy. But Claire has a lifetime to enjoy you. The gel's delighting in your company just now. Buck up, Claire. You'd let Clive help an old friend in a pickle, surely?"

Claire knows she must show Cynthia she's no fool to be ambushed by her. That she's spirited. Whichever way she jumps now Ma's perception of Claire will stick. Even married, she'll be deemed rigid, or weak according to what she does right now.

The conservatory has cooled somewhat; the fire's not been stoked by Alex, who's entranced by the drama unfolding on the hearth.

Suzy shakes her head slightly. Claire feels buoyed. Suzy knows what's right for her.

Yet Alex, sitting beside her sends a contrary message – he nods vigorously. What the…?

Claire can neither give in nor seem to have Clive on too tight a leash. She's been schooled to believe sexual jealousy a pathetic emotion. Programmed to be a good sport. What a con!

Cynthia is hoping for a bonus throw of fate's dice; a last chance to throw a six, to obtain a grandchild from their set.

Fortunately, 'fate' is not what your mama-in-law thinks should happen, Claire reminds herself. Fate is what actually happens.

Cynthia stands by the wicker whatnot admiring her favourite carnivorous plant, running her finger over its lip, awaiting Claire's verdict.

Claire gives the only reply a hardscrabble upbringing permits – compliance with a sting in the tail.

"Of course, Cynthia. Any friend of Clive's…"

Cynthia's glance barely lingers on Claire now she's given in. The gel's a pliable dumb-cluck, she decides. Her gaze wanders, bored, from Claire's face towards the kitchen door.

"It's okay, provided Hal comes as my partner. Bertie as yours," says Claire.

Clive guffaws loudly. "Good on you, Claire. You've outwitted Mama."

Hal looks up his eyes alight with mischief! "A domino couples' thing. We'll raise some eyebrows in the district. Capital!" He claps his hands together.

Mama's mouth curls involuntarily, as if she's swallowed something sweet with an unexpectedly sour filling.

Chapter 27
Fliss' Sandwiches

In June 1987, Claire first observes the Sins at play in their native environment. They've been engaged in Snakes and Ladders, a game supposed to remind us humans that goodness pays.

Felicity comes in with a plate of sandwiches. She hams up her entrance so much you'd think she bore a severed head on a plate. She wears snug-fitting jodhpurs – not that jodhpurs are normally snug but Fliss' hips have adapted to their habitat, taking up all available space and showing off her horsewoman's seat. Her bosom is unremarkable, Claire notices, pleased.

Fliss scans the room and singles Claire out; she wriggles her fingers and says in her sweet soprano voice, "Hi, I'm Felicity. Congratulations on your engagement, Claire."

Claire tries to struggle free of the low-slung couch. It's like a huge hand has her in its grip.

She hopes Fliss will see her awkward struggle and come over to greet her. But Fliss stands as if rooted to the cracks in the black slate flooring.

Eventually, Claire gives up her awkward wriggling. "Hello, Felicity," she says, "Clive's told me heaps about you – all good." Claire is surprised when her fib lowers the emotional temperature. Fliss smiles sweetly but she seems to be waiting for Claire to make a speech.

Claire's mind goes blank. Should she apologise for her prior carnal knowledge of Fliss' former fiancé even though she'd had no prior knowledge of her prior role in her fiancé's life till now? Claire has the floor, yet she's exhausted all discussion topics. She waits for Cyn to pick up the conversational yoke.

But Cyn is cross with Claire. She punishes her shy daughter-in-law by switching off the gushy river of chatter that she does so well. This minute is Claire's; it stretches on interminably. Claire starts to understand the theory of relativity.

At last Cynthia relents. "Yes, Fliss. Great news. Claire is from the bush," she says, making Claire seem an insignificant hayseed. "Alex's fiancée, Suzy's one of the Forsyth's of Berwick!"

"Ma," Alex intervenes, "Suz and I are friends. We don't believe in conventional ceremonies."

"Suz, this is our next-door neighbour, Felicity."

Now Felicity detaches herself from the slate floor, frees herself from the sandwiches by shoving them onto the antique table. She approaches Suz, who's occupying a double beanbag with Alex and hasn't a hope of rising gracefully. Fliss showcases her agility by squatting to speak to Suz. "Did you have a sister, Fiona, at PLC?"

"Yes," says Suz, pleased. "She married Tom, a diplomat; they're in the Middle East," she says. "We miss them."

"Remember me to her."

"I shall," says Suz.

"It's nice the gels are all pals," says Mama.

"Gosh, we'd better make the tea," says Fliss, "before the sandwiches dry out." She hands the first lot of sangers around.

"Let me help, Felicity," says Claire having arisen while Fliss and Suz were busy bonding.

"Or would you prefer that I helped with tea?" Claire's pleased at having used the subjunctive correctly under the strain of meeting her fiancé's former love. She hopes Clive noticed. And Alex. And Suz too. And then she wishes fervently she didn't care. Why are so many of the people Claire loves grammar pedants?

"Your help with tea would be super," Fliss says – she's no slouch in the pedantry stakes.

"Suzy might help too," she continues, picking up the subjunctive baton and running with it agilely. "I'll put my faith in Cynthia – hope it's not misplaced," she teases "– to hand these around even-handedly."

In the kitchen, there are more cucumber sandwiches; these are garnished with a huge curly specimen of the genus. Fliss holds it out to Claire as if daring her to take it from her.

"Impressive," Claire says, reaching across the bench-top. Her thumbnail caresses the cucumber's crinkly skin and explores the curl on its end as it lies in state on her palm. "Go on," Fliss says. "You've touched it now. It's yours. I've little ones on the way."

And yet Claire daren't take it from Fliss completely. They remain attached each to an end of this colossal agricultural specimen until Fliss lets it go. Claire holds it with both hands, wanting to rid herself of this freak while fearing she might damage it. Could Fliss be enjoying seeing Claire hamstrung and indecisive, she wonders. *No. Fliss is too sweet.*

Fliss busies herself with the tea caddie. Eventually, Claire centres the monstrosity on the plate and backs away respectfully.

"It's my biggest so far. I won't eat it however hungry I become," Fliss declares.

"Why not?" Claire asks.

"It's a blooming miracle, of course. I'll pickle it for the Royal Agricultural Show in November."

"It's your own produce?" Claire asks.

"Grown in my soil, but the seeds came from Bonnie's kitchen garden, I saved them, grew them under glass. I love it when neighbours cooperate to achieve something grand: a cucumber greater than the sum of its parts."

"I didn't realise cucumbers had parts. I thought *they* were part of something greater like a green salad," Claire says, hoping for a laugh.

"I'm aiming at self-sufficiency," Fliss says, ignoring Claire's attempt at a joke. "I've the best incentive. My parents died last year. Sad. They left debts. If I can't pay my way, I'll have to sell up, leave the district."

Now Claire feels awful for disliking Clive's former girlfriend on principle. She wonders if she should abdicate her attachment to Clive. It's hardly fair to lose a fiancé, parents and find oneself saddled with debts so young. Claire wants to pat Fliss' shoulder but fears seeming patronising.

"I'm okay," Fliss says, noticing Claire's concern and rubbing her arm. "I've a small riding school. It's growing via mouth to mouth recommendations."

"Gosh!" Claire says, wondering if Fliss meant 'word of mouth'.

"I try to be…versatile." She pushes a wisp of hair behind her ear then slices more bread. "I knew nothing about business until I enrolled in a distance education course. I'll soon know how poor I am. The bloke I was taking to the ball tonight is my tutor. He had a bereavement."

"It's okay with me that you're partnering Clive tonight," Claire says.

"Cynthia told me. Thanks muchly."

While Fliss deals with the kettle, Claire examines her rival critically. She is as wholesome as the weather on a fine day at the beach, with light to moderate breezes and five-centimetre swells. Her blonde hair has been coiled like rope on a trawler the way it's piled up on her crown. It's gone feral under the responsibility of tea duties but this minor untidiness makes her seem less soignée and all the more attractive for being natural.

"How did you do it?" she asks, turning Claire.

"Do what?"

"Get slippery Clive to commit."

"By not caring too much, I suppose," Claire says.

Fliss stares at Claire, her puzzlement obvious. "How clever of you," she says eventually, "I'm aware of that strategy but with Clive I don't have the genuine detachment to feign disinterest."

Boy, this girl is smart perceptive plucky. She has all the virtues and she's managed to put Claire down while being nice to her. She'd have killed their 'Snakes and Ladders' game.

"You'll find someone." Claire sinks into verbal quicksand to produce this cliché. "You're pretty." God, I hope I'm blushing, she thinks. *I can't believe I'm saying this. I hate how we women are only admired for our looks!*

"You're the pretty one," Fliss says, "with your dramatic colouring and exceptional height."

Now Claire feels like a great big red lump. "No," she protests. You're…"

"Short, dumpy and so fair it looks like I collided with a powder puff."

"But your colouring…your skin's as transparent as rice paper. You've a self-deprecating sense of humour. It helps…"

"…with life's disappointments?" says Fliss, finishing her sentence for her, fortunately because Claire's floundering was becoming terminal.

Suz is shaking her head as if to say, Claire, it's one thing to be nice but to flatter someone you can never be friends with – that's nuts.

But Claire won't play politics where love and friendship are concerned. Fliss is open about her feelings, and Claire admires her candour.

"Okay," says Fliss, "we'd better bring them in here closer to the feed trough. Better than risking Cynthia's last few antiques. The conservatory's a junk shop. When Bonnie's away, I tidy up. Otherwise, they get themselves in such a muddle. Always fighting bushfires, never planning ahead. And as for maintenance…Be careful the wiring up there," she points towards the upper floors and shudders. "Get a torch, Claire. Don't touch those Victorian era switches."

A frisson of fear runs through Claire like dodgy electricity. "Okay, everyone, tea's up!" Fliss calls through the door.

Chapter 28
Bonnie Home

While Suz and Fliss joke and flick soap suds at each other, Claire worries about the ball.

Bravado aside, how will she feel about Clive partnering Fliss? What will she wear?

The three girls are washing up. Suz and Fliss are getting on famously – a ridiculous expression – what's famous about getting on? 'Like a house on fire' is Claire's preferred simile – all that warmth and spark seem apt. But Claire can't throw herself whole-heartedly into the conviviality. So, she muses on the sidelines instead of acting all gossipy confiding and gigglesome. Fliss and Suz are snapping tea towels at each other, and swapping stories of disastrous first dates. Claire doesn't know whether to be exultant or horrified at how quickly women let down their defences when familiarity is on offer. Is she a friendship prude?

Claire can be playful, though she's shy and often considered stand-offish – an excellent way of putting it, she thinks. She's always to be found standing to one side of any gathering, observing her companions' behaviour. She aims to become the David Attenborough of human foot-in-mouth age. In any case, she doesn't have the heart for girl talk now.

The prospect of joining the Sins clan has her flustered. With part of her brain she's busy keeping Cynthia's Wedgewood safe from her famous butter-fingers while other regions of her mind are wondering about the ball. Cynthia has offered her a marquisate necklace to wear with her jeans and suede-fringed cowboy shirt.

"As useful as an ashtray on a motor bike!" Clive had said.

"Claire could go as Lady Godiva," Hal said. "I'll provide the pony, she the hair!"

"But my hair won't suffice," she'd told him, seriously. Hal had laughed like a loon. Claire thinks he's entitled to an occasional naughtiness when Mama's out of earshot.

Cynthia bustles in with an ugly woollen shawl. It's quickly rejected. What a shame it is, she opines that Claire hadn't 'been born better fleshed out', then she could have worn Cyn's best Balenciaga gown. *Been born better!* is Claire's take-home message from this judgement.

From the courtyard there's a clatter of quartz stones heralding an arrival.

Everyone but Fliss goes out to greet the newcomers – Bonnie and her brother, Bernard.

The girls' eyes widen at the handsome woman alighting from the battered old M.G. sports car.

The brother, a surly chap, doesn't help her up the steps with her case. He wears a flat cap of good quality tweed. When invited in, Bernard arcs his hand in a curt snub. He sweeps his eyes over them reprovingly, takes a last puff from a ciggie, grinds the butt out on the duco and lets it fall onto the driveway. He accelerates away in an explosion of quartz stones. One stone heads towards Cynthia, who flinches and steps back into the yew hedge.

How did he do that? Claire wonders.

"Oh sugar!" Cynthia says, as she's helped up, "Tell Bernie to leave decorously, Bonnie. Lovely to see you, dear, but you're not ON until tomorrow."

"Indeed, Mrs Sin. I got the pip stuck down at Boggy Creek…the piggish way the boys live, the stench of liniment, gaspers and beer. It's lemon meringue pie every night and me fretting for the twins and their lassies. So here I am; the prodigal gel. I'll do my duties unofficially."

This is code for: I'll work gratis. Claire finds Bonnie confident and talkative.

"Lovely to see you," says Cynthia smiling widely, "whether officially or not."

"Bonnie, we've missed your clever cooking hands," says Clive, taking her in a waltz hold and dancing her over the coarse flag stoned terrace to some Buxus plants that haven't quite joined up to form a hedge. They fall over laughing.

"Come, meet Claire." They dance up to Claire and, introductions made, the three join hands as if circling a maypole; they must look right chumps dancing on rough-hewn stone as if wearing concrete boots, Claire thinks, but the rich don't mind seeming silly. She feels drunk, although she hasn't imbibed. At least her anxious mood has passed.

"Bonnie, we're in gastronomic hell!" Clive says, in a stage whisper. "We've ploughed through a mound of Fliss' bloody sangers" – he lowers his voice saying this – "crisp enough but the blooming seeds are sticking to our teeth; if we don't find an antidote, we'll be burping and spitting all night. Fliss refused to give out her recipe, despite us threatening to draw her fingernails out. We need your fruitcake to disguise our sour breath."

Bonnie scans the gathering for Fliss.

"It's okay. She's a martinet about finishing the dishes," says Clive.

"Ah! Well, cucumbers are sour out of season, and worse grown under plastic in a drought…My fruitcake should help with your sour breath. I hid the cake from nibblers who sample 'til there's only a pile of crumbs, not that I'm telling," she stares at Cynthia and Hal, who act the goat pretending to herd together for mutual support.

The Sins seem to fear Bonnie, yet she's their employee. Claire intends pondering this conundrum later.

"When Alex called in to introduce Suz to me, me darlin' bhoy says, 'Come home, Bonnie, you'll be needed.' So here oi am."

"You didn't say you'd seen Bonnie," says Mama to Alex.

"You never asked. Bonnie is family as much as those who bore me," he says, letting, his words resonate with extra meaning but Cynthia, whom Claire expects to take umbrage, merely gives him a playful shove.

"Anyway Bonnie," Clive says, "Claire's the most beautiful woman in the world. An accolade you deserved in your day. I've seen the photos!"

Bonnie gives Claire an affecting hug. She's the first Sin hanger-on who touches her.

"You're as lovely as he said, darlin'."

"Who said?" Claire asks, knowing Clive hasn't spoken to Bonnie recently. So, if not he…?

Bonnie has dimples and a beguiling gap between her front teeth. It's easy to see her as a young beauty with her sinuous snake hips and olive complexioned oval face.

Cynthia looks peeved at the profusion of compliments flying about; none intended for her.

"Alex said so, of course," says Bonnie.

"Yes!" says Clive. "Claire's more beautiful than all former fiancées, whose number's legion…And whose fame's legendary," he says, ducking out of range of Claire's hand.

"Ooh! Ye kissed the blarney stone, Clive," says Bonnie.

"Long as it's only the blarney stone he's kissing'," Claire says.

"What will you wear to the ball?" says Bonnie.

"Oh, Bonnie," Claire says. "I haven't a thing to wear."

All have a good laugh at that. "What a cliché," says Clive. "My woman, the emblem of all women in having nothing to wear!"

"Wear jeans," says Suz. "Dada reckons Sins get away with anything. Play the hayseed. Won't be hard for you."

Claire wishes Suz wouldn't call Hal 'Dada'. "But you're not wearing jeans?" she says.

"No. I bought one of those bubble frocks in Myers windows. Passion red."

"She's a Remembrance Day poppy," says Alex. "Waiting to open up."

"You've had a preview?" Claire asks.

"I'm her principal advisor," says Alex, laying it on thick.

"You went shopping together?" Claire's voice rises higher as the sentence progresses until she all-but wails. She's giving away too much. All her ugly feelings of sadness, envy and betrayal are on show. No wonder she lost at Snakes and Ladders. What a seething mass of lust and envy she is.

"You never shop with me, Clive," she says, barely keeping a whine out of her voice.

"Our agreement states, I pay. You buy."

"You might have mentioned I'd need a dress for tonight!"

"I didn't know you'd want to go."

Claire sighs. It's true. It was her own crazy idea to engineer herself a partner.

"Now Claire, I've got the very thing," says Bonnie. "Come with me." She takes Claire's arm and leads her indoors.

Chapter 29
Bonnie's Room

Bonnie's room is surprising. It's thoughtfully furnished with elm-wood pieces, quite unlike the rest of the house that's chock-full of ill-assorted stuff.

Its washbasin has been plumbed in, judging by a slow dripping tap, an improvement on the arrangements in the bedroom wing upstairs, where there's no tap capable of leaking.

French doors lead onto a pretty walled garden shared by the morning room and the library.

A small study next to the bedroom has a fine desk and the best armchair Claire has yet discovered at Arcadia. A real chair to relax in! And there's a heap of books on a wine table.

Lucky Bonnie, Claire thinks. The room is painted a delicate celadon green. It's fresh and spring-like and not cool, as one might expect.

Bonnie opens a carved camphor-wood chest like the one Claire's mum uses to pack away winter clothes; she takes out a bolt of cream-coloured silk that's old but not discoloured. She holds it up to Claire's face. "Perfect!"

Claire touches the fabric tentatively. "Lovely," she says.

Bonnie bundles it into her hands. "Go on, love," she says. "I planned to use it once. It's yours."

"No. I couldn't."

"The cream is perfect. I didn't want a glary white against my skin. Yet you're fair. Anyone would think I had you in mind buying it. Your veins show through it pinkly; it's like you're blushing permanently," she says, brushing Claire's face with the back of her hand. It seems too intimate a gesture between new acquaintances but Claire doesn't flinch.

Bonnie unrolls the bolt. Wedding gown quality.

"Gorgeous," Claire says.

"The war," Bonnie says, brushing away any questions with a flick of her wrist. She takes the bolt and pleats and drapes it over Claire's shoulder.

Claire gasps at the dexterous way Bonnie handles the slinky fabric so she resembles a Greek goddess. Her every move is answered by a liquid silky flow. Her image in the mirror astonishes her.

"The secret's in the bias," Bonnie says. "Never put up with life's average warp and weft."

Claire nods, she understands about cutting on the bias – her mum sews. "Will it stay on?"

"Only if you want it to," says Bonnie, wryly.

She is the most surprising servant imaginable, Claire thinks. She produces some gold curtain tasselling, draws it diagonally across Claire's breasts, wrangling them into classic orbs.

Bonnie studies her protégé critically. "Bra off, love. Greeks didn't wear 'em."

Claire's eyes widen but she obeys. Once she's been transformed into a classical beauty, her bearing alters subtly to match her new sense of self. She always knew she had it in her to be Greek. "Bonnie, how clever you are!" she says.

"I studied dress design until life got in the way." Bonnie gestures eloquently, though Claire would prefer a more detailed explanation.

"Couldn't you find a use for this?"

Bonnie shakes her head.

"What if someone steps on my...train?" Claire asks. "I'll unravel like a ball of string."

"Ha! Down here folks have serious stuff to hide. If only a naked body was the worst of it."

"No kidding!" Claire says, her heart rate picking up. "I thought it'd be respectable and dull here."

"No! We all have something on each other. There's an unspoken agreement to keep mum."

The prospect of a story excites Claire. She's emboldened to come clean to Bonnie. Tell her what she's only told her diary and Alex so far. "Can I tell you something, Bonnie? I want to be a writer," she says. "Clive doesn't know yet. It was Alex speaking of his love for Shakespeare and realising I loved him too. Not Alex. I mean, Shakespeare," Claire blushes.

"Alex can be persuasive…"

True, Claire thinks. "Silly of me," she says, "to fight my way into a job where I'll always find work and then go and risk it all. I want to go from full on nursing to slow poetry. From a life that's 'red in tooth and claw' to the meandering life of poets in sylvan glades. Poets save no one."

"Mm," says Bonnie, through a mouthful of pins. She knots the tassel behind Claire's back.

"So?" she asks, indicating Claire's reflection in the glass.

"So, I'll be a poet, Bonnie," she says, irrelevantly. "I've decided."

"That's nice, love. Did the slinky gown give you the idea?"

"Why would a gorgeous frock inspire me to lock myself away and scribble nonsense?" she says, musing. "No. I've been dreaming about it for a while. Scared of being crap at it. Even before I met Clive, I had the urge…"

"Sure, you did, dear," says Bonnie drily.

"But Alex said we only get one go at life. It hit me. I couldn't tell Clive that first night."

"Today he's going on about all the kids we'll have. I'll be nursing them until my breasts drop off. Maybe a dual degree in nursing and literature might pacify him…"

"Two half-lives? No. Write. If you can't do what you love at 19, then when? I'd a chance at 19 and I let it go. Get some pencils. Get on with it. Clive will come around." Bonnie's voice comes out croaky as if Claire were an idiot determined to defy her.

"Thanks, Bonnie," Claire says. "But aren't writers meant to endure poverty and crap jobs to prove they've the right…to write?"

Bonnie laughs ironically. She shrugs.

"I want everything I want. And soon. Am I asking too big a helping of life, Bonnie?"

"No."

"Did you get everything you wanted, Bonnie?"

"No. I should have fought harder." She sighs. "It may be difficult to believe, Claire, knowing me hardly at all, but I've had more hopes fulfilled than most do." She speaks defiantly. "I've a family I love. All of them. Not just those easiest to love." She's sounding emphatic and cross.

Claire turns to Bonnie, hugs her tight. "The boys are lucky to have your affection."

"The boys had three parents and that, my dear, is why they're better than average. None of us doubted we loved them for an instant." Bonnie takes a hanky from her pocket. Her tears have marred the perfection of the silk. "Look what your kind words made me do."

"Sorry."

"Don't be. Life's about being used, so used that one day you're all used up."

Claire touches Bonnie's shoulder. "You okay?"

"Yes! And I've dangly earrings handed down from 'you know who'."

"Thanks," Claire says, pulling her hair back. "Maybe it *was* the gown that showed me how molten things can be. Made me think bold thoughts. Clive will let me write if he loves me."

"Yes. Come, Cinders. Your carriage awaits."

Chapter 30
Ball Part 1

Partnering Hal at the Bachelors and Spinsters Claire feels like a Doric column being ferried over the dance floor by a forklift on speed. Hal's complexion worries her. A yellowish cast shows beneath a sheen of perspiration.

"Hal, take it easy," Claire says.

"I have a goddess to live up to," he replies.

He's referring to Claire's Grecian gown that Bonnie sacrificed her wedding silk for; it's held together by pins and running stitches. A metaphor for Claire's makeshift engagement, perhaps?

Hal wafts her past his friends, acknowledging them with a brisk wave and a cocky shout: "Ahoy there, Percy! Did I not get lucky tonight?"

"You, old dog," say Hal's chums. "You intend monopolising her?" one gent asks.

"By Jove, I do," says Hal. "Rogues aplenty here tonight, my dear," he whispers.

In this abbreviated manner, she's met Jim from bowls, Henry from polo, Percy the entrepreneur who's accumulating land for a Retirement Village on the outskirts of town, and Jean and Jon from the Friends of the Warrnambool Botanical Gardens.

"Why aren't you introducing me properly to your friends?" Claire asks, hurt.

"You'll meet them at the wedding. That lot are my best chums. I'm saving you for mere acquaintances, those with whom I need cachet."

"Why do you need cachet?" Claire asks, deciding to make it her word of the night.

"Because we need to impress those we don't yet know."

"But if you don't know them, why care?"

"I may want to know them. And you make me *appear* interesting."

"Wouldn't it better to *be* interesting?"

"No. These chaps with whom I've a nodding acquaintance will see you are a looker and award me high points."

"You'll bask in my…glory?"

"I'm afraid so. We humans are deeply shallow."

"So, I'm just here to prove you're a dominant male?" Claire tries not to sound pissed off.

"Indeed. Your gloss will rub off on me. Sorry, but it's been like that since God was a boy."

"It stinks!" Claire feels her face reddening. "That it should take a pretty girl on your arm to earn respect," Claire says, then blushes, realising how conceited she sounds.

"You're lovely," Hal says. "An accident of birth, most likely. Still, it didn't stop you from using your looks to ensnare a dominant male. Men always want the prettiest girl. It's tough, but there you are."

The barn-dancers line up all scraggly but Claire doesn't want to dance. Hal's honesty about romance has upset her. She sees the truth of it. Ever since she started seeing boys, she'd known the dating game was superficial. She turns to him, "I hate this system, Hal. It's good that you're so honest about it. Still, it makes me sad."

"Why, my dear?"

"Let's sit this one out."

"Of course, I've run you ragged," he says, but his breath has a laboured quality to it. He leads her to some unoccupied chairs grouped in semi-circles around circular tables arranged so that one might talk or watch or both. Hellebores float in shallow bowls.

Seated, Hal takes Claire's hand in his two bony ones. "Why so sad?"

"Oh, Hal. I'm being a sook. My life's full of hope, opportunity, love. Meanwhile, Pat, my kindest friend, will never be loved. Ghastly acne – it's so cruel, random…"

"It's Presbyterian."

"Presbyterian?"

"Remember Pressies are born with a huge pressie – they're the Elect of God, who, in my opinion, doesn't exist in the form projected onto him by the godly. But Cynthia feels smug about her destiny."

"What makes her so?" Claire asks.

Hal hesitates while a Sinatra look-alike sings, *My Way*. "Nothing. Just self-belief. But it works."

"Do Presbyterians give money away?"

Hal shakes his head. "Collect it oftener. But they have their destiny. Pressies are our royals."

"Haven't all you Sins won life's lottery?" says Claire.

"Ha!" Hal gives a barking laugh. "We're in debt. No vast acreage. No private lake. A dam." Hal rises to his feet abruptly and stands at attention as the mayor – Malachi O'Neill wearing full regalia materialises before him. Hal lugs Claire to her feet. She manages a smile.

And it's all true, Claire realises. It's he whom Hal knows least, he seeks to impress. He introduces her to Mr and Mrs Mayor; he's portly, prosperous; she, a once handsome woman, clings to the shoulder-length hairstyle of her youth, although its thinning is well advanced.

If Hal is to exploit any aura of health or looks Claire's proximity confers, he must intersperse dancing with spells of moronic chitchat. He can't let the mayor leave until certain obvious things have been said. They discuss the Warrney Agricultural Show animatedly, the preponderance of Clydesdales over quarter horses, until Claire wilts with boredom. Once her relationship to the St Johns is explained, mayoral felicitations ensue. After a few more pleasantries, they're dismissed, and the representatives of the shire sit in the very chairs that had been theirs.

"They sought *me* out," says Hal, as if he'd met a rock star. Claire suspects the warmth of their reception has more to do with their need for a chair to soothe Mrs Mayor's bunions than to civic duty.

The Mechanics Institute is heated by six electric wall radiators that glow redly, giving an illusion of warmth. Alcohol and movement do the rest. 'The Ballarat Big Band' plays the standards, everything from *Sweet Caroline, The House of the Rising Sun*, *She Was Just 17*, *Sgt. Pepper's Lonely Heart*... Anything Bingish. Sinatra crooned. Ella sung. *Oklahoma*. Brubeck.

Claire's hasn't heard *Roll out the Barrel* yet. Hal likes slow tunes. When *Mood Indigo* plays, he holds her close enough to hear his laboured breathing in her ear.

Claire can't see lover-boy Clive – ah, there he is dancing as chastely as can be. Suz and Alex, too, are exercising restraint. It's cool not to appear romantically inclined. Hal, who doesn't understand 'cool', hums 'Sweet Caroline' in Claire's ear.

"Ah, here are Cyn's bestest friends, GwenLen," Hal says. "Their names chime so sweetly together, they only need the one. You'll have to meet them, dear girl, or I'll never hear the end of it. Recently, they moved from Warrney to fix up their weekender for retirement. Len's a solicitor, works part-time; he and Cyn closet themselves away for hours organising finances."

"I don't have a head for books. 'Now Hal, go play with your test tubes,' Cynthia says. So I do."

They cross the ballroom to meet the pair. "Gwenda and Leonard Law, may I introduce you to Clive's fiancé, Claire?" says Hal.

"Congratulations, my dear, you're as lovely as Cynthia said you were," says Gwen.

Len adds, "And now she's seen you up close, all Cyn's misgivings will have proven groundless."

"Shush, Len," his wife says. "Like all proud mothers," she explains, "Cynthia never thinks any woman worthy of her son but now that she knows you…"

"Now that she knows me, she's tricked Clive into partnering Felicity," Claire says, and then wishes she hadn't allowed these words to escape. She'd had no intention of mortifying kind GwenLen. The sentence had tumbled out without her censor checking it.

"Sorry, Gwenda," Claire says, "It's fine, honestly." But the look(s) on GwenLen(s') stony face(s) indicate(s) that her embarrassment mitigation attempt has failed. "We've first sitting supper tickets, they say, see you," they hurry off in search of something nice and bland like blanc-mange.

"Anyway," Hal continues. "I do play with my test-tubes. I'm working on a weed-killer for paspalum that won't affect healthy pastures. Trouble is the darned stuff must be applied in the cool before dawn and requires lighting so one doesn't poison viable pastures in the dark."

He's keen to impress her with his industry. "How clever!" she says. "Couldn't you invent a system that lets you sleep through the night?" His eyes cloud over. She regrets her honesty.

"Yes, Claire. Back to the drawing board."

Hal guides her into the centre of the room and twirls her around the dance floor as if he were a younger man. Claire strikes something bony. It's Fliss' ankle. Claire loses her balance and ends up on the floor. Did she lash out with subliminal intent at she who has temporary custody of her man? "Sorry," she says, as she's being helped up. "I didn't see you coming."

"We weren't coming. You were, honey. Too fast!" Clive picks her up off the floor. He checks Fliss and Claire for injuries. Shakes his head sadly. "Another fall, hon. I saved you again. Those heels…You promised…"

"I couldn't come to a ball in sneakers. These are Bonnie's."
Claire's voice sounds shrill.

"And they were Mama's before that," he reminds Claire.

"Not everything of Bonnie's was Ma's first," says Hal
cryptically.

Clive frowns at him. "Go easy, Dada. Don't make Claire dizzy.
Coming to supper?"

"No, we're in the next sitting."

"See you later."

Chapter 31
Potting Shed

There's sex in this chapter. Not sweet, soporific marital sex but urgent sex of the illicit sort.

Only three of the characters, Clive, Fliss and Alex are present in the potting shed of the Mechanic's Institute during the B&S ball on the 22nd June, 1986.

Claire is safely inside dancing with Hal (perhaps not altogether safely) while this charade is being played out, so for a time, she'll remain ignorant of Clive's true (lying, cheating) nature. She'll continue to delude herself that she loves him, whereas had she been present in the shed to witness his antics, she'd have stormed out enraged and there wouldn't have been a story worth the telling.

Outside, she'll have calmed down, provided her reaction is congruent with her past behaviour.

And, knowing the truth about her fiancé, Claire will be thankful for her narrow escape from an unfortunate marriage, or at least she will be once she's done with feeling humiliated.

She'll have implored Hal to drive her to Wangaratta on the morrow, from where she'll mourn her broken engagement while being spoiled silly by her mum, who'll forgive her for omitting to mention Clive. Claire will soon get over Clive, marry a local farmer and have lots of kids.

But this isn't what happened. Nor did the alternative possibility occur – the one in which Claire witnesses the potting shed farce, but is persuaded to give Clive one more chance.

In either of these hypothetical scenarios, there wouldn't have been a tale to tell. Luckily, for the sake of the plot, Claire is inside the hall and ignorant of Clive's antics. Witness accounts have given us an impartial picture of the event. The following account is Clive's knee-trembler 'stream of conscience' soliloquy, written as if from inside his head.

!!!!!!!knee-trembler alert!!!!!!!

its black-dark in here dark as sin all the better to feel you fliss you with the peach ripe bum wait ill lift you onto me properly girl not that theres anything proper about this enterprise squeeze your legs around me and bugger the velvet its sposed to be crushed thats fantastic fliss youre bliss

i did love you you know pity the city wasnt for you nor was the OT course and you so close to finishing it still credentialed or not you can occupy me therapeutically any time you want you must think im off my rocker marrying claire and hardly knowing her but that's the thrill of it i see her as a tabula rasa ready to be drawn on by me shes inexperienced grateful i noticed her sitting prettily on the shelf but shes sweet and comes from a big family shes educated but not a knowitall and yet she calls you the golden fliss its odd that she knows about jason can you get a classical education chez the nuns i guess shed be jealous if she were here but if she were here we wouldnt be engaged in such a sinful activity – had a skinful acted sinful that's the way it goes

absolute last time you get lucky *chez moi* fliss not that were *chez* anyone right now unless its the ratepayers of the shire and theres a bylaw against what were doing all fines payable to carl no-potting-sheilas-in-the-potting-shed-without-a-licence mc cance

anyway fliss i had to give you one last seeing to one last roll in the hay to say thanks for the memories i never minded your tiny mammories so stop apologising but claires will better suit our nursing neonates though im more of a hugh jarse man & i want you to know im not out here on a freezing cold dead o winter night out of selfishness this is for you my dear friend a rose pink thankyou note though i like high risk sexual antics anyway i hope it doesn't mean theres anything psychologically wrong with me of course theres not this is for you fliss for being a good sport there'll be no compulsion for me to snatch a quickie now ive got claire laid on like hot water and i can just reach out and turn her faucet on and she comes gushing out

still fliss youre not a bad ol tart youll end up with a mc cance marconi now im out of the picture youre not lowering your sights too much…naughty naughty dont pinch my maracas those maccas will be rich one day they're *tres* ambitious and with their organic this n that they'll strike it rich that carlo cocky little geezer might even make mayor one day but *pas de princes pour Felicite* a pity or you could withdraw pull out of the ratrace altogether like ill be doing in a minute though being a spinster would be hard for you hard haha subconscious minds a wunnerful thing

120

i reckon youll do whats needed to get yourself a man so train your sights on one of those dumb macca bunnies then gently squeeze the trigger and bingo grab your trophy skin im alive n throw im in the crock pot and cook his goose and even though the maccas are all fisheries n wildlife inspector scum marrying them is how you neutralise the pests locals will call you lady chatterley but at least macca will keep poachers away from your tight lil ol trout stream death to miscellaneous predators…like me…or you could be my bit on the side…no im a reformed individual…a pity life with claire will be eternal sunshine – has no vices i can find and her olds tucked away in woop woop primitive bush bashers she thinks a trip to the local chop sueys heaven shes a bit of a feminist though some women don't see the symbolism of our privates – we blokes pour our champers into their champagne flutes magnificent how were constructed urogenitally speaking tho im biased being a penis man but i can see the beauty design-wise gods a semiologist the physiology of reproduction chimes with the metaphoric side o things ill be sitting saintly with ma in the family pew tomorrow earn my inheritance Claire wont come ha ha get it she wont be getting any tonight once ive come im all done and now my cup of happiness runneth over and i can feel you smiling on the inside fliss now nicky woop hon before were missed into the lav n fix your hair…

Chapter 32
Alex and Clive Potting Shed

Alex's twin brother Clive has been doing that which he is best at. Okay, in case you haven't been paying attention, he's administered a heroic medical intervention to a girlfriend: it was gamely provided in the dark, under conditions less than sterile. The operation concluded satisfactorily.

Packing his equipment away, Alex's bro' hears his twin's wild howl. He's been sprung.

Alex drops to his knees. Instinct tells him to hide, although he's innocent. Despite the plush pile velvet black of night, Alex can see his brother's treachery. And, angry on Claire's behalf, he can't help but wonder, Is Clive's love for Claire waning?

"Okay, show's over spy," Clive bellows. "Better be the three wise monkeys rolled into one. Hear any evil? Then keep schtum about it, mongrel."

Alex snuffles miserably.

"Pervert, mouth breather," Clive calls. "Useless…"

"…prick?" Alex chimes in.

"Oh, it's you, bro, 'Ooonly yahooo'," Clive warbles tuneless with relief. "Gees, Alex, ya gave me a helluva scare. Ya coulda been anyone."

"From now on I'm anyone. Forget I'm your brother."

"Alex," says Clive, whining a little.

"Our brotherly smotherly pact ends now, mate," says Alex.

"Why?" Clive asks. He can be dense at times.

"Phff!" Alex says.

"Listen, bro, I worried about you at school. Ya went quiet in form four. Were you buggered at Timbertop the year I had glandular fever?"

"Don't pretend ya give a fuck about me," Alex says, his voice husky with emotion.

"I never liked to ask."

"Then, 'no': I wasn't buggered. Something minor went down. Why not ask me back then?"

"We had to stick apart at school or we'd have been compared."

"No. You were brilliant; I was kind," says Alex.

"You could do anything, Al. Now I'd like us closer. My kids'll need an uncle who knows stuff."

"You want an uncle? D'you even deserve kids? Right now, I'd knacker you 'til you sing soprano, ya lousy bastard." Alex's voice echoes around the iron shed and booms in his head.

"I know I'm apologising late but…there's stuff…I was stressed out at school. It's an honour being Head Boy. But you fear not measuring up. You run like mad to keep from falling back.

"Remember I had a month off sick when you were at Timbertop – some pesky viral thing. Doubt if I've ever been 100% since then. Mama saw how sick I was – we bonded. She bust a gut to get me well. Started the herb garden. Made up vile organic concoctions. She and Bonnie, always spiky together, bonded too…I was their joint project. Mama saw how much Bon loved me…

"Let's be friends, Al. This was just a thank you note. Is Suz here?"

"Na. Lucky me, to get here in time for your vertical gymnastics."

"What's to be ashamed of? Thank God no one else saw. I'll drive Ma to church tomorrow, thank Him personally," says Clive.

"Claire's another victim of your charm."

Clive's toe makes contact with a plastic planter pot. He lashes out at it.

Alex runs a spanner over the iron walls. He feels the corrugations thrumming in his soul.

"Don't imply she's 'just another' in a series," Clive says.

"Well, she is!" says Alex.

"Al, give me some credit. She's the woman who pulled me up short. Without her love, I'd be a lonely bastard like you. I'd never have plunged into marriage, mortgages and mini monsters.

"Claire's my cure for loneliness. Tonight was an anomaly."

"Shut up, Clive, or I'll put Claire in the picture."

"You punitive wowser! It wasn't an opportunistic fuck. I was saying thanks."

"Try a Hallmark card. Gees! What a con job we've perpetrated!"

"Appreciate your loyalty, Alex, honestly."

"I've spent a quarter of a century sticking my neck out for you; you save others but can't save yourself. Always gagging to be your best friend, confidant and faithful mongrel bitch."

"I never held a gun to your head, Alex."

"It changes now…ten pm, June 21," says Alex, unrelenting.

Time stretches twists like bubble gum. In the distance, the band strikes up a jaunty rendition of 'Moon River'.

"Ma says we're two halves of a whole; our twin-ship means I bathe in your reflected glory. I'm meant to hide your failures. Well, from now on there'll be no more rescuing!"

"You won't need to from now on. Now that I'm with Claire. Ha! The yin and yang twins! I'm the blond exuberant one. You're the smouldering log fire that's been pissed upon."

"Pissed on by you, you with the face of an angel, soul of a devil. I'm swarthy. I could be illegitimate. When Ma developed mastitis, she squeezed out droplets for her first-born!"

"Jealous?"

"Jealous of that air-kissing smoochy crap? No way. You smile and smile and kiss and you're a villain." Alex kicks the plastic pot to Clive. Despite the gloom, he returns it niftily.

"Always impressin' us with your Bard quotes. You and your corny Shakespeare club… you lot gave me the shits!"

"You were the handsomest; athlete, charmer, flawed hero. But if you hurt Claire with your Don Juan's progress, I'll…I love her."

"Aw, c'mon bro, you always think my girls are cute, but you're not inclined…You, your furniture restorer mates! They help you to sweet pieces off of shipping crates. Having an occasional girlfriend proves nothing."

"Bullshit!"

"The olds might be fooled. Not me. Suz is your prop. Thanks for bringing her this weekend. It helped Claire fit in. Claire thinks the world of you. All the way down it's, when will Alex come?"

"She likes me," Alex says.

"No way!"

"I'm fed up with your vile seduction scenes. I love the girl you're messing with now."

"Ridiculous!"

"Making love's not loving, Clive. I haven't had the pleasure. Yet I know her thoroughly. Her gentleness, her sensitivity. I love her rare bad moods."

"God, Alex? You fall for a girl you drive to Clifton Hill one Sunday?"

"Yes. I love Claire."

"Pathetic! Denying your own sexuality!"

"I'd have denied it years ago. But I felt for the gays at school. Shit they got for not being roughhouse Aussie blokes. If I ran with poets, misfits, dorks, I…"

"You did it to embarrass me."

"To avoid competing," Alex insists.

"Thanks for nothing', ya freaking phony!"

"That time you entered the cross-country, boy, I was pissed off," says Alex.

"Why?"

"My sport. You muscled in. That day…I pictured your victorious sprint to the finishing line, while I plodded along. I'd started late…my shoelace…"

"Typical!"

"You started strongly, but I caught you crying, exhausted in the thistles by The Little River."

"I've no recollection…"

"I wanted to comfort you, but I knew you'd hate to be found crying. I hung back. Waited behind an outcrop."

"The race was yours, fuck-wit!"

"No. Not once I'd seen you, vulnerable."

"But I'd muscled in on your race…"

"Mm. Sprints weren't enough. Ya had to win the slow race too." Alex thumps the wall.

"You should have taken what you wanted, Alex."

"I didn't want it badly enough back then. I do now. I'll fight you from now on. May the best man win," says Alex.

"He will," says Clive. "Despite my abysmal character. I knew how you saw me, I hated the me that I saw through your eyes."

"You knew what I thought of you?"

"I wanted to win everything back then. The night of the vanilla ice cream I saw my future. Ugly!"

"So vanilla ice-cream with sparkles is your antidote to an ugly life?"

"If it has Claire in it. Pragmatic marriages end up fairy tales."

Chapter 33
Cyn Plots

Arcadia

Saturday

I'm glad I'm home alone, getting in touch with my feelings. Anger splashes across the page when I press hard on my down strokes. They emerge fat and deliberate. Nothing wrong with well-directed anger. My rising strokes are buoyant, airy. Few see the lighter side of me.

A pity! I love my split nib pen. My split-nib self. No other pen could be more me.

How lucky Claire came this weekend. She appeared to acquiesce in my request re Fliss, but played me for a fool, niftily wrangling Hal as her escort. The dear old dodo was flattered.

Clearly, Bertie was unsuitable to partner me – he's outdoor staff and impossibly bashful. Does he fancy me a little?

Claire had had no prior knowledge of the ball, no clue that Fliss was waiting in the wings.

And yet she wrong-footed me. I was stunned. Is Clive marrying a prettied-up version of me?

Good luck to them all! Those heedless fools whooping it up at the ball! I'll spend my time wisely, by finishing my maiden speech to Toastmasters; it's an encomium on marriage: *Marriage*, I'll say, *is merely economics, domestic politics, and business deals closed in the bedroom...*

I lay my tools down on my correspondence set. I squeeze out a little Evelyn & Crabtree. I massage my hands. Writing helps me deal with negative thoughts, though Clive's opiates work better. He says, 'Go cold turkey, Ma.' He, who has never felt the chill of age.

This evening, leaving to pick up Fliss, he popped his head around the door: *'These sample pills are for emergencies, Mama. And they're the last you're getting from me. I don't treat kin!'*

My entire life is an emergency! I'm like a novice kayaker trying not to roll the death capsule.

Outsiders see our solid, busy lives; we're envied in these parts. There's our clever doctor son and the nice one. But all's gone awry. Our once fertile pastures are exhausted. Lush paddocks are infested with bracken fern. Paspalum weed has taken root. Livestock bloodlines are depleted. We butcher and eat our own dodgy beasts. We're already brittle with age. How many toxins must we ingest? We're in the red. Once apprised of her fiancé's meagre expectations, Claire will be off like a shot.

A successful marriage is like a company merger: wealth generated by the new entity should be < than its tributaries. We mustn't have two dry gullies crumbling into each other.

Love is curable once the romantic haze dissolves. Will Toastmasters want reminding of the facts of love? I wonder.

If Clive knew the truth; that Fliss is her parents' heir; if only he realised that, amalgamated, our two properties would yield up 50-hectare lots for hiving into hobby-farms, how then would he feel about Claire? But dear old Hal, he knows me well, he made me promise not to tell dear Clive or else!!!!

I pack up the papers. I love the ritual neatening of the documents' edges. I replace them in the concertina file, turn off the propane heater that Clive predicts will be the death of me.

And now to my ablutions. They're undertaken in the alcove off the bedroom, where a basin was installed in the '70s. It's still awaiting the plumber. At Arcadia, everything moves glacially!

I transfer water from my hottie into a jug and basin set. I won't mention my mode of dealing with the slops, though there's a clump of geraniums on the north side flourishing.

Something in me enjoys making do, saving the environment even. Hal calls it my ablution solution to ecology and pollution. He thinks I'm nuts: it's my Antipodean equivalent of Brits being mobilised against the Hun. *She'll fight them on the bleachers, she'll fight them at the school fete, she'll take the battle all the way to the CWA. She will prevail!* A card, my Hal!

Now for the ritual cleansing! There's nothing like a thorough-going scrub with a wind-dried scratchy face-washer to promote blood flow. So youthening! If that's a word.

I wanted a bleak boarding school in Scotland. Had to make do with PLC. I listen to music before bed: Wagner's stirring overtures won't do tonight. I'll need the '*Sound of Music*' to lift my mood. It's a CD I received from Clive, for my 50th.

We're an ill-assorted lot. Clive buys an entire sound system; Alex foists Sculthorpe's '*Sun Music*' onto me. Unnecessary in a world full of tunes ripe for the plucking! Modern classical music is like an Antipodean landscape – all scraggy paper-barks, and scrofulous reedy things cluttering creek beds. Our pioneers couldn't wait to rescue us from nature with rows of elms, stands of cedars, banks of rhodos.

'*Climb Every Mountain*' makes me want to career up steep inclines, waving my arms at the sky. If only God could have done for the Western District what he did for Austria, hill-wise. I wonder, *Did my forbears think they were off to Austria but were misdirected here? How easily God's major theme of tabletop flatness might have been modified to include an occasional high point. Even now a minor reactivation of an extinct volcano would give us 'our' own hill. Still, I'd never tell God what to do…Seated before the Queen Anne dressing table I see I'm blessed not to have been beautiful.*

It's so sad, seeing pretty girls ageing and forced to find within themselves the wit to tackle life plain. I was 'handsome in my way', a half-hearted compliment bestowed for my high colouring, thick hair. I could have given in to self-pity. My bedtime regimen's not as enjoyable tonight. I remove the pins holding my bun in place, and my hair, wiry with age, falls onto my shoulders. I make a come-hither moue towards the spectral Hal – the one I summon up from the far side of the mirror. It's how I tell him things without risking disappointment from his vague appeasing real-time replies. I ask and answer for him too. Thirty years ago, finding myself on the shelf, I dreamed Hal into being. Willpower saved me then. It will do now.

I relax my features. No serious pouting permitted when one's lips are grooved with more tracks and tributaries than the back end of a corgi. I suck in my cheeks to firm my jawline, though it hollows out my face! Delineates my skull.

Urgent Scottish blood surges through my veins; it feels as coercive as a tidal pull. We're fighters, we Scots. Mark my words, I tell my Toasties who have just now joined Hal in the mirror – the Warrney Town Hall's filled! *Melting pot stuff ends badly. If DNA resembles two fried bacon rashers intertwined, how long before we choose partners from petri dishes instead of balls in civic halls? What's wrong with testicles in vestibules?* Oops! One must eschew naughtiness in a maiden speech. I pause to let a victorious whoop erupt into the thin atmosphere. And then I attack my hair with the silver-backed hairbrush until each follicle stands out from my skull, electrified. *If love's not about manners, background, breeding, why make friends with 'our sort' when anyone with a pulse will do? Why have distinct social classes?* I rest my elbow on the dressing table. I buttress my chin with the heel of my hand. *Love is a volatile experiment,* I inform the mirror. *Procreation is already awkward, viz. all the undignified postures it entails. Our ancestors, having struggled to walk upright, must have wondered at the need to caper about like randy goats, and fall in love from a Café Specials list deficient in Fionas and Catrionas. We must unite with our own type!* It could be a chant for a protest march.

The noose of love proves fatal should the victim fall between two stools (oops, better leave stools out of it) *or lose his footing on the rungs of fiscal stability. A misstep might be averted by a will that disinherits the heir should he close on a dubious deal!*

Chapter 34
Ball Part II

Hal offers Claire his arm and leads her to the supper room. They queue in the doorway. The room is decorated with swags of coloured paper in a range of LCP blues and bunches of balloons.

She looks for Clive and Fliss on the dance floor, but there's no sign of them. Not eating, not dancing. Something within her curdles. A beery scrum of revellers joins the queue, distracting Claire from her gut feeling that something's wrong.

She meets Jock from the gun club. He's animated to learn she's from a farm in Northern Victoria. "Great part of the state," he says. "Good shooting up there!"

"Yes," Claire agrees. "Smithfield seemed dull arriving today. I'd never have guessed what a lively community there is tucked out of sight behind cypress hedges and boarded up shop fronts."

"Hear the Simpsons news?" Jock asks Hal. "On second thoughts, forget I said a word. Let's not put the kybosh on a pleasant evening," he says as Hal's focus sharpens.

"Go on, Jock, old boy, you've put your foot in it now," grumbles Hal.

Jock shuffles about as if his mouth needs the help of his feet to work. "Oh, it's probably not worth mentioning." He looks as cheery as the messenger in a Greek tragedy. "Well," he says, "the Simpsons have done it. Application's being considered now."

"What application?" Claire asks, elbowing her way in. She is marrying into the district after all.

"Oh, things aren't too flash, financially, Claire. Cynthia wants us to farm trout for tourists. We'd have to clear the creek bank of blackberries, lantana, gorse, enlarge the dam and set up a picnic spot for visitors, a kiosk and toilets. But a poo drop loo would be close to the creek." He wobbles his hand about. "Problematic!"

"Wow," Claire says, excited. "An elevated board-walk through the paperbarks down by the creek would let visitors enjoy the scenery without damaging the creek bank."

"You've quite a business brain, Claire! I didn't know you'd been exploring."

"Clive took me and Basil out walking at dusk. Beautiful."

"Romantic of Clive to show you the bank the bank will one day own," Hal says wryly.

"I think he was feeling guilty about abandoning me tonight."

Hal gives Claire a searching stare but says nothing. "Cyn wants a tea room in the old stables to sell local crafts," he says.

"Great idea!"

"Cyn's tea-making's not up to much," says Hal gloomily. "She's crafty enough though." He shakes his head. "Never warms the pot. Doesn't believe in tea cosies. I usually organise breakfast."

"Bonnie?"

"We can't pay her for breakfast duties, so she gets on with her French tapes in the morning and breakfasts in her room."

"She's learning French?" Claire sounds surprised.

"Do you have a problem with that?" says Hal.

Hal's put her in her place, deservedly. "No," she says. "But French is so hard. Italian's easier and more useful."

"Italian won't do Bon any good in Paris."

"I didn't know she was going to Paris."

"How would you?" Hal asks. "You've known her for five minutes." He's sounding sensitive on Bonnie's behalf.

"Sorry, French was hard for me so I…" Claire's words tail off awkwardly.

"Well, Bonnie can tackle anything," says Hal, and changes the subject. "I'm no better than Cynthia with kitchen chores." He licks his lips. "We'd persuade Bonnie to come in on the venture…" he says, his eyes fixed on a random spot in the cornicing. "But she's not keen on money-making," he says.

"Not keen on money?" Claire says. Coming from a hardscrabble mixed farm, she's aghast at the thought of liking or not liking money. You need it to get by on so you'd better like it pretty damn much. Her own father had hopes of striking it rich – he bought into a horse named *Golden Fetlocks*, but they'd had nothing but vet bills from her, she tells Hal.

"Well, Bon reckons money has never made anyone happier."

"Just better housed, fed and dressed, perhaps?"

"Bon would dress from the Op Shop. But Cyn insists she wear her cast-offs. Says they're better quality than Op Shop stuff. Not half as cool though. Bon pretends to be grateful, but she hates it.

Now, that silk you're wearing is worth a tidy sum, so don't spill your parfait over it."

"She must've loved her fiancé heaps to have saved so long for it."

"Who says she saved?" says Hal enigmatically. Claire lets the comment pass but marks it down for musing upon later.

"So that's another scheme dashed. We're fated to live beyond our means. The b…council would never give out two trout farm licences. Hopeless!" He draws his lips in.

"Don't get into a funk, Hal," says Jock. "I say, old chap, might I borrow Claire for a spin around the floor?"

"No, I'm with Claire. Once she's produced an heir, she'll be more popular than the Madonna. Sorry, Jock. Integrity of one's line, etcetera."

"But why did the boy entrust you with such a treasure?"

"Oh, here we are," Claire says. "Our turn."

As they're about to move into the supper room, a younger band sets up on stage. Hal scurries towards the group, funnelling his hands, he makes a request for '*Heartbreak Hotel*'.

If Hal is attempting to bridge the generation gap, he's failed. To Claire, Elvis is passé. She scorns the taste of older persons, but thinks anything's better than: '*Shine on Harvest Moon*'. On Hal's return, he beams in triumph. "I've got the music sorted, my dear. Now we can start jiving."

"Thanks, Hal." *Is he on yak testicle injections?* Claire wonders. He couldn't be less like the doddery old bloke who'd taken up residence under Cynthia's thumb earlier. And where's his dicky hip? Gone! He probably invented a dodgy hip to get out of wood-chopping marathons.

Now it's their turn at the feed trough. Hal insists on doing the foraging. Returning with two plates, he looks fragile as he's jostled by uncaring revellers. The choice he offers her is 'Devils on Horseback' or cocktail snags.

"Ta Da, tada!" she says.

"If you're a good girl, I'll let you ride my trusty stead *Beau Fils* on the morrow. Seven a.m. do you?"

"No, Hal. Cynthia is insisting we go to church, and I'm a poor horse woman."

"As long as you've a good seat…" His eyes brighten as he looks up at a newcomer.

"Dada, Claire, how are you holding up?"

"Fine," they chorus. Alex smiles at Claire but there's a troubled look on his face.

"Where's Suz?" Claire asks.

"Migraine. I had to take her home," says Alex.

"You are kind," Claire says.

"Kind's not what girls want. I'm the ute of all men. Good for transporting things. Can't compete with a Porsche engineered to whisk girls away at speed, can I?" He glares at Claire. She wonders what she's done.

Hal's rather interested in this enigmatic exchange. His eyes flicker from his son and back to Claire.

"So, Dada, how's your hip holding out?" asks Alex.

"What's sciatica compared with the pleasure of partnering Claire?"

"Nothing, I'm sure." Alex once again stares until her eyes weasel away from his.

"I'm glad about you and Suz, Alex," she says, looking at her shoes.

He raises his eyebrows interrogatively at her.

"W-well…you know…" she stutters to a halt.

"You mean you're glad two leftovers sought consolation in each other's arms?" He mimes a violinist bowing. Clearly, he's telling her she's glib.

"And what about your situation, Claire? It's okay with you?" Alex asks.

"I'm enjoying myself."

"Wake up Cinderella, your prince is at the ball with someone else!"

"With my permission," she hisses, and leaning towards him she whispers, "At least Clive and Fliss are behaving themselves!"

"Are you quite sure about that?" Alex asks.

"Of course!"

Alex looks at her as if she's an invalid or at least in*valid*. He shakes his head.

Claire feels a tap on her shoulder. "Hi, y'all. Havin' a ball?"

It's her beloved, a poet, and way too economical with words to greet fans singly.

A busy boy, two women on the go! But why is Alex regarding him hostilely? Claire wonders. Her unease of earlier returns. "Hey, Hon," she says, "where have you been hiding?" She snakes her arm around his back and gives him a hug.

"Me? I've been out back snogging Fliss!" he laughs.

133

Dada gasps. Alex's complexion darkens.

"Oh, Clive. You awful tease!" Claire makes to hit him with Cynthia's Oroton evening bag but midway through her swing, she finds she's laughing too much to follow through with it.

Chapter 35
Courtyard Claire and Suz

After the ball Claire awakes alone. Despite Mama's diktat against nookie between unmarried guests beneath her roof, Claire hadn't expected Clive to obey her. It seems he did. She rolls over and gathers her thoughts. Why are euphemisms for sex always cute kindergarten words: as in, 'I didn't get a chocky bickie with my nookie, waa!' And what's with willies, titties, boobies, bosies? Claire stretches. A lick of sunlight enters through a gap in the curtains. It disappears behind a cloud before she can decide whether to reach for it or stay put. Is this a metaphor for…something?

She luxuriates in the strength of her young caressable limbs. Honestly, she has no complaints about life just now. Claire knows this is a complacent train of thought, but she decides she might as well enjoy youth while she can. Cynthia and Hal have such a shopping list of ailments. Their access to medical information hasn't eased their decline one jot. She heads to the downstairs bathroom, taking care to hold the handrail; although she's wary of putting too much weight on it. She carries a duffle bag containing her toiletries, jeans and a fluffy cotton checked shirt – her usual outfit for weekends in Wang. Another cute little penis word: wang dong dingle. She uses the only functioning bathroom. It's a paean to the thirties – all matching sea-green fittings. The bath is rust-stained, so she showers hurriedly. No one is up. She daren't make herself a coffee this early in her friendship with the Sins. She explores the ground floor, noticing all and finding nothing boring.

The morning room's double doors give onto a courtyard enclosing a square of browned off grass. Grouped terracotta urns – more arty than classical are mottled by rust-coloured fungi and various lichens that, despite their lowly ranking in the plant world, add character. The urns are filled with succulents, and clumped against a reclaimed brick wall that's overgrown with ficus and Virginia creeper. She itches to move things about, to make improvements. She might have been a designer in another life. She tells herself to settle down; she mustn't flex her nesting instinct on

135

her in-laws' home. The clouds that had gathered part again. Weak early morning sunshine brightens everything. Claire is getting a better feel for the place today. A scrubbed pine table is homely.

There's an elm-wood buffet, a pair of sandy-coloured armchairs with linen slipcovers.

Cuttings from a holly bush in a vase make all the subtler colours pop.

She exits through the double doors, wishing she'd brought her jacket. As she's deliberating upon whether to go back for it, Suz hails her from the courtyard gate. Claire goes to greet Suz; they hug awkwardly. They didn't hug of a morning when they shared a flat. Just grunted at each other. Claire knows she's got to stop resenting Suzy for winning the 2nd best man on offer in all Melbourne. Claire practices the word 'lover' over and over in her head and applies it to Alex and Suz as a punishment for any jealousy she may feel.

It's no help. She's sorry, but she cannot imagine Suz and Alex as lovers. This is absolute proof of her poor character.

Suzy's choice of boyfriend puzzles Claire. Alex has an aura of the hippie about him; his personal style is scruffy, especially around Cynthia; it's an affectation and childish, she thinks, but it's a tic that's entirely forgivable in Alex. Although the idea of him in a relationship with her highly buttoned up friend Suz just doesn't gel. Claire ponders the incongruity of their partnering. The word 'partnering' brings to mind two kids tied together in a three-legged race, who are trying to pull away from each other. The image amuses her. She gives a yelp of mirth that leaves Suz staring at her as if she's nuts.

"Cyn loves citrus plants," says Claire, stating the obvious and groaning inwardly. How she hates effortful conversation but she has to try. She hopes she and Suz can be easy with each other one day. "And the poor cumquats," she adds.

"Yes. It's Cyn's attempt at an orangery like Versailles, according to Alex. Yet Versailles looked nothing like this when I was there."

"Poor Cyn! She tries so hard," Claire says.

"Well, there's nothing wrong with trying," Suz replies sharply.

Claire holds her tongue. She wonders if the word 'association' would better describe what Suz and Alex have together. She imagines them free-associating like fish in an aquarium, weaving around each other without touching. The image calms her.

"Enjoy yourself last night?" asks Suz.

"Yes, I did," says Claire. "Hal was sweet. And Clive behaved."

"He did?" Suz eyes widen, until they're threatening to take over her small face. She wants Claire to notice her surprise. What does Suz know that she doesn't? Claire wonders. "Of course, he did," she insists.

"Hm. That's good." says Suz doubtfully. The bitch! Claire thinks. She's with a great guy yet she takes pleasure in putting Clive down. "Headache still bad, Suz?"

"No. It's gone! Nothing like a good sleep and a lie in. The world looks brand-new when a migraine goes." Suz stretches and permits herself a smile suggestive of sexual languor.

"Is Alex sleeping in?" Claire knows he is, but she likes saying his name.

"He made me breakfast, then dozed off again. We're lucky, not being engaged. No pressure."

"Cynthia worries less about Alex's supposed 'homosexuality' with you here." Claire gives the 'h' word air quotes.

"Bullshit!" says Suz, her language bolder than it had been pre-Alex. "I could certainly reassure Cyn on that issue if I chose."

"Good," Claire says. "Not that there'd be anything wrong…" She wraps her arms around herself, fending off cold and other things.

"Set the date yet?" Suz asks.

"No."

"Get a move on then," says Suz.

"You think he'll go off me?"

"Possibly."

"Thanks for that, Suz. If you're right it's best we don't rush into anything," Claire says sourly.

"I reckon you're practising being in love while hoping for someone better to show up!"

"Unfair, Suz. I love Clive." Claire hopes she's injected the right degree of indignation into this remark. "Clearly, you don't think we're much of a couple," Claire says.

Suz shrugs, turns on her heel without replying and heads towards the door in the wall. As she gets there, Bonnie hurries through it with a basket over her arm; it's filled with spuds and carrots.

"Morning, Bonnie," Claire calls.

"Hi there, Claire! An' it's Suz, the darlin' girl Alex found himself! So slightly built and sweet and fair." Suz smiles and smiles.

"Yes," Claire says. "And guess who introduced them? *Moi!*" Shit, I hate people who say, *moi,* Claire thinks. Suz's lips scrunch

137

up tighter than a corgi's bottom at this claim. "Not that I'm claiming total credit," Claire says, hurriedly. Gees, she thinks. She's putting her foot in it this morning. Yet she feels compelled to add, "But if I hadn't met Clive, then Suz and Alex would never have met."

Suz glares. "It's always you at the centre of things…"

Claire is left speechless.

Bonnie rescues them. "Girls! Be nice. We might all be related one day." She laughs as if this were a delightful notion. "I'll make coffee while you two make up." She scoots off to the kitchen in her impish way.

Claire tries to usher Suz through the door ahead of her. Suz yanks the door wide open and waits for Claire to enter. Crikey! Claire thinks. It'll be lipsticks at ten paces soon.

Bonnie goes into the scullery for water. It's the business end of the kitchen; all the mincing and mucky pots are dealt with there, so the work area itself stays tidy for the leisurely stirring of soups and casseroles on the Aga.

Seated, Claire thanks Bonnie for the loan of her silk fabric. "Was there a groom?" she asks.

"A well-brought up young lass would never ask," says Bonnie.

"So sad – him dying."

"Who said anything about dying?" says Bonnie.

"Sorry, I thought…"

"You thought wrong."

"He left then. That's worse…"

"Not for him, it isn't! It means he isn't dead. And I'm glad." Bonnie is red in the face now.

"Of course, you're glad he's still alive." Claire is feeling chastened.

Suz shoots her a black look.

"Bonnie, sometimes it's therapeutic having someone to bring up difficult topics," Claire protests.

"So now you're a therapist! Here's the gist of it. My fiancé married someone else. She had the greater claim, being pregnant."

"He was a love rat?"

"No. Just over-scrupulously kind. You'll need to grow up a bit if you want to understand the subtleties of human behaviour, Claire."

Ouch! Claire's shrinks before this tart reprimand, but her curiosity is growing, not diminishing. She knows she should rein it in but, bursting with curiosity, she asks, "Is he still in the district?"

"Enough, Claire."

"Sorry, Bonnie. But mine isn't a prurient curiosity," she insists. 'Prurient' is a word she's been dying to get into a sentence.

"The bloke is happy with how things turned out."

"No hope, then?"

"For us? No. It was for the best."

Claire frowns but says nothing.

"I don't blame you, Claire," says Bonnie. "Writers are perennially curious. One day you'll learn that apparent tragedies often turn out okay."

"You're happier than otherwise, then?" Claire persists.

"That's hypothetical," Bonnie shrugs. "Marriage is unromantic. You're darning socks, or stewing mutton, scrubbing floors. It's drudgery. Living here, I'm paid. I've two lovely boys and no husband to get sick of."

"You put the best slant on things," Claire says. "I couldn't be so philosophical." Suz nods in agreement.

"Well, you'd better gird your loins, girls. Life's goodies aren't shared fairly. However carefully you plan, circumstances collide to alter things and change the way you look at them. Life's not just about love. It's about work, family, friends, community, gardening, politics, books and learning. Fun! Husbands aren't everything. At your age, I thought they were. Now if ye'll let me take a breath, I'll enjoy my coffee, ta!"

Chapter 36
Horse

"Ready?" Hal asks, coming into the kitchen kitted out for riding. Claire's lingering over a coffee, relaxed and congenial with Bonnie, though less so with Suz. There's no sign of Clive on the horizon.

"Hal! Please tell me you're not going riding?" says Claire, beseechingly.

"I'm not, you are, Claire. Let's get your gear on."

"Riding gear?" Claire wails, but Hal's immovable. Once she drains her coffee mug, he hooks his arm through hers and marches her off to the stables. They find Wally, the outdoor dog – a kelpie, curled up in a patch of sunshine. Claire tries to pat him but he growls. She supposes he's a fine working dog and not susceptible to females of her species. Not even a dog would want her in jodhpurs. They're from the cupboard containing Cyn's old riding gear, actually.

Claire inserts her foot into the cradle comprised of Hal's interlinked fingers. He bunks her up.

She wavers half-on, half-off the stallion. Hal boosts her rump until gravity and old habits take over and she can't help but swing her right leg over *Beau Fils* and slide into the saddle. What if I'm found dead in jodhpurs, she frets. Claire wouldn't be seen dead in jodhpurs normally, but then 'dead' is not a word normally paired with 'normally'. Dying is normal – we all do it – but not regularly enough for it to become normal and never on nice drizzly/ sunny mornings like this – the mizzle's just come on in the last few minutes.

It's not the dying that worries Claire though. Once dead she won't know, hopefully. Bugger!

Wrong use of hopefully! She prays she'll live long enough to commit more syntactical blunders.

Even tooth-chatteringly scared, the whole Vatican couldn't force her to renounce her recent atheism. And what if there *is* a heaven just when she's become a fashionable atheist? Could a reasonable God toss her out of heaven for following fashion shallowly? That's what humans are mainly, shallow narcissists. He made us so. Plus He failed to sprinkle enough decent evidence of His existence about. But surely, religion is about belief, not reason. Less than two billion out of seven believe in Xianity. That makes it a boutique religion.

Alex once said she might as well believe because either way there'd be no blowback. He was joking. But what will Claire's friends say when they hear she's died wearing jodhpurs, tied with string to keep them up; pants with empty flappy wingy things?

"Ta Da! Oops! 'ta-da'!" Her words and their fake triumphalism mock her. She fidgets in the saddle until her feet slip as easily into the stirrups as necks into nooses. She's sick with nerves. If she dies, will she receive intimations of non-being? Is death at the first hurdle a poor legacy to leave in horsy country? Will it provoke superior smirks in Fliss and Cynthia?

"Are you feeling a little queer, m'dear? If so, I've a remedy for that," Hal says, taking a flask from his hip pocket and passing it to Claire.

She throws her head back and takes a draught. Ta Da. She passes it back. Hal takes several swigs before replacing the screw top.

"Hal, if I fail, fall, please make excuses for me."

"Naturally."

"And do let me ride on the flat."

"The entire Western District is flat. Courage, Claire. You'll be back in the kitchen in a jiffy."

Yes, it'll all be over and done with, she thinks; I'll be indoors enjoying freshly brewed coffee with pale yellow sunshine drawing fingers of golden light across the floor-boards and exulting – me that is not the light – in the after-glow of having faced my fears. I bet skydivers enjoy the having-dived more than the diving.

"What doesn't kill you makes you stronger," says Hal.

"Don't be a sap, Hal. Sorry that was rude. Please tell Clive I loved him…"

Hal gives *Beau Fils'* rump a tap. He moves off sedately but going through the gate Claire's running shoe – she'd refused Cynthia's crusty riding boots – catches on the bent nail of the gate latch; she's held fast while the horse moves leisurely on. "Stop!" she calls, but now he barges on, muscles clenching and unclenching. She feels a winded jolt as she thuds onto hard-packed earth. What happened to last night's molten mud? Her innards are displaced; her heart and lungs collide. There's pain.

Someone leans over her: "Hells Bells, girlie. You came a cropper. Let's get you up."

"No," she groans. Hal, worried, calls for Clive, who arrives in his church duds and starts palpating her. Fracture, he tells crowding heads, looking like petals from Claire's vantage point.

"Now back off! Ambulance, Da! Stay with me, Claire."

Next thing she's being jolted about until she lands on something firm. Wondrous, the dreamy floatingness of the world.

There's questions. Things are said. Answers? Clive climbs in. He takes her hand. He says niceish things, she knows this for his face is soft and flab wobbles under his jawline. Cynthia scrabbles at the door, a sulphur-crested cockatoo for church. Clive pushes her off. They go. Claire laugh laughs. Then dozes. Dreams. "Dear Mary Mother of God, forgive my sins," she gabbles soundlessly: "Clive and I did it 27 times in our first month, until our rate tailed off; I put each f…in my diary, with asterisks. Relations occurred without the church's blessing. But since we didn't take precautions, heaven will smile upon our union, though if I'd known I'd die, I'd have sinned oftener. I hope my shirt didn't fly up, leaving my belly roll for Suzy to gloat over.

"Sorry folks, for my awkward funeral. Wedding-baked meats etc. I won't see Alex again.

"Sad.

"Sorry, Mum and Dad. I was creative with the truth; left you out of my seismic emotional life.

"And now you're in your little Target Sunday bests. Will they segregate you from the groom's lot? Marmite!

"I'm dying without funeral etiquette. Without philosophy. Never having tasted durian. I won't get through 'Grey's Anatomy'. Read Nietzsche. Climb a monkey-puzzle tree.

"I'll let the living deal with social class issues. I'll be in the democracy of the equally dead.

"Will Hal sing: '*Immortal, Invisible*', to annoy Cyn, it being a 'Methodistical' hymn for hard-scrabble miners? Added up and averaged out, my marriage would have failed. Dada is a pet, Ma a tyrant, Alex kind, Clive somewhat sexy.

"My accounting system goes: Dada (+ 1 point), Mama (− 1), Alex (+ 1), Clive (+ 1) = 3 plusses and 1 minus = 2 points out of 4. It would have been worth getting married – just! But eventually, I'd have found myself with an unattractive stranger."

"'Don't chalk, darling,' says Clive, all thick and weird. Think and wired.

Chapter 37
Leaving Hospital with Alex

After Claire's operation, it's decided she stay at 'The Lodge'. Woozy from the procedure to set her tibia, discussions about her recuperation proceed without her.

"You'll be right as rain, Claire. Besides, with my finals coming, I'll have no time for you. It's a boon," says Clive.

"Great!" says Claire. She's a sad winged bird. Her full range of movement is not even guaranteed, yet Clive is happily abandoning her.

"Cynthia hates me," says Claire. "Let me go home with you," she croaks.

"Darling, I knew you'd understand."

She flaps her hands ineffectually but he concentrates on filling a vase with those horrid artificial felt-petalled flowers, the ones she always forgets the name of...

"Gerberas! Gorgeous. They'll last forever," he says, admiring his handiwork.

Only because they're already half dead. Like me, Claire thinks.

"They're gorgeous. I could've been a florist if I'd wanted to be," Clive says.

"You could have been lots of things, Clive...Right now, you're a..."

"Now you be a patient. Okay? Got to go. Alex is staying to help out."

"Thank God!" says Claire.

"Yes," says Clive. He kisses Claire and goes to consult the nurse.

Marooned in the lumpy bed, she thinks about Clive's complacency. His assumption is that Alex is all innocent brotherliness, but Claire knows he likes her far too much. Clive wouldn't believe Alex capable of the sort of feelings she's glimpsed.

Clive is a gas BBQ – when turned on, he fires up. He's no high maintenance wood-fire; he needs no poking, prodding or (dare she even think it?) blowing. Guaranteed one bonk per week, he's content.

Clive returns; he affixes her clipboard to the foot of the bed.

"Love me, Clive?"

"You raise my happiness quotient massively. You're my Himalayas!"

"You want to climb me?"

"No, Hon, you make me feel I'm soaking in minerals at Hepburn Springs."

"Shouldn't I be exciting you?"

"I'm stimulated at work. I'll miss your healthy cooking, though. I'd started losing my pot belly!" He pats his mid-riff, proud as a peacock. "But you'll be as safe down here as in a chastity belt at Pentridge. Goodbye, darling!" He blows Claire a kiss from the doorway.

Alex picks Claire up from hospital the following day. He wheels her to the car, helps her into the jeep; he arranges her broken limb on the back seat, snaps on her safety belt and packs the wheelchair into the boot.

He belts up but keeps his hand on the ignition key, thinking. "Who do you want?" he asks her, "Clive or Ma?"

"Clive," she says, wishing she had a third option.

"Well, he comes bracketed with Mama. She'll be part of your marriage. It's potent, oedipal stuff. You sure you want to occupy one corner of a love triangle?"

Claire shrugs. "I've never found myself in a love twosome before."

"Love isn't for 'finding oneself in' but for falling helplessly into. It's stepping in dog shit and not caring. If you're not ready to decide, go see the world. Grow up," says Alex.

"Clive says my innocence makes me special."

"Especially naïve and malleable," says Alex.

"Which bits of the world should I see?"

"Take a stab at the atlas. I ran away. Left uni. Learned a lot."

"Why did you come back, then?"

"Everywhere is as interesting as anywhere," says Alex.

"Then what's the point of leaving?" asks Claire.

"Ha! You've a good bull-shit detector, Claire."

"What do you want from life, Alex?"

"That's private," he says quietly. He leans forward, turns on the ignition. The jeep judders into life. Flat suburbs zip past them. They leave the landscape of Claire's moral certainties behind, along with the convictions she's lived by: 'Thou shouldst love one man for life' has been replaced by 'fall in love weekly, provided thou keepst it in the one family'.

She sighs and studies Clive's signature on her cast with an index finger. What a skite!

It has fat loops – serifs. Alex's is sketchier. A high-peaked tent-like 'A' flows into a valley from where it rises gracefully. Al~~~d~. Claire feels Arabic tracing it.

Why, in 20 years on earth, has she fallen in love only twice? And why have these outbreaks of insanity occurred more-or-less simultaneously? Is an epidemic underway?

Alex takes more pleasure in manoeuvring Hal's jeep through the Warrnambool back streets than Clive does in the rush of his Porsche along highways.

He rubs his chin. "Since you asked, Claire, I might as well tell you. *You* are what I want." His eyes seek hers via the rear-vision mirror, piercing her calm.

She can't speak for ages; when she does, she repays his honesty with nothing but juvenile false modesty. "I'm ordinary," she says. His image in the mirror blurs.

"Do you love him, Claire?"

"I…I don't know. We made love 27 times in four weeks but that was because Clive was tired. A point 9 average. 'Not too bad,' he said." She claps her hand over her mouth.

"Ha-ha!" Alex laughs mirthlessly and pounds his thigh with his fist. "Point 9 of a fuck."

"I'd never short change-you like that. With you, I'd be tireless."

Claire is speechless. She knows something significant is happening, but she sits there in a bubble of silence. Alex too.

"Why?" she asks, once they hit a long, flat streamer of road.

"Why what?" says Alex.

"Why do you feel…you know?"

"That I love you? Romeo said it for me:

" *'But safe! What light through yonder window breaks?*
It is the East and Juliet is the sun'."

Alex, wheeling his arm, hits the cabin light, turns it on.

"The cabin light of my life is turned on, Claire. I'd happily be 'crabbed, cabined and confined' with you."

"Imprisoned?" she asks. Apparently Alex decides her retort's not worth a reply. "Juliet's a love goddess. I'm a nobody."

"You're like a sunset; one diffused by long, low streaky cloud."

"Like a bacon rasher?" she giggles.

Alex drives on, his face masklike. Claire wipes her eyes on her sleeve, fluffs up her hair. Odd, she thinks, even with our emotions in turmoil, we women want to look our best.

He angles the rear-vision mirror so he can catch her expression. "Forget I said it, Claire. It was wrong."

"Said what?" Claire wants to hear him spell it out. Her cast is beyond help now. Tears and *tears*.

"Said what I said. It's ten," he says. "Let's visit my sacred site."

"I mustn't get off on the wrong foot with Ma…" she says.

"That's hilarious, Claire," Alex says, swinging his arm over to pat her cast.

"I'm not getting into Cyn's black books just to keep you company."

"Then hurry home, and she'll snap her trap on you like one of her carnivorous plants. She'll watch you dissolve."

Claire goes quiet while Alex negotiates an intersection.

"Okay," she says, once they're back on track. "Let's phone. Fliss is coming for lunch. I can't offend her. She seemed nice…"

"She's good at *seeming* nice."

"Okay," says Claire. "Show me your sacred site."

Alex takes a sudden right. They leave the main road. He drives in silence. At the signage point for a tourist drive, they head towards the coast through undulating sand hills scattered with grass, spiky as hair plugs. They meander slowly as if they've a lifetime to arrive.

The road behaves eccentrically, Claire thinks. What shire engineer would countenance a road that's not Euclidian, in being the shortest distance between two points? Where granite boulders strike up through the sand, the road veers ever more recklessly. At last they pull into a lay-by beside a rocky outcrop and park.

"The view from the lookout here is fabulous," Alex says.

"I can't see…"

Alex eases her out of the seat. "Weight on your right foot," he orders. He picks Claire up as if she were feather-light, he nuzzles her hair, luxuriating in the smell of her. She feels as if a boundary's been crossed. She doesn't mind. "It's a pleasure to carry you, Claire. You're like a pile of sheets from the clothesline drying in the sun."

Chapter 38
Beach

Alex has been candid about his feelings for Claire. And now she feels her will's been sapped; that she must follow the grain of her life, wherever it takes her.

In the late 1980s the science of pleasure is filtering down to laypersons. Until recently, love had been about vague and fuzzy 'vibes'. Nowadays, endorphins – potent euphoria molecules – are known to act like drugs on the brain's pleasure sensors, sometimes even overriding logic to convince us we're in love.

Despite the strength of her feelings for Alex, Clive was the twin Claire saw first.

She's confused, guilty. She's no love maverick. Neither convent school's 'thou shall nots' nor the subtler indoctrination of family have fitted her for loving two men at once.

Alex lifts her onto the bluestone seawall and jumps down onto the sand. She wobbles ungainly on one leg and two crutches, watching him running about, wheeling, hooning, and imitating seagulls until he's scared all wildlife off the beach.

At the water's edge, he plays tag with frilly wavelets, looking like maidens' petticoats.

They chase him off the firm wet sand onto the softer, drier stuff. He backtracks as soon as another set gathers strength for an onslaught. Niftily, he dodges the waves, predicting the strength of each surge. It's a territorial dispute; he's winning it for now. His Blundstones remain dry.

He turns towards her. "Claire. I love you!" he shouts.

"No!" she yells into the wind. *Yes, you must,* she tells herself, silently. *And forever.*

"Too late!" he replies.

"Stop immediately."

"Easier…earth…turn…ay." Scraps of his sentence reach her on the breeze.

But focusing upon Claire is Alex's undoing. He loses his skirmish with the sea. A wave rushes up his calves, drenching his boots and jeans. He charges up the beach, swooping in to land beneath the rock-wall.

"Get your jeans off," she says, worried he'll catch a chill.

"You want me nude?"

"No, I want to be nursed by a healthy man."

"Heartless girl. Come, enjoy my great, big beach."

"I can see it from here. Gorgeous. Cliffs like two big encircling arms."

"You need to see it up close. The beauty is in the detail, Claire. My private rock pools are full of lettuce, sea-weed and sea cucumbers."

"A mixed salad," she says.

"Lean into me, I'll help you down," Alex insists.

"I'm cold."

"He wraps his arms around her working foot plus the poor disabled one. Better?"

"Yes, that feels nice."

"It could be nicer…"

"Let's go, Alex. It's time…"

'Yes, it's time." Alex leaps up onto the wall. He unbuttons her coat. It's warmer down there sheltered by the sea wall.

"Okay, you win. How do we do this?"

He jumps down. "Throw your coat, drop your crutches. Trust the universe to give you a soft landing."

"If everything turns out for the best, then how come I fell off that bloody stallion?"

"The best isn't necessarily about you, Claire. Clearly it was the stallion's time to send someone flying. His fate. And yours. And mine. You had sick leave. I don't have a proper job. Clive does. It worked out perfectly. I'm here and fit. And you've only your unimportant bits disabled."

"If that's your seduction spiel…get fucked…"

"Okay," he says, grinning.

"I've promised to marry Clive. I'm committed."

"Committed! Great word for a relationship, a madman or a felon. Don't invite me to your committal hearing, Claire."

"I'll be in oyster silk or champagne taffeta," she says. "With Mendelssohn."

"The full cliché."

"At least it's my cliché."

"It's everyone's, that's the point of clichés."

"So why did your Presbyterian God let bloody *Beau Fils* maim me? He brushed up against that nail on purpose. I saw evil intent in his eye. And why did He put me on the tram tracks for Clive to save, not you?"

"Because Clive wouldn't have saved me," Alex jokes.

"Ha-ha!"

"I don't know, Claire, maybe He was trying to organise time for us alone."

"Does God use stallions in His plans?"

"Maybe. Even a Hindu god would favour real love over a fleeting month of lust. Maybe you needed a wake-up fall. All right then, marry Clive if you must, exasperating woman!"

Alex rips his pocket lining inside out, spills scallop shells onto the sand. He forms them into patterns. 'I *heart* CLA', his message says.

"Who's CLA?" she asks, smugly.

"I'm writing a letter to my favourite sea-creature – the clam – it's tight and secretive, hard to prize open but worthwhile. Shit! Ran out of shells. He grins at Claire, taps her cast. Come, drop your crutch. Let yourself go. I'll catch you."

"I'm afraid of letting go," says Claire.

"You know you have the urge. Give in to it. Come."

"Okay," she says.

Alex holds his arms wide. She drops her coat and her sticks clank onto the bluestone.

Does the hospital fine you for rough usage? she wonders.

But their timing's out by more than a month. The instant she leaps, Alex turns to follow the flight of a heron.

Overbalancing, she screams shrilly, picturing her newly set tibia being wrenched apart, plus minor bones becoming infected with the novelty and fracturing too.

'Don't build on sand', Claire remembers from the Bible. Sand won't withstand the elements.

'The centre cannot not hold, mere anarchy is loosed upon the world'.

Pretentious ramblings but Yeats was Claire's VCE poet of choice; he came to mind as she launched herself. Marvellous, she thinks, thinking and falling, how one idea leads to the next in a daisy chain of tenuousness.

Mid-fall, Alex senses movement. He's too late to brace himself for her weight. His mouth forms a 'no' but having begun falling, no advice helps while laws of physics hold.

Her destiny isn't unfolding, it's exploding in her face.

Landed, at least she's horizontal. Once more she's fallen only to find herself face to face with a lovely man. Alex's chest has been filled out handcrafting furniture, and not turned into a talking point by a false bosom apron.

"You okay?" they ask each other.

"I think so. The pain's no worse," she says. "Did I hurt you?"

"In loving Clive, not me." He closes his eyes, goes quiet for a bit.

"Alex, I hate hurting you. I want everyone happy."

He's silent. "Alex, talk to me." She pries one eye open. His eyeball has rolled into its socket. "Talk to me, Alex!" she yells, slapping his face.

He opens his eyes, leers at her and winks. "I may never have children," he says. "You jumped me when I wasn't looking. You couldn't wait to have me, could you?"

"I could so wait."

"So, you'll wait for me?" he asks.

Claire beats her fists on his chest. "No, I'm not waiting."

"Got to have me right away?" he says.

"God, Alex. Stop twisting everything. I want everyone happy and everything fair."

"I heard you. Hoped I was hallucinating. Everyone happy? Go buy a Barbie doll."

"I thought you were ready for me," she says.

"I am ready for you, Claire."

"You didn't catch me. What if my fracture's come unset?"

"Then I'll be your personal slave forever." He frees his arms, drags her duffle coat over them both. "Warm?" he asks.

"If I end up back in hospital, it'll be okay provided you win the double-meaning game. You twins…so bloody flippant…"

"But lovable?" Alex plucks a handful of sand, lets it spill through his fingers.

Claire takes a tendril of seaweed. "We don't fall for everyone we find sexy. Robert Redford's sexy but…" she pops a bubble on its string of pearls. It feels good. She pops manically until her fingernails hurt. She could pop polyps forever. "What next?" she says.

"It's up to you. You have the upper hand."

"I'm disabled. I can't hop up and run away."

"Ease yourself up gradually, roll sideways. Move your good leg first."

"Now you're getting rid of me." Saying this Claire's aware of how illogical she's being.

Alex grabs her hands to still them. She's been drumming her fists on his chest, an unconscious reaction to their predicament. He brings her hands to his mouth and kisses them. "Oh, Claire, one minute you don't want me. Next, I'm in trouble for helping you go."

"You're staring, Alex."

"Your head is in my face! Your nose has 17 freckles? Don't hit me. 17 is a prime number. But point 27 isn't! Remember that next time Clive…"

"I wish I hadn't told you that." She makes to hit him but strokes his stubble. "What next?"

"That's up to you, Claire. You could plait my ponytail. I liked your French plait that first night. French kisses. French manicures. French letters. Why is everything racy French?"

She shrugs. "It's not my sole responsibility."

"Being French?"

"No, Dopey. Deciding…about us…"

"We could flip this shell? Let the clam decide. Heads we kiss, tails…?" He flips then palms the shell before she sees how it's fallen.

Chapter 39
Bacon and Eggs

If two falls aren't bad enough, it's my third fall – the one from the seawall – that lands me in hot water – morally, if not literally. Alex is family, our intimacy violates a taboo. On the peaks of Mt Parnassus Greek gods are rubbing their hands in gleeful anticipation of my comeuppance.

Despite my bung foot, I didn't sin inadvertently like Oedipus. But how gravely I've transgressed!

Diary Entry 1:
I'm convalescing chez Cynthia. I write when not shelling peas or darning socks or soaking up sunbeams during rare sunny arvos in the courtyard.

My fracture's healing slowly. Cynthia threatens to send Alex home. Luckily, I'm too heavy for her to manage or Alex would be gone by now. We behave with circumspection – she's not buying it.

Nor is Hal. His questing tortoise neck twists from A's face to mine, verifying what he knows & dreads.

Goals
1. Stand up to Cynthia.
2. Forget Romance. HEAL!
3. Write

I get four hours a day of congenial company from Alex. He's giving me the classical education I missed out on chez the nuns; he encourages my writing, greets me each morning with a brotherly kiss on the brow.

"How's Joyce James?" he asks. He jokes, teaches me chess; he leaves during phone calls with Clive.

Ministers tactfully to my needs.

"Why aren't you getting on with your chair?" I ask.

"When I'm with a woman like you, I'm not tempted to spend all day in the workshop," he whispers. "Once you're off your crutches, we'll drive to Port Fairy, to the island where the Shearwater nest."

Cyn's often in the kitchen. It's beside the lounge – my sick bay. Bonnie's being overwhelmed with help.

In Alex's demeanour, I see nothing beyond what's brotherly but there's a humming in the air between us as if we're connected by an invisible string that vibrates subtly.

Returning from the beach that day, we decided to bide our time.

Alex has an opinion on everything. I raise topics to challenge him. "Alex, I say, I can't heal until you've taught me all you know."

"Okay, I'll up my erudition a notch each day, so you'll never quite catch up. Then you'll need me forever." I can't help blushing at this romantic notion. "Scheherazade with a pony tail," he says, "concocting tales to fascinate or I'll lose my head. Too late, I've lost it already."

Reluctantly, he plays with his prototype upending spine-extending chair; he'll apply for a Design Council grant once the idea coalesces. Now he's distracted by thoughts of me! Is he really? I hope so, and I dread it equally. I receive one hour a day from Cynthia so the ratio of Alex's company to _her_ bossiness is 4:1. Happy ratio? No. Cyn delivers her hour of lavender scented malice most efficaciously.

Example:

"Claara," Cynthia calls, "I'm frying bacon. There's room in the pan for you." She materialises in the lounge, in a pink candlewick dressing gown, matching rollers, her face is flushed from the Aga.

"Oops," she says putting her hand over her mouth to simulate regret at her ill-chosen words. "Silly me!"

She taps her temple, miming a level of idiocy that we both know she doesn't possess. The corners of her mouth droop in mimicry of a clown face. "You can't eat bacon. The Belgian lace is for a hand-span waist."

Bonnie barges into this exchange. "Now, Cyn, there are too many thin girls. It's a downhill race to become a broomstick or dead, and all for some shallow man."

Cynthia looks fed-up.

"Surely, Clive enjoys Claire's curves,'" says Bonnie.

"No smutty talk, dear."

Alex drops in with kindling for the firebox. "Two streaky bacon DNA twists for you my girl plus a big fat fried egg." He heads towards the kitchen.

153

"Remember how I had to lace you up on your wedding day," says Bonnie. "And you passed out."

How does Bonnie get away with her cheek?

"Bonnie," I ask, "were you here when Hal and Cynthia married?"

"Yes, I started at 17. I knew Hal well" – she pauses a second here – "before Cyn came on the scene."

I tense up, awaiting Cyn's retort to B's claim of prior knowledge of Hal. Cynthia's mouth sets in a hard line but she says nothing.

"Poor Cynthia," I say. "You must have felt like a cow being crushed by her own ribs."

Cynthia inhales, examines her image in the mirrored sideboard. "Ideally, you're too tall for Clive," she says, parry for thrust.

"Better go in and get my legs shortened," I say. Bonnie laughs raucously.

"Alex is making you a bacon sandwich," Ma says. "Enjoy now. Grieve later. At least exercise your arms." She wheels hers as if semaphoring her witches' coven.

Aromas invade the drawing room. Cynthia trundles off to supervise as fast as her Hush Puppies allow.

1 Ma: 0 Claire!

Clive and I mouth platitudes during phone calls. Lots of platitudes like, 'missing you, hon', 'take care', 'keep your chin up'.

"Bought any new silk duvets recently?"

"Turned your face into a pav yet?" Clive retorts.

"Don't drink horizontal on the sofa. It'll cure your hiccups by killing you, Hon!"

"I'm learning to write with my foot," he says, and I laugh so loud, Cyn comes in to see what's up.

"Good to hear you two getting on," she says.

I don't know enough about Clive to ease our conversations along. Clive and I have spent a total of nine hours talking since we met. No wonder we're awkward. Our love is too recent to have evolved its own catch phrases. Born hurriedly, it already needs mouth-to-mouth resuscitation. Any free time we had was spent drinking, eating, snogging, but rarely talking.

So, if I don't know my fiancé's concerns, blame hospital timetabling. Does Clive vote Liberal? Read classics? Barrack for Collingwood? Read philosophy? Asked what existed before the 'Big Bang', he'd said, "Whoever thinks he knows the meaning of life is a wanker." It was our longest spurt conversation yet!

Despite my delinquent obsession with A, I'm torn. I've a duty to try loving Clive, knowing 'duty' and 'love' shouldn't exist in the same sentence. I doubt I ever I loved him, but I can't let him go yet.

Here in the country it's hard to keep Clive in the forefront of my mind, A being so, so…I need an omni word here. I'll leave a gap…A wouldn't need to. He'd know the word already; Clive wouldn't care.

Clive is sure life has no meaning. A is sure he doesn't know. But he speculates, wonders, mulls.

Mama's more likely to gull than mull. She drops rocks into the tranquil well of my peace of mind via anecdotes about Fliss *et al* Clive's other gels. She trumpets their riding exultant to hounds. Asks: "Claire, do you ride? Oh, silly me, it's why you're in that horrid cast, fallen before the first hedge."

As far as soundings of my heart go, presence trumps abscess, oops, absence, every time. A bird in the hand in the bush is worth an aviary of peacocks in Melbourne town.

Now I can wheel myself from the lounge room through the kitchen to the conservatory, where I lie on a daybed, trying to summon up the image my fiancé's face. All I can retrieve is a caricature of Clive's moon-face, the corners of his mouth quirking up in a crazed grin while he picks pasta ears off his bosom apron, whistling through them before swallowing them. Was I ever that girl? The middle of his face is empty; thinking of him brings on macular degeneration in me. The skylarking, so funny *that* night, seems totally naff now.

Dada is an angel. I can't fault him. He guesses the complexity of my feelings towards his sons, and though I chatter fatuously about how great it is that Clive's coming down soon, and how we'll have more fun than anyone's had with three legs between them, Dada shakes his head, smiles sadly, eases himself out of his armchair and heads to the sideboard for another Scotch. And it's not even teatime.

Mama guesses something's not right. She studies me with puzzlement. "You don't mind Alex helping you to the lav?" she'll ask, squinting at me. "Nursing toughens you gels up."

I smile sweetly. "We all have bums, and they all need wiping and I'm capable of doing that alone.

"How lucky that A's here to lift the chair over the uneven floors. You with your frozen shoulder…"

Mama frowns. "Marriage to a professional is like having an absentee spouse, you know," she'll say. "Early in my marriage Hal was always off at dawn to assess bridge stress in peak hours. He'd buy a cold pie. I've no doubt Da was off early home late – he'd assess stress levels brought on by the prospect of Ma's cold collation."

"I'm throwing myself headlong into my career," I say.

"So, you *are* going on with nursing?"

My bowels clench. My diary! When A. took me to the old volcano, she…! I can't think about it!

I smile sweetly and grind my teeth. Failure to react to her malice is near-criminal. What if she knew her prize ram had been superseded by the black sheep? She'd be glad Clive's been saved for Fliss, perhaps.

Chapter 40
Cyn at Church

If guests can diarise, then so can I. I took Claire to church today. I'd planned to 'church' her last Sunday but she fell from *'Beau Fils'* instead. I was just leaving when I heard piteous cries and phoned for an ambulance while the boys made a makeshift gurney and carried her in.

Did God, moving mysteriously, have anything to do with Claire's fall? I mean, who falls from a near-stationary horse without divine intervention?

Home now, Claire has been resisting my attempts to raise her religious profile; she's an atheist one day, an agnostic next, Buddhist in the evening. Just as I'm throwing up my metaphorical hands, I resort to the insider info discovered within the pages of her diary to give me an insight into Claire's state of mind.

"You know, dear," I say, "a dose of church might be the thing to help you decide."

She flushes at the word 'decide'. "Decide what, Cynthia?"

"Decide upon your future," I say, leaving it vague.

"Oh, Cynthia, I'm giving up on…"

"Marrying?" I ask.

"Nursing," she says, unready to confess her feelings for Alex yet. "I want to write."

"Goodness," I say, appearing surprised. "Does Clive know?"

Claire looks so miserable, I'd give her a hug but it wouldn't be the thing, so I keep my arms folded across my chest.

"Clive will be displeased, but you must follow your heart."

"Yes," she says, looking frantic.

"Writing's an urge," I say. "And a woman must follow her urges – I mean the decent ones."

"Cynthia," she says eventually. "Perhaps I will come to church."

Poor girl. Brought up in a loving family of the sort that leaves one as vulnerable as shelled snails in a Parisian restaurant.

Alex shakes his head. He thinks she's capitulating, but he pushes the wheelchair onto the turning circle Hal supplies with quartz so it won't revert to a bog.

I'm wearing my favourite hat, all brim but little crown. One needs a crown in today's gale. I clamp it to my head, leaving me one hand for the wheelchair. Alex calls: "Ma, lose the silly hat!"

But I battle on, praying it'll stay in place. It's a 'picture' hat. Supposed to set my face off, though with this horrid horizontal wind, its brim decrees that I walk hunched over like a crone or end up in a pothole. In church I'll have to throw back my head with sunflower-like abandon to be seen.

"Claire," I say, "do your bit or we'll get bogged." The gel has strong arms so we make decent progress.

The church is a tent pitched in a windstorm. In consecrating this makeshift edifice, God was evidently trialling environmentally suitable building styles. Wise of Him not to waste bluestone on a site that mightn't 'take' since it adjoins the ugly BP.

We brave the scrum of Marconis – the father Italian, the wife Maureen, Irish. They assemble in the forecourt in long woollen coats. Why not talk later while masticating their Aberdeen Angus lumps of beef as big as plates? Maureen hails me – we're neighbours now.

The warmth of my response is congruent with Christianity – just.

I settle Claire into the aisle beside my pew. The organist plays, *Shall We Gather at the River?*

Claire's a rock-like obstruction in the river of life. We'd have been better at the end of the row but fewer congregants would then have seen Clive's pretty fiancée. The pew's heated rail is my footrest, and I allow its warmth to percolate up through my skirt.

It's a loose silk undies day today, but God doesn't need to know this. What would the minister think? It'd give him a blush to go with his stammer.

Once I'm sure nothing of interest will be said, I slump into alert semi-consciousness.

Who needs Alex's yogi vouchers with church so close? It'd be a waste of petrol travelling to observe cheesecloth and ashes hippies contort themselves into pretzels. I remove the hatpin, confident it won't be needed, despite Mr Preeps being a windbag and needing a little prick. The boys would be shocked to see the bawdy side of their Mama. Hal wouldn't. Each generation thinks it invented naughtiness.

Now I assume an attitude of gratitude in hopes of His beatitude. I've a pencil handy to jot that down. I never waste felicitous phrases.

The McCance/Marconis in their shiny suits haven't a clue; it's the holes and patches in Hal's worsted jackets that make a gent of him.

And now it's all things wise and wonderful. All fur trims, great and small. All coats come from Georges. Draped bodices for all. He loves things teal and shapeless. He made our twin-sets wool. Hooray for pearls and opals. Hooray for horse-brass scarves…

Wearing a full fur coat (a little *arriviste*), Gwen sweeps in late on the arm of big bluff square-jawed Len Law. Handsome pair! They're like the awful Whitlams as to bearing. I'm honoured they've befriended me! Oops! No, it's the other way around. I raise my suede-gloved arm in greeting. Such an aura of health comes from wealth or good sex, although if that were true, Maureen Marconi would look like Lady Muck. She catches sight of my fluttering fingers, and waves frenziedly. I cover my mouth as if to say: 'not waving, yawning'. I must discourage Maureen, or we'll be invited over for margaritas soon.

At last the minister spreads words of comfort over us like margarine on Granny Davis bread in a voice that suggests he's juggling marbles near his epiglottis. Restrained piety is the note I aim for. Doctrinally, I feel a knot of grievance tighten in my chest when the minister reads inflammatory Pauline passages. St Paul has turned me into a blamey feminist! One morning, I twisted around, expecting to see faces contorted in scowls of an intensity similar to my own but the flock was busy wool-gathering, except for Gwenda, whose glower of pain and rage was remarkable.

Much later, after we'd befriended the Laws, I learned that Gwenda used prunes to alleviate bowel complaints and although striving to coordinate her 'voidance' with her churchgoing, sometimes the parson's oration cued the prunes in to make a break for freedom – just when she could not. Her anguish was hard to conceal, given clenching of facial muscles among others.

Gwen made this confession to me while taking cognac one night, after a dinner party; hearty laughter cemented our friendship.

On the day in question, Gwenda hadn't a clue she'd been taken for a rebel. Over a cup of tea in the Sunday school, I grumbled about 'that awful man' and Gwenda, thinking I meant the parson, laughed aloud as she too found him a bore. Thus, deep friendships may flourish even in the meagre soil of misunderstanding!

Gwenda was pleased to be singled out by me. A pharmacist, Gwen had remained friendless for want of suitable candidates. I, too, despite community work, was one friend short of the full complement, so the friendship suits us both.

Despite the misunderstanding at its bottom (tch! how wickedly the sub-conscious mind works), Gwenda was elated, indeed elevated, to be singled out by Hal and me. She had little time for gentry before we took her up. As for me, I'm glad to be chums with such a sensible, unpretentious woman from the middle classes.

Just as Mr Preeps is beseeching the Lord to "Be with us and remain with us in the week to come", the heavens open and there's an almost tropical downpour. An excess of drumming and thrumming on the corrugated iron roof – comforting when comfortably curled up with one's hottie – bodes ill; is God reviling this, His measly church hall?

I call for help in manoeuvring the wheelchair towards the hall. Some young ones oblige. I exit with "Lead kindly light amid the encircling gloom" ringing in my ears. Maudlin, these non-conformist hymns. It reminds me to change the batteries of the bedroom torches.

Blast! The walk downhill has done for my ankle. Now a word in Gwen's ear.

"Gwennie, thank God!"

"I'd hug you but my limb has been commandeered," whispers Gwenda, trying to disconnect from Maureen McCance/Marconi Her Octopussyness.

"You seem liverish, Gwen. Is it your usual theological issue?"

We laugh. "I'm fine, Cyn. None of us is getting any younger," Gwen says.

I wish she wouldn't use platitudes. It's Toastmasters for Gwen. "I've a brainwave," I say. "I won't disturb you and your new pal." I poke my tongue out at Maureen's back.

"What's up, Cyn?" she asks.

"You're invited to lunch. I've solved Clive's romantic problems, ours as well."

"Didn't know you were having romantic problems, Cynthia. The thing is we're invited to the Marconis' for lunch and as you didn't invite us this week, we'd no excuse." She bunches her mouth up as if trying to shrink it to a pinhole.

Chapter 41
Post-Church Lunch

Thanks to the heavens opening, GwenLen, guilty about lunching with the McCance's, drive Claire and Cynthia home. Rain has made the road's narrow shoulders deadly, and Claire's accident has left her with a sense of dread. Her former love of novelty has gone; change no longer means happy excursions into the unknown; exciting adventures are likely to become exiting adventures. She's too young to die; she'd hate to see anyone she loved getting hurt or bogged.

Does this include Cynthia? Has their joint church going bonded them? Has their zizzing off side by side made her feel cosy as if she'd crept into bed of a Sunday morning with her mum?

Pew!

Claire admires the masculine efficiency of Len as he lifts her into the front seat, snaps the wheelchair shut and packs it in the boot. Gwenda holds her brolly over Cyn while she climbs into the back. They join a queue of cars going nowhere fast. Len must be driving by radar as visibility's zero.

"You'd think some of them would drop into the Parthenon for lunch to ease the traffic jam," says Cyn, employing the self-serving logic she's known for. She herself would never be seen dead in a Greek Chippy, though she sends Bertie down for supper on pension day. It amazes Claire that folks who own broad acres can draw a pension.

They laugh about God orchestrating inclement weather in order to cause maximum inconvenience for His flock. Does He disapprove of them so much He must begin to punish them immediately? On the slow drive home, they speculate about what has displeased Him. "I reckon someone's committed one of the Seven Deadly Sins," says Len. "Which one, Cynthia?"

"Adultery," she says. "Those Marconis didn't come by stork."

"Now, Cynthia, be nice! We're going there for lunch. My money is on avarice," says Len.

"You'll learn all about that at lunch," Cynthia says, niggling away at the Laws for accepting an invite to Villa Malodoro, as the Marconis' place is known locally.

"Gwenda," she says, "please promise to measure their balustrading for me."

"How could I do that? I'm socialising. Besides, I've no measuring tape."

"Just stand on the patio with your arms outstretched, as if overwhelmed by the view – you will be since it's the view of our lovely creek flats – then twirl about a bit counting as you go. Look as if you're exulting in the scene."

"I'd feel a right twit doing that!" says Gwen. "It'll look like I'm dancing."

Len gives a hearty guffaw at this. "Reminds me of that joke: why are Methodists prohibited from vertical sex? People might think they're dancing. Haaaaa!" He thumps the steering wheel rhythmically to show amusement at his own joke.

"Oh, Len! That's rather smutty," says Cynthia, hiccoughing.

"The Marconis had the smarts to exploit your view. Your house merely faces the road," says Len, a comment even Claire thinks tactless. "And don't give Gwen a hard time, Cyn. She's only being neighbourly," says Len.

"Which sins tempt you, Claire?" says Len, trying to draw her into the chat.

Claire blushes but quickly recovers herself. "Oh, we've all borne false witness," she says.

Len catches her eye. "Do you fib?"

"Maybe I'm living a fib," she says and wants to bite her tongue. *Was there a truth drug in the communion grape juice,* she wonders. "I mean we all exaggerate or omit to tell the whole truth," Claire amends. "Sometimes we're being cowardly, sometimes kind." Phew! She thinks, I didn't know I thought that. Sometimes opinions one's unaware of holding emerge when thinking aloud.

Gwenda mentions the wholesome smell of wet wool on a rainy day.

Cynthia says, "Yes, but every silver lining has a cloud. God neglected to tell you to wear wool today. Your fur is quite ruined. Pity."

"Foxes dry out. My fur will too."

No one mentions Cynthia's picture hat that's landed in the Service Station's Goodwill bin.

Everyone seems to give Cynthia a wide berth in such matters for fear she'll… *Do what? Explode?* Claire wonders.

Len speculates as to whether rain on Sunday isn't God reminding us not to grumble too much about droughts.

"We want rain when we want it, not when we don't," says Cyn tartly.

"And what's your opinion, Claire?" asks Len, as they turn into the drive.

"I think God did Cynthia and me a favour or we'd have pegged out coming home." Now when did she fall into thinking of Arcadia as home, she wonders. Claire can't wait to hear Alex's theology of weather. He'll accuse her and Cynthia of not praying hard enough. Why else would He turn them into drowned rats? At the turning circle, Len hops out of the car and carries her gallantly to the front door, and returns for the chair. Cyn waits to be ushered on Len's arm. Her farewell jibe at Len is: "Now Len, do remind Gwen we've a permanent arrangement Sunday or she'll accept any old invite. Roast chicken today. Too much for the five of us but Bonnie makes chicken *vol au vent* with leftovers. Don't reproach yourselves. Hope it's not too nouveau over there! Ta-ta!"

Alex opens the door and shepherds them in. "So, Claire, how was church?" he helps her into the wheelchair.

"Uplifting in a way," she says.

"In a mysterious way?"

"Now Alex," warns Cynthia, aware that Alex is about to wind her up about her own Sabbath-day-only piety. In Claire's weeks chez the Sins, she's become expert in assessing what causes bad blood between them. She quite enjoys a minor skirmish.

Claire's feeling emotional; it's a peculiar thing about church, she thinks, however resistant you are to its blandishments, it's hard to leave without the feeling that something somewhere inside you has shifted; as if the singing of stirring hymns whose words you might find naff has somehow made your innards subtly shift; the hymns tug at your heartstrings even against your convictions.

Once their wet clothes have been abandoned, they go to lunch in the morning room. Bonnie has set the table with the best dinner set. Cyn lets Bonnie know via significant eye movements that two placemats can be removed.

"Lost your best friends for good?" Alex says. "If not, you'd best promise them a permanent gig. As grace, I'll offer up a prayer that the Macca boys aren't as entertaining as we Sins."

"Of course, they're not," says Bonnie, stoutly loyal, as she serves the cauliflower soup.

"We'll have no prayers from hardened atheists," says Cynthia.

"I'm not even a hardened agnostic, Ma. I'm tabula rasa. I don't know the meaning of life, nor do I care. Sincere ignorance leaves the universe with leeway to surprise you."

"The universe will surprise you whether you're ignorant or not," says Hal. "Just being alive is bracing, awe-inspiring and surprising. I, for one, wouldn't be dead for quids. Two four six eight. Bog in, don't wait."

They all tuck in.

"How was the monister, I mean, minister?" asks Hal.

"As exciting as usual, thankfully," says Cynthia. "I had a most relaxing time. I tuned out as soon as he started in on God testing Abraham and my headache went. A miracle."

"So, what was the outcome?" asks Alex.

"Of God's test? I don't know."

"Poor Abraham," says Alex. "His only sin was to love his favourite boy more than God. And yet it was God who created Abe, made him a loving father." Here Alex stares at Ma but she won't be drawn in.

"Now you're speaking like a believer – a disgruntled one," says Bonnie.

"Haa!" Hal erupts in a sharp bark of a laugh. "Good on you Bonnie, you've bested our 'intellectual'."

"Bonnie's a worthy opponent," says Alex.

"And the rest of us?" Hal asks.

"Still awaiting your Mensa scores."

"You know," Cynthia says, surprising Claire, "I don't like that part of the Bible. How could God ask anyone to kill their innocent son? Luckily, I slept through it. I'll bet no new information was tabled."

"If Jesus died for our sins then we ought to be sinning merrily to make it worth his while!" says Alex.

"Some of us are," says Mama cryptically.

"Most of the Bible's invented," says Bonnie, "just about everyone had their oar in." Will Bonnie's remark will be considered opinionated in an employee, Claire wonders. But all grunt in approbation. Despite her wise contribution, it's Bonnie who clears away the soup plates.

Cyn helps with the main course.

Hal busies himself at the sideboard; he's organised the wine. The 'good' wine has already gone back to the cellar. "I wish the minister gave out the water into wine trick," says Hal. "I'd pay top points for that."

Hal has an odd way of being around alcohol. One minute you see him with a full glass. Then it's empty. Then without seeming to move, he's set up the next one, and helped others to theirs as well, but Claire never seems to catch him in the drinking of it. It disappears as if by sleight of hand. He's like a cat, innocent looking one moment and up on the kitchen bench the next, but somehow you miss the glide that connects one state with the other.

Rain starts up again. Pellet-shaped shrapnel pepper the courtyard.

"For God's sake that's the Macca's BBQ done for!" says Cynthia. "*Quelle dommage!*"

"Don't you mean *quelle damage!* Mama? Why should He who created sub-atomic particles bother being vindictive towards the Maccas? Wasn't Marconi a genius Italian? Would He spend His Sabbath ruining a single family's Sunday lunch (not to mention the collateral damage to our garden) just because you don't like them?"

Cyn's plating the roast lamb. She gives Alex his plate. "It does seem cruel of God. It reminds me of you boys – falling out and paying each other back. But the Marconis have gone too far – they're stealing our best friends."

"I've never heard such a lot of ego-centric twaddle in my life! Do you believe one God is busy watching every one of billions of friends falling out of a Sunday so He can patch things up?" asks Hal of Cyn.

"It's better than watching billions of sparrows falling from their nests. Now that would be mega-boring," says Alex.

"God's in the details. Even the raindrops are falling aslant at precisely the right angle to squeeze under our new-fangled patio awning thing so it'll get mildewed," says Ma.

Hal covers his face with his hands. He may be laughing; He may be crying. "Oh, my dear woman, what would I do without you? So, God's paying you out for meanness to GwenLen by damaging your awning? What next?"

"Well, if God is in the details," says Alex, "I wish He'd find a CD of Bruch's violin concerto in E minor for Claire's wedding."

"Who is Brook?" asks Cynthia.

"Not Brook of the babbling variety, Mama."

"I assumed you'd have The Mendelssohn, dear," Ma says to Claire.

"Oh, Cynthia, the arrangements aren't far advanced. Alex is just stirring. I like Pachelbel but Alex won't attend if I choose a clichéd tune."

"But he's best man."

"That's what I keep telling Claire."

Now Claire's flushing. She'd swear her face is clashing with her hair. Bonnie gives her a look. She examines the silver napkin rings. Hal shifts in his chair.

"Alex thinks I'll have a naff wedding without him, I mean without his advice," says Claire.

Cynthia smiles at her quite kindly. "Don't let him force his bang thump music onto you."

If only I *were* marrying Alex, Claire thinks, and gives herself goose bumps at the idea.

"Look, the rain's abating," says Cyn. "I do wonder what the McCances' mansion's like? I wouldn't mind a shufty one day. They say it's a mock Palladian mansion circa 1980. Who'd blame God for the wash-out considering their taste?"

Chapter 42
Claire in Library

As weeks wear on without her telling Clive their engagement is off, Claire's anxiety lessens.

She'd wanted to pull the plug quickly. But now she couldn't care less. When speaking on the phone with Clive, she hears giggling in the background. Her diary jottings mention 'the bawdy braying sounds that type A males make when hopping to mate'. She leaves the typo uncorrected.

Clive misses her. Dreadfully. Or is he just behaving dreadfully? He pleads loneliness. He must surround himself with friends or 'go crazy'. Claire gets it. She's too unsophisticated to be all he needs. Like a baby's skull, her personality's component parts are only just now joining up; she's changing weekly. In losing her, Clive won't be losing the compliant girl he'd chosen.

Nevertheless, she wishes her fiancé were capable of constancy, even though she herself is not.

Constancy in a partner would reflect well on her. Wow! How twisted I am, she thinks.

Clive overdoes the Snuggle-pot cutesy nicknames from their true love's songbook. If emotions were coloured, Clive's would be beige; his soundtrack staticky, like trampling on dead gum leaves.

She's single again. Almost. She must talk to Fliss – a great girl. She visits Claire. They are becoming friends. Fliss is everything to everyone. She flatters Hal that he's encouraging her, although actually she's boosting him. She asks Cynthia for motherly advice she doesn't need.

Surely Fliss will know someone who'll want a boarder, someone who'll give Claire a job with some leisure to write!

Claire's determined to make a change, even if it means sprouting mung beans and eating cress.

Her former life as the saintly, blood-taking, injection giving, meds dolling, bum-wiping, despair-averting, BP recording, clip-board filling, ugly shoe-wearing nurse is done.

She'll live in the country, perhaps near Warrney. Not in Wang, where people hold firm opinions about her. Down here she could help Fliss with her horsy enterprise, she thinks, then remembers why she's immobilised. She laughs so hard, she empties out her tear ducts and must sip some water. The end of her nursing career frightens and enlivens Claire. It's like she's bungee jumping on a dare, or like a bud bursting open before spring has warmed things up sufficiently; she's full of forced optimism, ready on the blocks. Mixed metaphor!

Surely, new doors will materialise along her narrow corridor of existence. Surely, she won't have to endure Mama's dictatorship forever. She breathes, throws open her arms, which gesture lets her diaphragm expand, allows her lungs to fill.

She's sad today. Alex has been cross since Claire's last phone call home. Claire's mother, Thelma, had pumped her for details of 'Your Big Engagement, the one you waited a month to mention'.

"What's Clive like, really?" Thelma had asked.

"Clive? Perfectly charming, of course," Claire had said, falling into Thelma's trap.

"There's no such category as perfectly-charming-of-course," Thelma had said, running the words together. "Tell me, would he rather suffer pain himself or have to watch you suffering?"

Thelma believes true love means putting the comfort of one's beloved first. It's her gauge of love. Claire responds honestly. "He'd observe my pain with mild concern," she whispers, sensing Alex lurking nearby.

"Then he's not for you!" says Thelma triumphantly.

"Maybe," Claire says, her mouth going wobbly from her nearly tears. In that moment, she receives a dollop of insight from the 'God of Writers'. It hits her with a wallop why tears and tears share the same spelling. While you're tearing up, your innards are tearing up. Homonyms!

"Claire, please. No more decisions before my visit. So, what's the brother like?" she'd asked abruptly. And although Claire scorns belief in the metaphysical, she wonders if her mum has a sixth sense. "Oh, *he's* gorgeous," she'd gushed, "he's the kindest, sweetest man you could meet."

"Then marry *him*," Thelma had said, brusquely, and hung up.

Claire heard the kitchen door slam. Alex had left abruptly. The import of this incident hit her.

Alex, having heard one side of the conversation, assumed she'd said that *Clive* was gorgeous!

He's been treating her coolly since then. No more head pats. No stolen kisses. No clown faces.

He drives alone to town on errands for Mama. He's dutiful but distant.

Although the other night, musing while stoking the conservatory fire, he'd expressed a wish that she was an atheist/empiricist/humanist like him, because marrying a religious nutter would test him.

Marry, she'd thought.

"Is empiricism to do with empire?" she'd asked. He'd laughed, said empiricists believed in what they see, touch, smell, taste and hear – "Depend on the evidence of your senses, Claire," he'd said, adding, "I wouldn't mind some proof that you exist!"

"Do you want to lick me or do you already know you like me," she'd said, smiling when he laughed. Their feelings are labile. (It's on her list). They build to a crescendo like surf, expend their power and melt away to single molecules. Despite Alex's snit, he's deposited her in her favourite room, the library. It's huge and lined with books, including a reference section and a curved and carved mezzanine. "Alex, could you wheel me to the romance section?" she'd asked.

But somehow, she'd ended up in the reference section, "Better I deposit you here. I can refer to you if necessary. Might even take you out one day."

So saying, he left her with history books when she'd longed for something light; a bodice-ripper would have been better than *'The Decline and Fall of the Roman Empire'*. As she's about to plead with him to stay, he says he's off to Warrney for golf with a friend. But he has no clubs with him.

Is he fibbing? Has he left her in this remote wing so she'll appreciate him more?

"But you don't play golf," she'd said. "You can't have gone from '70s hippy to 'Great White Shark' overnight, surely?"

"Don't pigeon-hole me, Claire," he'd said, sternly.

Why does he react to her jejune rebuffs? Can't he see through her bluster to the truth of how she feels? But she's being unfair. Of course, Alex has flaws; he's human. He places her close to a bell-pull to summon Bonnie. He leaves with a long stride and never a backward glance. Her throat aches.

Now Claire wishes he'd wheeled her to the loo. Her phantom need distracts her. She'd be happy to see Cynthia just now but she's at CWA. She had left earlier carrying a basket full of cuttings: a bough of cedar, she-oaks, ivies, ilex, snowdrops and winter roses looking unlike roses, plus lily of the valley.

She's competing at Ikebana today and carrying secateurs. "What a shame you can't come," she'd said, testing the secateurs' spring, on off on off while pointing them at Claire.

"But I'd have loved to come," Claire had said.

"I'd have wrangled you an invitation had I known you were the flowery type."

It looks like Cyn and Claire are stuck in an everlasting conditional tense. Claire knows it's tosh. Cyn would have snuck her in quick-smart had she thought Alex and Claire would be left alone, unsupervised.

And Hal? He's organising a Point to Point with his chums Jock and Malcolm.

Chapter 43
Claire Driving

Claire's in the library. She hears what sounds like an armoured tank strafing the yews that line the turning circle. The din suggests barbarian tribes are besieging a redoubt. Soon the noise resolves itself into Cyn's old Bentley. It has an asthmatic wheeze.

She's learning to recognise the Sins' various idling engines. Mama's Bentley keeps them "stony-broke without a single crown", says Hal. And judging by Cynthia's dash up the drive heedless of pebble damage, something's up. She's forgotten something vital to her Ikebana win, Claire decides.

It turns out that the delicate specimen she's left behind is Claire.

"Girlie," Cynthia calls from the doorway; she's in such a state she's forgotten Claire's name.

"Ye-es?"

"Ah. You drive a little, don't you, dear?"

"I'm not licensed," Claire says.

"But you do drive on farm tracks?"

"Only in emergencies." Reflexively, Claire has backed the wheelchair well into the reference nook.

"Good, because we've an emergency. I'll be needing you at the lecture, my dear."

Cyn cuts off Claire's protest, signalling like a traffic cop. "Gwen was suppo-osed" – she grants this word an elongated vowel to emphasise Gwen's treachery in catching a cold on the very day she was to have helped. "Me?" Cyn shrugs. "Colds won't ground me. No wonder Gwen's sick. Lunching in rainsqualls on dubious food. I don't get it, her namby-pamby policy of always being agreeable."

"Some people are just nice. It's not a policy," Claire says.

An expression ripples across Cynthia's face like a cloudbank briefly reflected in a lake. She thinks Claire vexing, and Gwenda a dill. If only everyone's storm warnings were as easy to read as Cynthia's, Claire thinks. Then she'd be an excellent writer; then she'd understand people and their inner thoughts and motivations! "But Cynthia, unlicensed driving's a crime," she protests.

"This so-called 'crime' will require you merely to steer. And to apply the brake occasionally. It's well away from prying eyes, despite running alongside the best public gardens in the district."

"It's stealing," Claire bleats, knowing she sounds as pathetic as a new-born lamb.

"It's borrowing cuttings. No one will see you," Cyn says, a politician answering questions she's not been asked. "Only horticulture students go there. Von Mueller founded the Gardens."

"And he's too dead to tell on you," says Claire.

"True, and Hal established the pinetum. I maintain the metal edging around the flowerbeds. Hardy perennials need segregating from pretty annuals. Mustn't be overrun by the wrong sort."

Am I the wrong sort? Claire wonders.

"Girlie, I'm merely borrowing flora I planted!"

"So, you'll return plants after use, then?"

"Don't be facetious. Your job is to roll downhill in neutral while I scavenge."

"Steal?"

"Tosh! You'll brake occasionally. It's illegal by default to ignore a runaway car gone out of control."

"But, nicking plants!"

"I'm withdrawing deposits made into the Botanicals over eons. How lucky that your left leg was broken," says Cynthia, smiling beatifically. "I'm merely requisitioning your good leg."

"I suppose my accident was fated so you'd win the Ikebana comps?" says Claire.

Cynthia frowns and approaches Claire like a wildcat about to pounce on its prey. She releases the handbrake, draws the wheelchair out, pushes it through the double doors onto the lawn, where the Bentley's been run up over the bluestone edging for a quick get-away.

Cyn pushes her over the lawn by wrenching the chair this way and that to by-pass the larger stones.

Claire feels she's been commandeered by an Amazon and not the feeble woman who needed help getting her to church recently. In three shakes of a lamb's tail, Claire's belted in, and they're over the wall! Cyn pulls up in the turning circle and examines Claire. "Fix your hair, dear. It's lank and greasy."

Claire twists her hair into a knot…She refuses Cynthia's cyclamen lipstick though.

They travel in silence. The countryside is beautiful despite the weather threatening to turn or perhaps because of it.

The queer yellow light directs a corona of golden spars beneath banks of cloud. Stands of she-oaks are lashed by wind-gusts that disturb the frill-clad paperbarks. They line creek-banks along their route. The trees' bark looks like it's been ripped, torn, then roughly stuck back on by infant hands.

Cynthia drives, her face pressed up against the windscreen as if inclining forward will get them there sooner. "Remember, Claire, this is me pruning my own garden," she says.

Cynthia could wrestle her way out of an iron box under water while handcuffed and emerge, her do undamaged, Claire decides. "How else could I keep ahead of the pack without purloining the occasional fine old botanical specimen, dear? Who has a stupendous dogwood in their grounds?"

"You do."

"Yes. And I'd never savage my heritage trees. Just imagine the shame of losing to a cream-brick unit; me with my advantages! We'll be late but the girls enjoy unstructured time to compare hubbies' prostates. They want Clive down for a talk."

"Clive must get his surgery hours up," Claire insists. "And he failed an exam, Cynthia."

Cynthia regards Clive as a facile genius who needn't study because he's of 'The Elect'.

Claire knows how hard he struggles to do moderately well.

They stop beside 'Hal's' pinetum. Even a novice garden lover like Claire can admire the clever planting; the various species' profiles blend aesthetically to make the whole greater than the sum of its parts. Spindly casuarinas are clumped together; nevertheless, their wispy outlines make them seem pencilled in. Claire wishes she had the vocabulary to describe the beauty before her.

While Cynthia forages, she gets out, tests her bad leg. It's stronger. She feels her health and strength returning. The world looks rosier. She's happy suddenly. She doesn't want to trust this feeling; joy can be fleeting. But in this instant, she realises she loves Alex; she resolves to tell him so as soon as possible.

There's a yoo-hooing of private school voices echoing from the gardens, and Alex emerges from a thicket of trees with Fliss. They look scruffy. Leaves are clinging to their hair.

Chapter 44
After the Botanical Gardens

After the Botanicals, neither Cynthia nor Claire feels up to a CWA meeting. Cyn phones the town hall from a payphone to apologise, muttering in her mouth full of marbles voice about family troubles. At the café, she vets other patrons in case she knows someone.

Seated at last, her shoulders slump. "Claire, you are a dear girl, but you lose your heart too easily." She fans her face with a napkin. "You don't know which twin has the Toni, do you?"

What's the Toni? Claire wonders. Ah! She remembers. It was in an ad from her Mum's childhood for a home permanent product! Cyn's judgement of her as indecisive would be spot on, except for a brief interval – 17 ½ minutes ago – when she'd decided in favour of Alex. But before she'd had a chance to tell him so, he'd turned up with Fliss, looking sheepish at the questions in her eyes. And she'd retreated into indecision.

"Fliss wants to marry one of my sons, too; no, not two." Cyn raises two fingers. "I mean too, also," she shakes her head at the treachery of English. "Now, despite the touching scene in the Botanicals, I can assure you Alex isn't interested in Felicity. Fliss loves Clive. Very much."

"But Cynthia, you don't want me to marry either son. You and I…We don't…get on."

"I may seem like hard toffee to break one's teeth on, dear, but deep down I'm a soft centred Polish sweet that seems hard but collapses in the middle."

"I hadn't thought of you as lolly," Claire says. Her hand goes to her mouth to stifle a giggle.

Cynthia bares a run of teeth with a dash of lipstick on them. "If you want a son of mine then marry the one *you* want and not the one you don't want out of guilt. Follow your heart and the sums will come out right."

"The one *I* want?" says Claire, astonished that her feelings are so transparent. And even more surprised that Mama would accept the jilting of her favourite with such sang-froid. "Don't you mean the one I'm spoken for, Clive?"

"Not necessarily. Don't look shocked, dear. Marriage isn't about romance, it's pure maths. Take one son, his ideal partner, add them together and multiply by two and you end up with two happy couples." She shakes paired fingers on each hand at Claire. "But if one son misses out on his ideal mate, you're left with a mediocrely happy couple plus two sad loose ends." Here she joins together both index fingers and lets her middle fingers curl sadly. "Now Claire, there's group happiness and individual happiness. No one's happy when his clan is unhappy."

Cynthia stares at her as if boring holes into Claire's pupils. "I warmed to you for standing up to Alex over church. You're strong. Alex's rustic charm belies his strong will. The decision is for you and the boys to mate, make, but Clive and Fliss have been friends forever…" Cyn shrugs.

"And Clive inherits Arcadia right next door to Fliss' property," Claire is moved to say – the words having formed themselves into a sentence without her help. Where did the piecing together of these disparate pieces of information occur? Did the words queue up on the tip of her tongue, forming a theory on their own? Maybe some ideas do creep up on us invisibly like an infection, so there's no absolute not-knowing to them, no sharp borders around them.

This idea must have been growing within her like Bonnie's mung beans in their gauze-covered jar. Add water and a germ of potential life turns into something nourishing. Claire wonders was she influenced by her talk with Fliss that first evening upon learning that the plucky gel had taken on her parents' debt. A solution was obvious even to an outsider like her: Fliss' property and the Sins' being adjacent, their amalgamation would enrich both parties, council permitting. At the ball Hal said their land was too small for development. Had her brain unwittingly figured out a solution to the Sins' dilemma? The same solution Cyn had worked out too?

Why not? Why should she begrudge Clive, Fliss, Cyn and Hal their lucky win at Monopoly?

Let them end up happy and rich. She'd go back to square one. She'd not been so unhappy there the first time around. And if, in withdrawing from the contest, painlessly disengaging from a man she doesn't love and his brother, whom she oughtn't love, she could save their family, then, all the better. With the slate wiped clean, she'll have endured a pointless feeling fest but at least she'll have gained a wealth of experience.

Cynthia's face flushes redder than a Rothko. She fixes Claire with a sharp look. "Have you been going through my papers, dear?"

"Me, Cynthia? Never! Though I wonder if you are planning to do something funny with wills."

Cynthia shows her disdain for this comment by ignoring it. "Ah, coffee." The waitress sets the pot down. "And how did you feel upon seeing Alex and Fliss together earlier, dear?" Cyn asks, keen to probe Claire's feelings while they're raw.

"I felt awful for Suz," Claire fibs.

"Hm!" Cyn says, her head shaking, her mouth twisting wryly. "Suz was a red herring. We both know that. But I've seen the way he looks at you."

"You have?" Claire's gobsmacked at Cyn's perspicacity. "But Suz talks about Alex constantly," Claire protests disingenuously.

"She's trying to make you jealous. You *could* be made jealous over Alex, I suppose?"

Cynthia pours the coffee and examines Claire shrewdly.

Claire blushes up through Cynthia's turtle-necked naphthalene smelling cast-off sweater. "Possibly," she mumbles. "No, you deserve the truth. I could be…I am a bit…"

"Ah, the truth!"

"I love Alex. Today I felt sure until I saw him with…"

Cyn flaps her hand emphatically. "Loose ends. Just loose ends. He's been friends with Fliss since kinder. If he needed someone to talk to, who better? Alex may be feeling hurt to see you wobbling all over the place, trying to decide."

She beckons the waiter. "We ordered scones!"

"So, sorry, Ma-am, the scones are ready now and another coffee is complimentary." Cynthia appears as happy to receive free coffee as the queen to inherit a new castle.

"You look pretty, flushed," Cyn says. "You'll make a lovely bride. The question is, whose?"

"I was happy before I met Clive. I had my work…"

"But you're giving up your work as well as Clive. Nursing's a perfect calling for a gel! You are a contrarian like me when young. I wanted to be an airwoman," says Cynthia. "I had to face facts."

"You'd have been a good pilot, Cynthia," Claire says. "You've got the nerve for it."

"Are you saying I've a hell of a nerve?"

Claire smiles at this unexpected evidence of humour in Cynthia. "Nursing doesn't engage me fully. I'm not passionate about it.

"It's not enough to start things so you can give things up, Claire. Writing's a pastime. I've spent my life doing community work. Hal and I support an orphanage in Vietnam. I don't tell people this…"

But you have just now, Claire thinks, but says nothing. It hits her how hopeless it all is.

She bows her head and weeps. Mid tear-fall, she realises her crying sounds uncannily like hysterical laughter. She starts to laugh in earnest. It's cathartic.

Cyn's arm snakes across the table to give her hand a squeeze just as a plate of scones thumps onto the table and the consequent spillage means any chance for a tender moment between her and Cynthia has been squandered.

"Listen dear," Cyn says, leaning in as close as her shelf of a bosom allows. "You're alone too much now Alex is focusing on his wood-work."

She means, 'now that he's tired of you', Claire thinks. Alex's pretext for staying at Arcadia after the accident was to help-out and to design a chair from which to hang upside down and stretch one's spine upon.

"What about your little friend Mary, who's so bubbly on the telephone? Could she spare you a few days?"

"Maybe."

"Then call her, Claire. You need someone to talk to."

"Thank you, Cynthia. I shall."

"I'd be most interested to see your writing." She gives her tea a thorough stir, clunking the spoon against the china. "Cheap tea set," she says, "doesn't clink."

Chapter 45
Mary Comes

Mary's fed up with exam prep. "Sure, I'll come," she says.

Next day they argue about who'll pick her up from the station. "Not you, Alex, dear, you're susceptible to the fairer sex just now," says Cyn.

"But what about the less fair sex?" he says.

Mama won't answer. Claire disguises her laughter, hiccoughing. Alex gives her a gentle whack on the back and although its intent is practical, she enjoys the contact. She now realises Fliss was merely counselling Alex in the gardens. Regarding her, Claire!

"What's wrong with having female friends? Ma? You were suspicious of me and Fliss. But, nothing doing. We got talking on the grass." Alex jiggles his ute keys at Claire. "Let's go. It's the 2.00 pm."

"Alex," she asks, when they're in the ute. "I need money for…things."

"What?"

"Stuff my brothers won't buy me."

"'Hygiene items'?"

"Mm," she says. Eight weeks is late for Claire. She experiences a pulse of fear.

"Hm," he looks at her speculatively. "Well, I'm glad I'm not your brother." He rubs his eyes with the heel of his hand. "That would be intolerable." He engages first gear.

"It'll be a squash in here with Mary," she says.

"Slide across," he stops at the road and eases her along until their bodies are aligned. Claire smiles. Alex too. He turns to her and grins hugely. "Glad you're back, Clarabelle. I was…" He raises his hand then lets it drop. "Jealous. I'm an idiot."

"I said nice things about you on the phone," Claire says.

"I know. Mama was listening on the extension."

"Thank God she's a snoop."

"She still hopes Clive and Fliss will get back together."

"You should have trusted me." She pounds her fist upon his thigh.

"Can't you say you love me without resorting to violence?"

"I do," Claire protests.

"What?"

"Love you."

"More than Clive?"

"More than Clive loves you? Probably," Claire says, teasing. "Of course, I do! Hang on, Alex, Something fishy is going on. Ma's spent a month keeping us apart. What's changed?"

He shrugs. "It'll be about money."

"Mm. Cyn no longer cares whom I love. She'll have her reasons." As they're about to pull onto the highway a sleek car slows. It's Gwenda with Maureen.

"Alex," she says, restraining his hand, "we've been seen!"

"Let's give Gwenda something to talk about." He turns towards her and kisses her whole-heartedly on the lips. Mid-kiss, he pulls away to wave. Gwen and Maureen return the wave gleefully as they glide by in the Lamborghini. "See, kissing spreads goodwill," he says.

"And gossip. How do we dump Suz and Clive painlessly, Alex?"

"Impossible. Come on. Let's get girlfriend number two."

"Do let Suz down gently, Alex."

"There was no chemistry between us."

"She talks about you constantly. 'Alex called. Next time he's in town, blah blah.' You two, did you?" Claire asks.

"Fuck? Of course."

At the station, Claire weeps to see Mary. Alex leaves them in a café to talk.

They order coffees with French vanilla slices. "Snot blocks!" says Mary.

"How's nursing?" Claire asks. Mary gives her a summary.

"Gosh, I'm well away," she says.

"But you were conscientissimo!"

"I fell out of love with nursing. Down here Ma makes me exercise my back fat; I dry dishes from my wheelchair. Alex wheels me to the loo."

"Ooh la loo!" says Mary.

"The floor's uneven. There's dry rot, rats at night. I sleep with the radio on so I can't hear their skittering. Alex goes to pubs when there's a band playing. I plead with him to take me. He won't.

"I play chess with Bonnie or the olds; TV's on the blink. Alex sleeps in the hall in case I need help."

"So 'help' is what you call it. And your days?"

"There's the herb garden. Sewing outer sides to inner sides of old sheets."

"Yeah?"

"Economising. We make potato and zucchini parings soup stock. A veggie diet's healthy. I've lost my puppy fat! Bonnie makes corn bread to save petrol. There's Ikebana. Church."

"You've become the sort of girl who makes me want to puke! So industrious!"

"Better than dressing wounds. I snip box hedging. Peel spuds with Bonnie. She's my friend."

"Lucky, you. No meds, no deads. How's your leg mending?"

"I fell off a cliff my first day out."

"No! How come, dummy?"

"Was on a scenic drive with Alex." Claire reddens at the memory.

"Suz's Alex? He's heaven. Horny tradesman's hands. An air of knowing all. A B.S. act, I bet."

"He knows tons," Claire says, cross.

"Aha! So, you're two-timing both Clive and Suz!"

"Mm." Claire tries to hide an insistent smile.

"Your face speaks volumes and it's talking bodice-ripper romance. Wicked girl. No wonder your leg won't heal. You need your injury to disguise the pain of being rejected at heaven's gate for choosing fornication and fulfilment over duty."

"But nursing was my dream!" Claire insists.

"Will Clive need comforting?"

Claire shakes her head. "Not by you."

"You couldn't care less. Heartless thing," says Mary.

"I was the solution to his existential problems for five minutes. Now he's fooling around. The house is full of drunks, and Giggling Gerties. Hopeless! Still says he wants to marry me. But I'm done with others' problems."

"No hope, then?" asks Mary

"No hope for Clive and me," she says, wondering at how her feelings have firmed up overnight. Earlier she'd told Alex she needed to see Clive once more before deciding. It's no longer true.

"Do you want me to get you any hospital scuttle-butt on Clive?"

"No. I couldn't care less. Why do people queue up to marry?"

"Our hormones, luv. You think it's sexual attraction on its own. But sexual attraction is all about finding yourself a suitable father for your kids. It's about babies, babies, babies."

"You're on Ob Gyn rotation, right?" Claire says accusingly.

"Yes. It explains why sex is so great. Who'd guess babies would be so gorgeous? At sixteen all you can see is drool and yellow poo. Sex is the lure but you need good providers who are kind. How does Alex make his house payments?"

"He does a bit of this and that!"

"Then stick with Clive. He's good enough."

"I don't want good enough! I used to think that was all I deserved!"

"Gees, Claire!"

"Mary, you're a tonic. Marry Clive after all. Be my sister."

"I may prefer the charismatic Alex!"

"No way!" Claire slaps Mary's wrist playfully.

"Okay. I'll have a pumpkin parings hol. It'll be a change from Suz's everlasting Spaghetti Bolognese. You'll have to ring the Head Girl, though. She'll be displeased. When you left she fell into a deep hole." Mary swipes her hand across her forehead in a Suz drama queen way.

Claire snorts coffee from her nostrils at the idea of Suz's affectedness.

Chapter 46
Cynthia, Claire – Will

Cynthia is waiting at the door, having heard the ute arrive.

Bertie trims shrubs out front. His faithful kelpie accompanies him. He's eager for an eyeful of Mary. Her famous well-defined legs under flippy skirts have made spot pruning compulsory.

Mary's hairstyle has taken a 'punk' turn since they left the café. It's extremely short on the left, yet a hank on the right forms a gravity defying purple spout.

It's an outlandish wig designed to wind Cynthia up. To no avail. Today is a 'Good News Day'. Cynthia is all smiles and hugs. She simply adores Mary's 'punk aesthetic'!

What's Cynthia on? Claire wonders.

"Sorry Ma-am, it's a wig," Mary says, removing it and finger combing her straight black hair.

"Well, purple hair or not, you're most welcome. And call me Cynthia."

"Bertie," she calls, "you've had a good squiz at Claire's gel-friend. Stop torturing the hedge. Go set up the camp bed in the sitting room for goodness sake! Then there's a firewood delivery from yesterday that needs stacking."

Bertie slinks behind a yew but Claire sees dark eyes gleaming from the shrubbery.

"You're in with Claire, Mary. Would you do the evening loo-run? Give Alex a decent sleep."

Cynthia lingers over the word 'decent'. She's convinced Claire and Alex have been 'up to no good' in the dead of night, when really they've been behaving with utmost restraint. Except for an outbreak of staged-managed snogging recently, Claire's been a model guest.

Cynthia rings the bell by the front door. Calls for Bonnie to rustle up tea. Earlier Claire had discovered the biscuit supply had dwindled to Cyn's 'rock cakes' that the horses like; they take more energy gnawing than they confer in calories. Claire will have to tutor Mary in the dunking process.

Next, Cynthia introduces Mary to the ancestors – the Rogues' Gallery has been reduced by one since Claire's own arrival tour. In the conservatory golden rays of sunlight infiltrate the bamboo, lending an impression of lushness. The bamboo's been cut back without Claire's intervention.

The murky windows are hardly noticeable.

"Oh!" says Mary, clapping her hands with delight. "How lovely."

And it does seem to be so, Claire thinks. New eyes on an old scene can transform reality even for the most jaded viewers. It's as if Claire's spectacles had just been updated.

The architecture of The Lodge is testament to generations of owners who dreamt wild dreams of how a grand home should look; luckily, their plans stayed mostly in ancestral heads, rarely being transposed onto architectural blueprints, let alone realised, or things would be more of a muddle than they are.

The conservatory walls are bluestone on one side, while recycled square timber sixties' window-walls clad the rest. The ceiling is half-glazed in atrium-style, adding to the room's schizophrenic character. It's as if two rooms of opposing character had been glued together.

Cool and dark in winter. Warm and bright in summer. Perfect only at night when there's a blaze in the fireplace and on fine nights when the light is out and stars are visible. A warm lounge is one luxury the Sins don't stint on!

The furniture is from the Sins' beach house in Port Fairy. The house had to be 'let go', as Cyn puts it. She makes it sound as if a domesticated creature needed releasing into the wild. Claire would love to tell Cynthia that, freed from its heavy cargo of brown furniture, the room could appear quite chic.

Earlier that day, Claire had been summoned to the study; she'd wheeled herself in, grateful to be negotiating her way through the rat-run of corridors on her own.

Cynthia had pretended not to see Claire waiting in the doorway. She was all business, lips pursed. Claire can see why literary mouths are often said to be 'pursed'. Cynthia's mouth resembles an old-fashioned coin purse whose leather pouch is gathered into folds by a clasp. Eventually, she looks up, waves Claire towards a chair, forgetting that the gel comes supplied with her own built-in seat.

Cynthia hands Claire a letter. It's from her brother in NSW; he has terminal cancer.

Cedric has deeded his estate to Clive, on the proviso that he should marry and produce an heir before his benefactor's death, otherwise the proceeds of the estate will go to charity.

A small investment portfolio goes to Alex of whom Uncle Cedric says he's 'very fond', having been 'honoured to be present at his birth'. Claire's nose wrinkles. How odd!

If he was present at the twins' births, why mention one fondly, while endowing the other twin with his fortune? It doesn't make sense.

The boys aren't to know about these provisions. Cedric won't have Clive changing his life in order to fulfil the requirements of a will. Cynthia intends to abide by these stipulations. "With treatment, Ced has 12 months to live," she announces flatly.

"Why involve me, Cynthia?" Claire asks. "Do you want me to wise the boys up on the sly, so that I'll be the one disrespecting your brother's wishes instead of you?" Claire seems to have hit a nerve, Cynthia's face darkens; she waves her hand as if brushing away a blowfly.

"I needed a witness, dear."

"Why not Hal?"

Cyn stares wide-eyed at Claire as if examining her face for signs of idiocy. "Hal's the last person I'd trust with this. He'll get all high and mighty on Alex's behalf and pester Cedric to make changes."

"The will does seem unfair, but it's none of my business," Claire says.

"Precisely, that's why I've chosen you as witness. When things come to a head or if I should predecease Ced, there'll be someone disinterested who knows where the papers are stashed and understands their import. You!"

"But you're in robust health, Cynthia," Claire says.

"One mustn't congratulate oneself on one's good health. It challenges harmless cells to multiply crazily. Now Claire, I've been frank. Promise me…"

"I won't break your confidence, Cynthia, but I want you to know it's over between Clive and me. He's drinking, partying…"

"Clive's sowing wild oats. Married to a good woman and with a darling babe on the way he'll…"

"Be rich."

"…change his ways."

"I don't care if he 'changes'! It's too damn late."

Cynthia's eyes widen at Claire's overt hostility. "I thought you might rethink things, dear. Now that you know how things stand financially. In such sensitive situations, one oughtn't be seen to love two men at once."

"So Gwenda saw Alex and me canoodling, I suppose?"

"Yes. Even Maureen Marconi told me. Decent of her."

"It's Alex I love, Cynthia. I think you guessed as much before I knew for sure."

"Doesn't today's news change things?"

"No. I don't want a man with a big bequest – just someone to love and peace to write," says Claire.

"That costs. Today while you were in town, you left your diary on the table. I tidied up. Saw your poetry."

"I didn't give you permission to read my diary!" Claire protests.

"I thought you'd left it there on purpose. I found asterisks denoting your menses. There's been nothing in two months."

"I haven't been keeping it up to date," says Claire, flushing.

"I'm not prying, dear. I'm just asking you to reflect on certain issues…"

"Issues about issue?"

"Very witty, dear, but loving first this one then that one leads to ambiguous offspring. Do be fair to the putative father of your child."

Chapter 47
Claire and Mary Courtyard

At dinner on the evening of Mary's arrival, Claire watches her tucking into the lamb roast Alex splurged on. Mary, a thoughtful girl beneath her hyper-confident exterior, thanks Bonnie for the delicious meal. Bonnie in turn thanks Claire and Mary for helping with the apple crumble made from Hal's cold storage Pink Ladies.

"One day," she says, "you'll make bonzer wives. Of course, Claire's promised to our own dear Clive," she specifies, after Cyn sends her a significant look. Her encomium stutters to a halt when Alex sends her a contrary look. Hal squints from face to face, guessing there must be a sub-text resonating in the air, but he misses their expressions in the instant they form and catches them only on the wane, when less trustworthy. Still, he knows something's up.

Lady Muck reminds them the lamb wouldn't have been worth two bob if not for her mint sauce.

"How do you make the spuds crispy?" asks Mary, to get the focus off Cyn and back onto Bonnie.

Claire's happy to have feisty Mary around.

"Dead easy," says Bonnie, pinkly pleased from all the flattery. "You par-boil them, scrape them with a fork, roll them in flour, then pop them into a hot oven."

Bonnie's appearance tonight is what Claire's dad calls 'fetching'. Her hair is piled high on her crown, she's applied a blush of lipstick to her shapely mouth, and highlighted her cheekbones. Anyone would think she was planning a night on the town.

"We'll do the dishes later," says Mary. "Let's check out the moon."

"Yes, girls. A blood moon tonight, according to the ABC," says Hal. "A rare celestial event – a lunar eclipse coinciding with a full moon that's orbiting so close to earth it picks up earth's reflected light."

"Let's go before the wind starts up in earnest," says Mary.

"Good idea," says Hal. "There's a weather alert out for the Western District. High winds. Potential for storm damage. *Beau Fils* is locked in for the night. And Alex, you'd be safer in Clive's room." Alex nods. "The girls will be fine. But you and me, Cynthia…up there in the tower…we're the ones under the hammer."

"Maybe we all should take a bedroll and sleep on the floor of the Great Hall," says Cynthia. "It'd be a hoot! Structure's sound enough. Your forebears hadn't started gambling when it was built. When the boys were young, we'd go pretend camping in there," Cynthia tells them all.

"These days you'd never clamber off the floor for the lav, my dear. Anyway, you enjoy a rollicking good storm," says Hal.

"That was when I felt invincible, Hal." Cynthia's looking somewhat defeated tonight, her hair is dull and it appears to have resisted the styling tongs.

"Oh, I love a little *Sturm und Drang*. You're safe with me."

"I'm always safe with you," says Cynthia, implying she'd rather be somewhat endangered.

Bonnie looks displeased but she conjures up a pair of duffel coats and pushes Mary and Claire out. Mary wheels Claire through the courtyard to the folly, where they can shelter if it rains.

Settled, she lights a cigarette. Claire lets her enjoy it guilt-free.

"So what's wrong with Clive?" Mary asks. "Indulge me."

"Mare, you've never asked me to elaborate on blokes before. The twins are good guys. Clive lacks empathy, I think. It's like having a low IQ. Not his fault. He needs remedial classes." She sighs. "It's irrelevant who's the better person. I want to be with Alex. I like the me I am with him."

"Wow! I've never felt that with a bloke," says Mary. "Ha! Bloody blood moon. Nothing to see!"

"You're never with men long enough," Claire tells her.

Mary sighs, "So many men, so little time. I'm so used to being outrageous because people pay me attention and that encourages me. I'm like a type-cast actress who only gets the goofy, daggy roles."

"At least you're you," says Claire.

"Well, I envy you. Every woman needs an Alex in her life." Mary stares at Claire intently. She draws deeply on her poison. Holds it in. Takes time to savour it. Then she stamps on the rest of the cigarette and stuffs it back into the packet.

"You'll have to throw the others out now."

Mary nods. "It's my strategy. I buy a packet a day. Take a drag on one, then force myself to throw the rest away. It's breaking me."

"Smoking like you did would be dearer long term."

"Sensible Claire. I deal with men similarly. Feed my addiction, throw them out before I'm damaged."

"You used to wear them once and take them back for a refund."

"Shh!" says Mary.

There's a crunching of quartz stones. A shadowy figure turns into Alex.

"I come bearing '58 Grange Hermitage," says Alex, proffering a bottle. Its label's hard to read but clearly, it's cheap plonk. They both shake their heads.

"What discerning women," he says. "Dada has some actual Grange hidden away. He refuses either to sell it or taste it. Grange keeps you immobilised by indecision; meanwhile, the stuff keeps going off. I told him to liberate the cash, give Bon her back pay."

"The cracks were showing tonight," says Claire.

"Yes, Ma and Bon often schedule their tiffs for Friday nights."

"So, is Grange like an asset? Can you buy a house with it?" asks Mary.

"Don't ask me." He turns away.

"Stay, Alex," Claire says.

"No. It's a perfect evening for girl talk. Better come in before the wind starts."

"How will we know if it hasn't started yet?" asks Mary.

"You'll have to use your female intuition, girls," he laughs, turning away.

Once his footsteps fade, Claire says, "I want a fuller life than Clive's broodmare wife will have, always in foal or just out of it…"

"You and Clive would have gorgeous babies, Claire."

"Then you marry him. He's free."

"Oh, God. Look. There's the moon! A rusty colour and so big."

"Wow!"

"Claire, Mary!" Alex hurries back. "Mary, I've a favour to ask. Bon's brother Kevin's had a bad turn. He's in the Koroit hospital. Bonnie wants to be with him. I can't leave the olds tonight. Would you mind driving her? You'll have to stay there overnight, though. Too dangerous driving back through the storm!"

Chapter 48
Storm

The Lodge is battered by vicious squalls; sleep is impossible. As a reminder of human frailty, nothing's better than an honest to God decent storm. Without storm's savagery, we may be tempted to believe that thanks to the government, the SEC, the local government sector, our strict building regulations, the big four banks and Victoria Police, we're safe.

Storms showcase nature in its rawness. But Claire isn't enjoying this one. The rattling of sash windows grates upon her nerves; a cedar creaks in the wind. She prays it won't fall. She doesn't want to die tonight, just when she's ready to be happy.

She stares up at the ceiling. This was once a lovely room. Flashes of lightning reveal its generous proportions. It has oak panelling. A chandelier hangs from its coved ceiling. Of a morning she watches the crystals come alive as sunbeams dance across the plasterwork. Tonight, there's a tinkling of crystals in the volatile air currents. She hopes the chandelier is well anchored to its rose. She rolls onto her stomach to protect her face. Too uncomfortable. She rolls right way up. The musty smell means water damage is underway. Have her senses been sharpened? The drawing room's decay wasn't apparent by day. Now the rain, gentle during the evening, builds. Hal and Cyn, their bedroom being underneath the tower, have volunteered to go down with the ship. Claire's thankful that Alex sleeps nearby.

Through the muslin curtaining flares of sheet lightning illuminate banks of cloud; each flare is followed by a thunderous boom. Unlike the remainder of the roof that's slate-clad, the portico has a corrugated iron roof. She loves the squeak and thrum of iron sheets rising and falling in time with wind gusts; it's a familiar sound from childhood.

She sleeps fitfully until awakened by a branch from the monkey-puzzle tree outside the sitting room; it scratches at the windowpane; Claire envisions a wood sprite clawing at the warped old glass for entry with its long fingernails. She has awakened from a troubling dream. She wishes she could latch onto the dream's webby trail and follow it hand over hand back into the vortex of her dreamscape.

No. Let it go, Claire. Fall back into sleep's deep furrow, she tells herself. But, she can't. She's wide awake. A boy was flying a kite on a beach. A wind gust lifted the kite, then let it fall to earth.

Earlier in the evening, Alex had carried her to the recliner chair in the conservatory; he'd adjusted its mechanism, organised pillows and a rug before attending to the fire.

Cynthia and Hal were jousting at chess. Eventually, they'd gone to prepare supper.

Alex, crossing to the board, had given her a wink, then shifted a chess-piece of each parent.

"Now I've disadvantaged them equally," he said. "Things will get lively." He'd returned to the fire. "Are you bored?" he'd asked.

"No, I love watching flames. I'm glad there's no TV. It leaves my thoughts content-free."

"You make your own content," said Alex ambiguously.

"It's a luxury musing," she said, flipping through a 'Country Life' magazine. "If sloth is a sin, I'm morally bankrupt; I'll never win at Snakes and Ladders. But I'm up for a chat if you want."

Alex wastes no time in bringing a beanbag to her side. They chat and play furtive footsie games.

Wheeling the trolley in, Cynthia doesn't notice the disarray of the board. "You're on light rations until the wedding, Claire," she'd said, her voice fluting girlishly.

"But I'd rather have the cake than the wedding!" said Claire, shocking herself. How full of cheek she's become! Yet Cynthia seems to respect her now she's asserting herself.

Hal gives a surprisingly loud cackle, considering his slight build. "Atta girl, Claire."

"Why pin one's hopes upon a single day?" Claire had said. "I want a long, happy life."

"Heirloom wedding lace anchors us in the past," said Cyn.

Claire had made a grimace at this remark. "I need freeing not anchoring."

Alex had taken some cake, mimed the eating of it and folded it in a napkin and hidden it.

"Aterlo," he says in pig Latin.

"Oodgo," she'd replied.

At bedtime, Mama, anxious to see them tucked into their respective beds, clanks cutlery and stacks dishes in the kitchen until they're settled. She retires when Alex, on his bedroll, pretends to snore.

Cyn smiles sweetly at Claire and wriggles her fingers, "Goodnight dear, I'm not trying to starve you like poor Gretel. I've your best interests at heart," she says, closing the door and mounting the stairs laboriously.

Claire's wakened by a loud boom. She'd been dreaming but she can't get back to sleep. Her bladder is sending communiqués from the front line. Bloody bladder, she grumbles. She lies there ruminating over the day's events.

Why does Mama accept quite equably that Alex and she are in love one minute, yet next day, she's once again adamant Claire should marry Clive? And why is Clive the sole heir to Ced's fortune?

"Sometimes first instincts are right after all," Cyn had said during their pow-wow in the study. It strikes Claire that Cedric's letter must have arrived that morning; the very same morning she had read Claire's diary and she'd wondered if Claire might be pregnant.

Claire had been wondering too; but she'd managed to push her fear of pregnancy to the back of her mind ever since it wormed its way into her consciousness earlier today. Yes! Of course, Cyn hopes she's pregnant to Clive. Once a child is born, Clive will be Cedric's heir. Shit!

She reaches for the bell. She rings it softly. Bas, the dog, stirs and nuzzles her hand. She calls out, "Alex, come quick."

She hears a yawn, a groan and a drunken stumbling issuing from his side of the room.

"Claire? You want me?" Loaded question.

"Yes, Alex, I'm desperate for the commode."

"If you've got to go, you've got to go. Just a sec." He stands over her trying to get his balance. She can just make out his features. He lifts her onto the commode and leaves. But his legs buckle as he deposits her back in bed.

"Hop in, Alex, or you'll catch your death." She holds the bedclothes open.

"Oh, Claire. I've been feeling like Basil, forbidden the mistress' chamber. Except he's allowed on the bed. I'm not." He pats the dog who's taken a shine to Claire, much to the disgust of Cynthia who spoils Bas but he never finds her worth fussing over. Bas snuffles in his sleep. "I promise not to lick or paw you."

"Don't you lick me anymore?" she jokes. "Just lie here beside me, Alex." Claire pats the blanket.

"You're shivering." He rubs her arm. "Is it the storm?"

"No, a dream." She tells him the gist of it. "What could it mean?"

"A beach is wildness, liberation. The kite means freedom. Submitting to the elements, risk-taking. The broken kite could be you, injured. You flew too high, you fell in love, and then the wind changed, dropped you back to earth. Are you accident-prone? Should you fly again?"

"Of course, I should!"

"Good on you, Claire. I love the new courageous you."

She smiles to herself in the dark. He loves me, she thinks, feeling smug. "Alex," she says, "Did my subconscious mind invent these symbols? If so, how come I need you to decode them for me?"

"Your subconscious mind is wise. Trust its insights." He gets up. Leaves the room. Comes back with carrot cake. He breaks off a piece and feeds it to her.

"The icing's the most delicious part but it's no good without the cake."

"Why?" she asks.

"Life needs it's high and low points. It's like over-dosing on love, way too rich!" He sighs.

He hands her the slice.

She feeds him tiny crumbs. He curls his tongue and rolls them around his mouth. "Sweet of you to share your cake." He kisses her hand. "There's something better than exquisite food," he says.

"I know there is, and I want you, Alex."

"No, Claire. First you must tell Clive about us."

"Are you withholding sex like those Greek women?"

"Yes!"

They lie side by side, two friends holding hands.

The storm grows wilder. Its epicentre seems directly above them. Alex opens the curtains. "Look!"

"It's the deities' sound and light show," he says. "Promise me you'll never sleep through another storm."

He rolls the divan towards the window. The clouds have shifted. Lightning splits the sky into jigsaw pieces. One second later thunder booms. It's wild, exhilarating and frightening all at once. Alex reaches for her hand; they lie there, hardly daring to breathe.

"Alex, could you at least hold me?"

In the morning Hal wakes them on his way to the stables to check on the horses. Alex's arm is still slung across Claire's flank when he opens the door. He stands for a moment in the doorway. Coughs loudly. "What a night! Good of you, Alex, to comfort Claire," he says. "Well, I'm off to see if any trees have shed branches. Now hop up quick, Alex, Mama is on her way downstairs. We wouldn't want her to get the wrong end of the stick, would we?"

Chapter 49
Cyn at Dawn

I climb the tower; open the sash window giving onto the lookout. I fight my way through to the flimsy platform overlooking the gnarled stumps of vines planted in a triumph of enthusiasm over realism. I lean my weight upon the rusted wrought iron railing. What would happen if the railing gave? The view is to die for but I'm not one to give in without a fight.

Over the Western District plains dawn's progress seems glacial. Shouldn't it come all-of-a-rush? Once over the Great Dividing Range, there are few topographical features to impede the light.

According to predictions in *'The Age'* of yesterday, dawn is late. Or is it Papa's old watch that's gone bung?

Whatever, dawn always inspires awe. Even the most jaded of us wonders what the day will bring. We go from still-but-only-just night to almost-but-not-quite day so subtly it's imperceptible. It's like that mathematical paradox in which a door can be open or half-open. Or a quarter open, one-eighth, one sixteenth and so on. On that basis, the door can never quite close. And yet doors close.

Somehow. Are mathematical principles unreliable or what??? I'll ask Hal when he's up. I moisten my lips. From my vantage point in the tower you can see earth's curvature. My breath fogs up the windowpane. At last a proof of life.

Last night was midwinter's eve! And my life's nadir. "You're no 'lioness in winter' just a 'grizzly bear' all year long," Hal said last evening, but with fondness. Overall, I've been lucky with Hal. Little passion. But a solid partnership.

The house is falling to bits around us – the pipes are rusted out, and our son a plumber who'd rather play around being creative! Then there's Hal's prostate, and he too embarrassed to raise the issue with our urologist son. I try stifling a yawn but I give up. Why cover my mouth? No one is watching.

How generously we rearrange our lives to fit in with Bonnie's family dramas. However, last night being a Friday, Bonnie wasn't well pleased at how things turned out.

Events have overtaken me since my chat with Claire in the café two days ago. That day I'd said, follow your heart – marry Alex – but since then the world's done a 180-degree turn; now it's her duty to Clive that counts. Poor thing's confused. Me too.

The chess win Hal grants me of a Friday evening mustn't be mentioned or the game would be up. No one would win if our charade were known about. Bonnie doesn't notice the sleight of hand we use to ensure Hal loses, despite him being smarter than me. It was less fun tonight without Bonnie's stern eyes on us. And Alex had wrought some mischief with the board before supper. Made it harder for his father to lose. But eventually, Hal succeeded – in losing, that is!

I struggled out of bed early this morning but not before giving Hal a smart tap on the shoulder. A tendon in his neck twitched. I'm onto him. There's no malice in me really. Just annoyance at our situation. We're like three circus clowns balancing on a rubber ball – we stay aloft, provided our blamey feet keep moving unceasingly.

It was nice to have Hal to myself last night and him *seeming* as faithful as if he actually *were* faithful. I achieved my obligatory chess win. But the 'win' wasn't so enjoyable without Bonnie's sharp eye surveying the scene. I even won Hal last night. A storm-brought bonus!

While Hal snores from the whiskey he tippled, I take my torch from the bedside table, where it's lived since the pull cord conked out and remains broken for reasons too tedious to mention.

Descending in the semi-dark, I miss a half step by the angle turn and step off into empty space.

Landing, my ankle twists. "Blast!" I exclaim, crumpling onto the stair tread. Luckily, my centre of gravity is low or I'd have rolled downwards, killed myself. I sit holding my head in my hands. It's hard making our 'situation' work. To what end? So, we three can pretend to live normal lives? The truth will out eventually.

Frustrated, I weep tears of the dry heaving sort that involve one's body in a workout. I stagger downstairs, intending to limp up to Alex and whisper the things I ought to have said long ago.

Young Alex was the more loving son, though his boons weren't boast-worthy. He wasn't the spitting image of Michelangelo's David, nor had he prodigious exam success. Today Alex would be deemed 'creative', thanks to his cleverness in taking things apart, and learning how they work.

He talks philosophy as if he knows about it. None of us is qualified to contradict him. Did we fail Alex?

I shine my torch on Alex's camp bed – he's not there. He's in with Claire. Of course! We sent him in last night when the storm worsened!

I rehearse my guilt about Alex; had I compromised my integrity by insisting on certain legalities back at the time of the boys' births? Is it therefore my fault that Alex wants to bed Clive's fiancée? Was he denied the mothering he needed? Alex wasn't mine. It was wrong of me to pretend otherwise.

I sigh and sink onto the ice-cold flagstones by the lounge room door. I listen attentively.

There's nothing to be heard. I'm not spying, just being a mother. Should I play the avenging angel flinging wide the door, sweeping off sheets, confounding evil, being a prude?

'Prude' is the wrong epithet for me. Early one morning in the late fifties, here, at Arcadia, during a house party, I, Cynthia, a virgin at 26, arrived at Hal's door begging a Craven A of him but hoping he'd offer so much more.

But that was then. Now I'm celibate, not by desire – an unfortunate word 'desire', considering Hal's medical problem! Is Hal's merely a plumbing problem or a partner specific problem? I wonder. I'd never ask for fear he'd tell the truth.

I limp back upstairs to the alcove off the bedroom – my office cum dressing room. There's always something practical to do. I'll go along with Cedric's plan to entail his estate upon Clive – the presumed father of Claire's son. Hal knows nothing of my recent efforts to secure our future.

I hope he won't be cross on learning I've invited the Marconis for an informal lunch. I'm not even trying to put Gwenda's nose out of joint for betraying our friendship, as one might reasonably expect me to do. No. I'm just covering our backs in case Claire goes home pregnant – marries no one. We need a second string to our bow. Cedric was adamant that without a child, whose middle name was Gordon after 'our lot', the bequest would lapse.

Yesterday when she phoned me gleefully to give me the gossip on Claire and Alex, I sounded out Maureen Marconi on a business proposition. Would she be interested in the sale of our creek flats to them? Would she what! Hal is reluctant to carve up his land but Maureen and Beppe are salivating at the possibility of creek access.

We're meeting in the dining room at midday for a preliminary discussion. By the time Hal has tippled several glasses of French Champagne, we'll have carved up his birthright and convinced him it's a bargain.

Chapter 50
Morning After Alex and Hal

Alex and Hal busy themselves with outdoor chores, orbiting the garden like planets destined never to collide.

Hal watches his son's lithe form as he deals with the cedars that bore the brunt of last night's battering. He sorts fallout from the gale with an efficiency of movement that's a sight for sore eyes, or would be, under different circumstances. Limbs are sized, removed to the woodpile by the shed with despatch. Marvellous how Alex tackles outdoor tasks! Could have been a dancer, his movement is so fluid.

But what dispiriting circumstances! Hal thinks. Storm damage might be a metaphor for their lives.

Ruined trees! Damaged families! Extinguished hopes!

"Over here, Da!" Alex calls. He beckons Hal over to a particularly fine specimen of the genus.

Upon inspection it's found the tree is rotten to its core.

Hal feels physically ill. "The blight will have them all," he says. This scourge attacks trees as silently as ill-judged lust undermines families, he thinks; it leaves the outer foliage intact, while burrowing down to the core and once you're cored…

"What do you reckon, Da?"

"Borer," Hal says. "Got to come down. But not today. It'd kill Cynthia. Tidy them up so they're okay cosmetically, Al," he says.

"A tree surgeon might save them," Alex says.

"He charges extra for hopeful diagnoses," Hal says. "It'd look like a mouth with missing teeth." Hal wishes Alex didn't always look on the bright side. It's as if Alex is critiquing his own hopelessness. Hal carries smaller off-cuts to the pile, telling himself they're branches and not limbs.

Hal is glad he's old. Old age insulates one from disappointment. It protects one from emotional entanglements, except those pre-diarised for Friday evenings in the room off the library.

In his mind's eye, Hal safeguards his image of 'B' as a lithe young girl. She still has the power to light up his synapses brighter than the Manhattan skyline after dark.

Eventually, Hal pushes away the image of young B or nothing would get done. In any case, he'd never swap the mature B for her younger tomboy self; B, the woman, has magnificently fulfilled the template of her youth. Her perfect oval face is hardly lined, she's slender yet womanly, her complexion hasn't faded in the way of olive-skinned persons. She's gracious, confident, at ease and even if at times she regrets the decision made all those years ago, she never says so.

In a way, she'd been right. Better the cherished mistress than the humdrum wife who's always monumentally there. B had yielded to Cynthia's superior claims; guessed she would not be accepted as mistress of Arcadia – she, a mere diary farmer's daughter. He'd tried to sway her decision but to no avail. Eventually, he'd gone along with the scheme Cynthia had cooked up to conceal the mess he'd made of all three lives. How weak of him!

Their pact at least allowed Bonnie to help raise their son as his and Cynthia's. Bonnie had naïvely accepted Cyn's claim to have become pregnant first, a furphy as it turned out. The enormity of the lie rankles with him still.

Cynthia's pregnancy had resulted from a night of awkward fumbling in the bedroom upstairs.

She had initiated the encounter at 2.00 am after a party, on the pretext of botting a Craven A from him.

But Cynthia, the silly not-so-young filly, had never smoked; hers was a ploy to endear her to the most eligible bachelor present – Hal! He should have been partnering B but she'd had a family emergency.

Cynthia had been invited by his sister Eudora – a friend from PLC; Eudora had known of his attachment to Bonnie and of their engagement; nevertheless, Cynthia had set her cap at him. Two dutiful dances with her host had convinced her he was available.

But that night in the bedroom! What a fiasco! After her first attempt at the drawback, Cyn had erupted in an almighty coughing fit, and Hal had invited her to sit on his bed while she caught her breath. Her stole had dropped, unveiling a pair of plump pink shoulders.

He'd sat beside her, patting her back in an avuncular way. But poor dear C, more an ocean-going vessel than vestal virgin, had taken his kindness for lust; she'd lain on the bed, her arms wide open as if crucified, her eyes closed against untoward views of the masculine anatomy, and waited for him to ravish her.

He pitied this clumsy, desperate girl – all she had was her pluck, so he'd obliged her, confident that his dear B, once she knew the circumstances, wouldn't mind too much; that indeed she would regard his behaviour as an act of punctilious kindness on his part. And, so she had done.

Today he's sad to see so many fine trees destined for the woodpile, but, hell's bells, what a fuel bonanza! Nothing lifts the spirits like a fire ablaze from one's own gleanings. These off-cuts were pruned by Mother Nature – a cosy winter is now guaranteed. But are they plugging the dyke with a cotton bud, he wonders.

Knowing how much Hal loves these cedars planted by his Four Bears – a family joke – Alex hates to see his father eager to sign the death warrant of the oldest of them all. Sad that its death has turned into a firewood windfall. Finances must be worse than Alex had imagined.

How he'd love to help them while letting them maintain their pride. He could always beg racing tips from loquacious windbags in the pub, who ingratiate themselves with punters for a jar or two. Invest his savings, all $3,000 of it, at the racecourse. He'd probably lose it. Better that he should give the cash directly to Hal, pretending to have invested it on his behalf and made a tidy sum on a long shot. Now that'd do the trick although he wouldn't be able to produce a betting slip if asked.

But fancy letting Da find him tucked up in bed with Claire! Hal will have had his suspicions but today wasn't the day. He could have said nothing happened. It was true. Yet also in a way a lie.

Such a wallop love gives you! It fills Alex with awe. Now he knows why men are fools for love.

Why Antony put the Roman Empire in jeopardy for Cleopatra. Love is all-consuming, awe-full, or is it just awful? So far, he's got through life content with daily pleasures: a day's work done well, a natter with a mate, a carpentry problem solved; now all he wants belongs to his own brother.

He wants Claire desperately, desires her infinitely, lusts after her basely. Such love is death to one's peace of mind. But would he go back to where he was two months ago? Never.

Chapter 51
Bonnie Back

Bonnie spends her time off in Koroit with her brothers. However, Friday night's visit was an unscheduled one. Her brother Kevin, trudging back from the milking shed, had fallen and aggravated an old injury. The boys had insisted she come home to help with his care. Young Mary had driven her through the storm to Koroit and had then gone on to Port Fairy to stay with relatives.

The boys neglect their health. Emmett has diabetes, curse of the affluent, although they're no longer well off, with milk prices falling. They eat only junk food! As soon as she gets home, Bonnie's first chore is to empty their only vegs – potato crisps – into the pigswill.

She knows she's meant to revel in her time off but given her brothers' neuralgia, arthritis and nary a wife between them, though they've had others' wives aplenty in their day, she's guilted into looking after them more often than she should be. But these days, with everything oozing neglect, they're campaigning for her to move in back home. Become their housemaid! Good luck with that!

Mud-caked boots dry by the fire; the liniment pong in the parlour smells like a footy change room of a night. Their vinyl recliners circle the telly like it's a holy shrine. Bonnie gets it all – the drinking, the arguments, the winner-take-all card games – it's quite common, these are symptoms of primary producer's malaise.

The truth is her *real* family needs her. She fits into the Sins' lives like a piece of plain blue sky fits into an intricate jigsaw puzzle – she's the insignificant bit that's essential to complete the picture.

It's too late to make a life in Koroit. She's prepared to see the boys once a month for the stories they provide. She returns from her downtime bearing anecdotes for the Sins. Her tales of hoary dairy farmers battling to survive against the odds entertain the Sins. She exaggerates to give the Sins a better perspective on their own lives. She laughs along with them, delighting in her own inventiveness, though feeling somewhat guilty for having made her brothers' misfortune a source of merriment. The Sins' glam-shabby manor house offers a certain amount of job security, and mainly pleasant, if eccentric employers. She embarks upon her time-off reluctantly even though the Sins haven't paid her in a while.

Cyn has started insisting she's family now that they're almost broke, hoping that Bonnie, flattered, will forgo her pay. Hal, as usual, deals with things by pretending they're not happening.

On Sunday Emmett drives her back to Arcadia. Kevin's crisis is over and he's grudgingly agreed to shell out for some home help.

Although the winter landscape unfolds before her appreciative eyes, they snag uncomfortably on the yellowed paddocks and the bloody Scotch thistles. Idiot who introduced them here needs whipping! Bonnie thinks, shaking her head. They need Brett in to spray. But now that Cynthia's a born-again conservationist, she deals with weeds like Hal deals with lack of funds – by wishing the problem away.

As the ute clanks over the familiar cattle grid, Bonnie relaxes. To anyone else the noise would sound like a prison door clanking shut. And certainly, it brackets Bonnie's down time from her reality.

But returning home, her spirits lift. Here, she's valued, however lowly paid. She has a role in a drama.

It's more a long-running soap opera than Shakespeare, though some of its plot lines are reminiscent of Macbeth.

At Arcadia she never questions whether she's spending her life well or badly. Koroit seems a dank swamp. Despite all its draughts and drawbacks, at Arcadia she feels she inhabits a gothic fairy-tale castle.

This time however she returns to find the cedars brutalised and the emotional landscape altered too.

They pull up at the front door. "Glad to be back with your toffs, eh?" Emmett says. He gives Bonnie's cheek a sandpapery buzz. The stench of roll-your-owns and the residue of stale saliva make her want to retch. She'd wipe off his kiss with her lawn handkerchief but she controls herself.

"Get with it, Sis," Emmett says. "You look like a Latin teacher. All the barmaids I know have gone blonde with age."

"I'll bet you've known more than a few," she retorts.

"You can talk! See ya, Bon! And do think hard about coming home." Emmett drives off.

She doesn't exhale until he's well away, having sprayed gravel over the yews. "Phew!" She sighs, shakes her head at the storm damage. The cedars have been restyled to resemble short back and sides' haircuts.

As she picks up her case, she senses something untoward. Hardheaded countrywoman Bonnie may be, but when the front door of Arcadia groans open, to the sight of Bertie's permanently worried dial she picks up a change in the vibe even before knowing of anyone's distress. She doesn't hold with supernatural tosh but moving through the portico it feels like someone's walking over her grave.

Bertie comes at a run instead of simply materialising as usual. He takes her case indoors and leaves it near the library annexe. "Someone in trouble," he says, pointing upwards. Bonnie can hear a soughing sob. Drawn to its source, she leaves her handbag and hurries up the stairs.

She finds Claire crawling backwards up the staircase using two arms, one bottom, and her good leg, which leaves her bad leg waving in the air like an insect's antenna. "What is it, love?"

Claire wails histrionically.

"Come on, Hon, nothing's that bad. Where are you going?"

"…tower…pregnant…"

"Ah! I see you're in a spot of bother but why the tower? Can you get unpregnant in a tower?"

"No, I just felt like being dead, I guess. The tower seemed…My period is late."

"Oh, well. At least you're being careful not to break your leg again. Your orthopaedist will be glad you took good care of it, despite you being dead," Bonnie says, drawing her lips in.

Claire wails, then starts to laugh manically.

"Quite sure, you're pregnant, dear?"

"Yes! I'm never late!"

"Get tested. An' if you are, then pregnant is good, isn't it?"

"I don't know whose…?"

"Surely, it's Clive's child?"

Not necessarily.

"Crumbs. Then come and help me get lunch. Don't despair until you've had a pregnancy test. You like babies, don't you?"

"I think so."

"Good. Can you peel Jerusalem artichokes?"

"Are they an abortifacient?"

"Not unless you eat them in a hot bath with gin and a knitting needle." Bonnie gives a tentative giggle at her own witticism. Claire looks at her wide eyed and then joins in.

Chapter 52
Cooking

Downstairs in the kitchen Bonnie dries her tears and sets Claire to work slicing vegetables.

She chops away at the Jerusalem artichokes, the vegetable Bonnie calls 'old men's testicles'.

Claire, amused, asks her, "Is chopping always so therapeutic, Bonnie?"

"Sure," says Bonnie. "For me it is. I take a zucchini. 'Hi there, you big Long Worry'. It's the aboriginal name of a town around here Longwarre. Chop! You're halved. Chop! Quartered. Eighthed. It's like homeopathy. Reduces worry to negligible levels."

Bonnie gives Claire a chopping board and a vegetable knife and seats her at the kitchen table with a footstool for her leg.

Alex bustles in with kindling. "Hey, girls, look at the wood we cut today. Died of natural causes. One day a windbreak. Next day a windfall."

"Hi, Alex." Claire smiles at him wanly, hoping he won't notice her puffy eyes.

"Hi, Claire. Good night's sleep?" he asks warily.

"No, I had a strange dream," she says.

"The one about the boy with the kite?"

"Yes, that one. I think I know what it means. That I'm ready for a disastrous fall."

Bonnie, busying herself with the stock, stirs on but it's clear she's listening in.

"Claire, don't get all worked up over last night's dream again. It was a bit ambiguous is all. If you took all your dreams seriously you'd never sleep."

"Find some watercress, Alex, dear," she says.

"It's not Cressmas."

"Then something green for the table."

"The spinach coloured tablecloth? Some lichen?"

Alex's witticisms provoke a weak smile in Claire.

Bonnie quirks up the corner of her mouth mirthlessly. "How are the Marconis' squash today?"

"Seemed well enough when I fixed the post-and-rail fence their stallion leaned on earlier."

"That's their eldest son, dear," says Bonnie, with a wicked grin.

"Both sons are of stallionic proportions," Alex says.

"Go and borrow our shears back. And ask nicely after their squash. It'll look lovely on the Wedgewood."

"Soggy excuse for a vegetable. Whom are we expecting?"

"How should I know? I just serve up. I fake a wide-eyed interest in their busy lives. How I hate pretending…"

"Pretending what?" asks Alex.

"That I'm thrilled to play Cinderella in your mother's Cuban heels when I'd rather be flipping through Margaret Fulton for new recipes, or checking race results."

"Sorry, Bon. They ask too much of you. Please tell me who it is so I can escape."

Bonnie shrugs. "I don't know and once everything is prepared, I'm going to my room as a protest. They don't pay me. So, I'll work for nix, but I won't socialise in your ma's paisley print frocks that weren't fashionable even when they were."

"I'll support you in that, Bonnie. At least tell me how to win at gambling," Alex pleads.

"Read the Form Guide. Though it's never helped me. Anyway I only pretend to gamble. Since when were you into the gee-gees?"

"I need a few quid. I'm in a tightish spot," he says.

"Ask me if it's a loan you need. I'll give you what little I've got."

"Oh, I get it. You can gamble, but I can't?"

"My system involves matchsticks. I add the winnings to my pot for next race day."

"How's it going?"

"I've saved a thousand matches recently."

"When will you convert to actual currency?"

"Probably never. Now, Alex, do stay to lunch! We need your cheek and liveliness."

"I'll stay if you go and rest, Bon. You're not paid enough to sit through Ma's excruciating lunches."

Alex hesitates. "They're still paying you?"

"Ye-es, of course."

"There's no of course about it."

"I've had a brainwave. I intend hanging around colourful racing identities in the bar of The Royal until they spill the beans."

"Crooks?"

"Probably. Then off to the TAB to cash in."

"Never!"

"I'm off gambling on the olds' behalf. Better keep that under your hat. But if I win, at least they'll have to pay you."

"I'm not their most importunate debtee. Times are hard…"

"Importunate? Big word. Jot it down, Claire. How's the list?"

"Growing."

"Bonnie, I'd rob my piggy bank to keep you here, pretending to be my friend."

"I've never had to pretend with you, love."

Alex takes Bonnie in his arms, frying pan and all, and waltzes her around the room. "Ta da-da-da Dum…"

"You are very sweet, Alex," Bonnie says, pushing him away and tucking loose wisps of hair behind her ears. "Anyhow, it's no one special coming or Cyn would have ordered from the fancy shmancy deli in Warrnambool. She said, 'Use whatever isn't mouldy yet.'"

"So, it's someone we must use up before *they* go off. Who deserves to eat squash Marconi's cats peed on?"

"And what do you smell of, Claire?"

"Gin and garlic."

"An abortifacient?"

Claire hangs her head over the peelings.

"What's up, honey pie? Da girl missing' her fee-on-say?"

"Squash please, Alex." Bonnie's voice emerges with an edge to cut glass.

Alex's gaze moves from Bonnie to Claire and back. "Mm. A brace?" Unanswered, he leaves.

Hal enters. He sits on the doorstep, drags his gumboots off and throws them into the mudroom.

"Where did Alex go?"

"Off for squash."

"Thought he'd given it up."

"What?"

"Squash!"

"He's not playing…"

"Just practising, is he?"

Bonnie sighs. Claire giggles.

"What are you girls on?" Hal says, heading to the pantry.

He returns with shot glasses and Scotch. "So, here's to a lovely warm winter," he says, pouring.

"Phew! That avenue of cedars. Never protected us from gales. Now there'll be heat all winter long. Cheers. Heat, sunlight and tucker," he sighs. "All humans need, well almost all," he amends, glancing Bonnie's way. "But we mustn't get too warm and cosy or Cyn won't want to warm her tootsies on the Methodist's foot-rail on Sunday." He winks and flicks his tongue to mitigate any impression of disloyalty.

"Good on you, Hal, for shooting those lapins for me," says Bonnie. "They've been marinated in plonk. Oh heck, the spuds."

"Poor bunnies. Still stunned from the storm," says Hal. "Not a fair fight. I fired a warning shot but then I thought it fair to science to let Darwinism win. Too dumb to breed. Like most humans."

"We all ought to be certified fit for breeding," says Claire, "but who'd be wise enough to administer the test?" There's a bitter edge to her voice.

"You all right, my dear?" asks Hal.

"Just a cold!" she says. "Okay Bonnie, the artichokes are done! Carrots now?"

"Yes. And set the table, please Hal."

"Certainly, my dear. Where's the cloth?"

"Here. We're expecting nine, three courses. Here's cutlery."

Hal puts the shot glass in his lumberjack shirt pocket, the bottle goes under his arm. Like Clive does, Claire thinks.

"Whom are we expecting?" Bonnie calls after Hal.

"I haven't been informed. I only pay the rates," Hal says, flicking the tablecloth over his shoulder as he leaves. "Ask Cynthia. She's in the study, doing the books."

"How come you're so good at it, Bonnie?" Claire asks.

"At cooking?"

"Getting rid of men. Staying cheerful."

"I've had years of practice, worse luck. Bread needs slicing."

"Sure, I just wish I'd had more…"

"Men?"

"No. More experience."

"You're having an experience now. Experience comes from experiencing things."

"That's an epigram, Bonnie. You're clever. Know anything about coat hangers and gin? I've created massive problems for this child. I'm unready for motherhood. If only its origins weren't so…"

"Uncertain? Would your love for the child depend upon the father's identity?"

Claire's eyes narrow. "No. I don't think so."

"Good! Stock's ready," Bonnie says, tasting it. She scrapes artichokes and spuds into the pot, adds chopped herbs and replaces the lid.

Chapter 53
Luncheon

It's a rare gathering of humans one can't learn from. At school, Alex learned his ABC.

Nowadays, he learns from everyone he meets.

This ability, developed at Melbourne Uni during his brief sojourn there, and stayed with him as he moved on to lesser things. Why, he'd asked himself, with his broad interest in life, the universe and almost everything, should he waste years on an obscure thesis? Angus from school had committed years of his life to '*Endogenizing the Exogenous*' whatever that meant.

Instead of specialising in arcane matters Alex collected glints of gold from his immediate surroundings. He maintained his awe and learned something of worth wherever he landed.

At uni, boring came in different gradations, some so mammoth they trailed their own microclimates like comet tails. He subjected himself to challenges: if he could remain vertical during his interminable calculus sessions, he'd reward himself by taking the afternoon off kayaking.

This strategy was only partly successful, his arms soon turned into tree trunks, while his brain didn't atrophy too much. However, the nubile female students, who might have been impressed by the sinewy arms draped casually across the backs of the metal seating units, paid attention to the lectures, not to him. The developed parts of his anatomy languished undiscovered along with the rest of him. His university days were numbered.

He gained one skill from mathematics: poetry. He wrote odes to the lackadaisical young beauties wilting in the summer's heat in the seat in front of him. Mediocre poems to swan-like necks accumulated in notebooks during fallow hours. Nothing was worth nothing it seemed, barring his own poetry.

Cynthia's surprise guests turn out to be the Marconis – sons and all. It amazes Alex that these taciturn, hunky guys, known as 'the Italian stallions' – despite being half Irish – would come to a tame neighbours' lunch on a Saturday. Surely, they had their own busy lives to live.

Why has Ma invited them? Is she hoping to off-load Claire onto one of the cocky, affable sons?

Is she hoping to buy, sell or swap pastures with them for their mutual benefit? Or is this payback on Gwenda for breaking the Sin/Laws friendship compact and socialising promiscuously?

Is Cynthia putting Gwen on notice that her best friend status is under review? In any case, Alex looks forward to observing the Maccas' grief when forced to eat the squash he'd nicked from their side of the common fence-line earlier. Will they eat with relish, knowing the outrage of the theft?

Maureen has dressed to a formula; it hits the right note. Clearly, she'd known in advance that Cynthia is no fashion plate and has toned down the haute part of her couture. She's a chameleon, Alex decides. She could dine with anyone and know how to impress her hosts; she'd challenge, bamboozle or seduce, depending on the circumstances.

She's up with fashion, though not a slave to it, whereas Cynthia hasn't a clue there's such a thing as being 'up to date'. She'd reject the very notion. For when did pearls and cashmere twin-sets ever date?

Quality is paramount with Maureen; she lets her prosperity show without being showy. Her well-cut frock hasn't come off the hook of any dress shop in these parts. It has a twist of fabric at the solar plexus that indicates the location of her breasts without unveiling them. It's as if she has an invisible arrow pinpointing the spot near her cleavage where her heart would be, in case a medical emergency occurred. She hasn't proffered her bosom for viewing by all and sundry, although she understands the advantage of a good figure in a woman. She is proud of her shape but she's not bringing it to the table, and Alex is certain that this is a negotiating table. *Has Cynthia gone off the idea of forcing Clive and Fliss to reconcile? Is she on to her next scheme?* Alex wonders. *Clearly, more than neighbourliness is afoot.*

Maureen assumes the role of moderator. Cynthia, a bit lack-lustre today, accepts her role as underdog. Maureen can speak intelligently on a range of topics: politics, the arts, farming or regional matters.

She's just completed a distance education degree from the ANU and cannot help but mention her excellent results; she's been accepted into an honours degree. Cynthia becomes animated upon hearing this and asks whether they offer philosophy courses.

Maureen promises to drop in with brochures. Alex sees Cynthia's prejudices start to melt away, since she has nothing against nouveaux if they admit they need improving.

Her second husband, Giuseppe Marconi, doesn't give too much away. Progenitor of the aforesaid stallions, like Hal, he seems overwhelmed by his spouse. He's the nuggety, silent type, not uncomfortable when hemmed in by strong women. Beppe and Hal have re-drawn Cynthia's seating plan and cornered themselves a pair of chairs from which to confer on proceedings sotto voce. Alex guesses the two codgers have already forged an over the side-fence mateship they've neglected to mention to their spouses.

The phone rings. Alex takes the call in the hall. He expects it's Bonnie's, who had had to return to Koroit almost as soon as she'd finished making the soup. Her brother has had a 'funny turn'.

But no, Mary is on the line; she's been staying with her Port Fairy relatives since her heroic drive with Bonnie through the storm-front last night. "Should she go straight to Melbourne?" she asks.

"Please don't go home yet," Alex says. "Claire's desperate to see you. Something has upset her. Late or not, come to Ma's luncheon party. We're eating hors oeuvres, it's more a meeting than "a lunch and there's a hunky pair of bachelors who'd love to meet a sweet young thing of marriageable age…I'll pick you up from the bus station."

"Me, sweet? Hope not. It'll take an hour at least."

"We'll eat slowly and save you a few scraps…"

"Hope the men aren't scrappy."

"They look as fit as Mallee bulls."

Cynthia comes into the hall and snatches the phone from Alex. "We need you here, dear girl."

"With Bonnie gone again, suddenly our menu's changed," says Cynthia. "I don't think Bonnie's bunnies will do the trick today," she says, half to herself. "Alex will need to pick up finger food for a grazing sort of lunch. So, we'll delay our second course until you get here, Mary. It's a business lunch, really, dear. Don't rush. We've a lot to talk about." The old black phone thumps back onto its cradle.

Chapter 54
Bathroom

At lunch, a pleasant enough affair, given the surprise of the guests, Claire whispers to Alex that she needs the bathroom. Her complexion matches the artichoke soup – greige. Alex wheels her from the room without delay. Cynthia tells him to be quick about it or he'll miss out on conversing with the boys. She points out that he's a few mates short of the full complement in Warrnambool.

"It's time Claire managed the wheelchair on her own," she says.

"No, Ma," Alex replies, "there's no way Claire could negotiate the oak door on her own; the weight of the oak alone calls for a body-builder."

"Mm. I suppose," she agrees, but with reluctance. "Well, get it over with quickly. With Bonnie gone, I'll need your help serving the rabbit stew. And then you'd better head off to pick up Mary."

"Why don't we take a break? You can introduce our guests to the ancestors and the orangery, Mama. I'll collect Mary from the bus station and buy something from the deli on the way back. That way we'll have Mary's company. Let's leave the stew. It will freeze and thaw again in time for the next emergency." Cyn glowers at this remark.

The guests' faces soften with pleasure at having escaped the threatened rabbit stew. "We'd love to have a wander around the garden, says Maureen. And visit your ancestors of course."

"I suppose so. It will give Alex time to pick up Mary. Claire's friend is a dear girl and most helpful," she says, "without Bonnie's help we do feel a bit lost entertaining these days…"

"Okay, Claire." Alex wheels her from the room

The McCance/Marconis stare at Alex's departing back. Cyn had pointedly introduced Claire as Clive's fiancée not Alex's.

'What's he doing taking his brother's girlfriend to the loo?' they're all thinking.

"Oh, it's all above-board," Alex says, turning towards them in response to their unuttered query. "It's not as if we actually ablute together," he says, intending to be flippant, but it comes out sounding crude.

Once he settles Claire into the downstairs bathroom, he can hear her retching sounds even in the hallway. He knocks. Hears gulping sobs, goes in.

"You poor old thing," he says. He wipes her face again but tenderly. She starts dry retching; he picks up the vibe of desperation she gives off. "Gees," he says, "you *are* pregnant, aren't you? That's why last night's dream, upset you so."

There is no response. Just a rueful expression on her sweet, sad face. Alex wishes he could be happy for her and Clive; hell, he wishes Clive were here and happy. Poor Claire! A pregnancy and everyone horrified at the very idea of it; he wishes she was pregnant with his child. "Theoretically, it could be mine, couldn't it?" he asks.

"Unlikely!"

He checks Claire's face. It's slick and green. The 40s bathroom tiles reflect their sickly sea-green hue onto Claire in the neon-lit room.

"God, Alex. I was a virgin two months ago. To be pregnant already – shit! It should be impossible. I'm still on my L-plates. It's so unfair!" she says.

He gives a cynical bark. "Don't expect life to be fair," he says.

"Maybe it's a bug," she looks up at him hopefully.

"You're off your food."

"I'm sick; sick of being here with Cynthia."

"Your period's late, and you're nauseated into the bargain. You could always have an abortion. Level with me, Claire. You're sure it is Clive's child?"

Disoriented, she answers honestly. "I've done the maths. It's got to be Clive's child: 30 to one."

"And mine one to 30?"

"Mm."

"I wish I were the father, your lover. I won't give up hoping yet. People buy Tatts tickets on slimmer odds." He rubs her hair.

"Don't mess my hair up, Alex, please. I've got to go back in there and face them all."

"Typical woman! One minute you're in despair. Next moment you're worried about messed up hair!"

This earns him a wan smile from Claire. "Listen, our baby would be wonderful," he tells her.

"Clive's will be too. It'd be perfect if I'd known you first." She goes quiet after that. She winds her arms around her torso and rocks back and forth on the varnished loo seat. "I can't bear the thought of twenty years with Clive. I could script our every conversation now!"

Alex runs possible scenarios through his mind. "Listen, Claire, will you come away with me, baby or not?"

"You'd raise your brother's child?"

"Of course."

"Oh, shit, shit, shit! I wish you weren't such a great guy, Alex, then I wouldn't feel so bad…about what I've got to do. About leaving you. Alternatively, if Clive was just a bit worse than he really is then maybe I could leave him."

"I should have been a right bastard to you, so you'd feel better about dumping me?"

"Don't be idiotic! Still, if you had been a horrid love rat, I suppose I'd have married Clive with less reluctance."

"And you'd be happy being only 50% unhappy?" He gets a smile out of her now.

"I guess no one's totally happy."

"Then I want you partially happy with me, not Clive."

"Mm, me too! It's what I'd want, ideally."

"Let's run away!"

"No. I've got to face this. If I ducked out, I'd be ashamed. I'll never regret knowing you, Alex. It's so sad for the three of us. There's four of us now." Claire rips out a wad of tissues. Wipes her eyes. "Alex, I'd be with you in a second if I had it in me to be a cruel bitch, to deprive Clive of his child. But would you want me then?"

Alex shrugs. "No. Yes. What about me? I'll be forced to play the best man, when I am the best man…to love you." He sinks onto the ledge of the bath. "Let's not blame each other. It's fate."

"We're star-crossed lovers?"

"Mm."

"You'd rather be a handsome, dead Romeo than…"

"Than what?"

"I don't know. I…we should have managed it better."

"How do you manage love?" Alex grasps his head in frustration.

Chapter 55
Pub

Q. Why does a pub feel more like church than church?

A. Because pubs are shrines to the gods of geniality. Here no sceptic struggles with his faith. Pubs are sanctuaries where blokes, guys, chaps, sheilas, senoritas, hombres congregate for solace, even happiness. All communicants welcome if they'll have a beer.

Alex leans against the doorjamb. This is his local, outpost of a worldwide faith: The Believers in the Blessed Ale. No barman's blood was ever shed for the punters – unless they were involved in the dust-up in Warrney last week. Oh. They were! No matter, they're welcome anyway! Come. Drink. Eat. Slake your thirst, at least.

Pubs are a buffer between the rock-hard givens of home and work! Havens from blinding sunlight! Even on corrugated outback tracks, there'll be a ramshackle pub aquiver in shimmering air-currents, a beacon in a post-apocalyptic wasteland. Without, all is parched and dire. Within, it's as cool as a temperate rain forest.

A cheesy air current wafts Alex's way. When did 'chook pyjamas' become the national dish?

Did we vote on it, he wonders.

Mary's imminent arrival had provided Alex with an excuse to bail on Cynthia's luncheon with their neighbours. She'd phoned from Port Fairy to say she was just hopping on a bus. It suited Alex to go and pick her up so he'd told Ma 'a little white lie' about Mary's e.t.a., thereby carving out 20 minutes of peace for himself from this absolute bugger of day. Might he yet salvage something good from the day? Would 20 minutes' respite cure his shitty mood?

The news is dreadful! Claire pregnant! And to Clive! Who doesn't love her. Meanwhile he, Alex, does! Wheeling her back from the loo, his shoulders sagged under the weight of her news.

It was cruel of him to leave her back there with his family at lunch, her tears plopping onto Mama's Wedgewood. Alex admits he isn't perfect. But he'd reminded himself of those airline safety instructions advising parents to look after themselves before saving their dependents.

Alex is glad no one knows him. Here in The Royal, his being anonymous is a boon. The St John Smiths had become infamous six years ago after applying to hive off creek flats after a shire re-zoning went their way. When the story hit the local paper, his father had insisted they wouldn't profit from it. He'd said, no; it wasn't worth the bad blood. Their name had turned to mud anyway. Locals had hated the effortless way things favoured the St Johns. Made it even worse they didn't bother cashing in their luck. Others would have had to. One night, Alex had been worked over in a Timboon pub.

Today it's the din that assaults him; it rises like a solid wall. Breaking out of his reverie, Alex finds himself stranded in the doorway. He tries moving, he imagines loping across the room with his usual free-swinging gait. But he can't move; he's stuck. His legs require instructions from his brain; his will needs priming even to perform this basic feat.

Alex trains his eyes on the bar as if the intervening space were a stretch of turbulent ocean.

He makes the crossing somehow remaining upright. At the bar he props his chin on the heel of his palm.

The grubby flannel shirt he'd worn to lunch to anger Mama attracts puddles of spilt beer. It's a sensation he would usually find unpleasant. Today he wallows in its ickiness.

Fanned across his brow, his skinny fingers hold his head up, like fragile stone arches supporting a cathedral. He shakes his head at the absurdity of this insight. Now the mirrored shelves behind the bar fracture the image of his ugly mug. He feels emotionally fractured. And Claire has a fractured tibia. He laughs mirthlessly.

He catches the barman's eye at last.

"A pot, ta."

He watches the barman pulling beers, loving his dexterity. It's harder than juggling, the balancing of the amber fluid with the head, so the fewest possible drops of beer are lost. The barman angles the glass towards the tap, he flicks the handle around. As beer spurts around the glass tornado-style, he brings the glass up straight, snaps off the tap and holds the vessel up for inspection before placing it in front of Alex.

"Brilliant!" Alex says. The barman grins.

Today, he's after numbness, not companionship. He hopes by rubbing shoulders with the multitude, he'll salve the pain of singularity. Forget how utterly Claire is lost to him.

Before he'd met her, Alex was ignorant of love's power to sap ones will, to turn one into a sap. But this was aeons ago. BC, Before Claire. Before, life was about work and friends. He'd felt content when his life was *con*tent-free. Now he wonders, *Does contentment even rate a position on the happiness spectrum?*

In Melbourne, he renovates, mixes with furniture restorer mates, dates tepidly, feels sanguine about his aloneness. He must donate 'sanguine' to Claire for her list. It might cheer her up. It means cool-blooded, which she's not.

Everything changed for him that day on the beach with Claire. He'd never met anyone he wanted so much it hurt. She, with her crutches, her pain, seemed a stick puppet from a Hindu shadow play. But even as a broken tern, she was more alive than all the squalling seagulls on the shore.

"G'day, mate. Did I see ya in a red ute buying in feed from Jackson's yest'd'y?"

"Yeah, mate, I'm Alex." He offers his hand.

"From 'round 'ere then?" the bloke says, shaking Alex's hand forcefully. "Todd."

"You're Todd and I'm *on* my Todd." The bloke fails to respond to this witticism; Alex continues, "Melbourne these days."

"Not on the land?" Todd asks, slow-witted.

"On it – sort of – the olds are past it. Mainly agistment now. You?" Alex asks.

"I'm at Dookie. On a break. Workin' on the folks' place. Dairy."

"Hard yacka!"

"Yep. Looking into oenology!"

"Great! Drink, mate?" Alex offers, longing to be alone with his non-thoughts.

"Yeah. Ta!"

"Another VB. And…"

"Same."

While Alex pays, his friend yells at someone who's downwind of them, judging by a waft of chemicals.

"D'ya wash that stuff off a youse?" Todd asks. "We been spraying Roberts' joint with somethin' shit awful," he explains.

"No kidding! D'ya get a permit?" Alex asks.

Todd shrugs. "Comes in ten gallon drums from Cow Chemicals. Big firm. Must be kosher."

"They're the bastards that made agent orange!" Alex says. "Dioxins. Hope you've got protective gear? Where you spraying?"

"Around the creek flats," Todd admits.

"Great, so that's the fishing stuffed for the season!" Alex says.

"Excuse me, mate." Todd heads off, keen to escape Alex's misery. It seeps from his pores.

The barman tries to weasel conversation out of Alex. Fended off by Alex's surliness, he gravitates towards heartier patrons.

Why can't I be normal? Alex wonders. *If only I had the litany off-pat. If only I could grumble drolly about drought, iniquitous land-tax, crop yields, paspalum infestation, poor carrying capacity, fisheries and wildlife scum, I'd be accepted, because 'Life's a bitch but we're all in it together'.*

But Alex suffers discreetly and discretely. That's bloody public school for you!

Encourages spelling puns, gives you a posh accent. Turns you into a diamond in a cowpat.

He grabs his glass and heads for a table. Shit! The chairs are bentwood, his *bête noir*. Men built like boab trunks should never squat on bendy sticks, their glutes tensed tight against collapse. It's obscene. Makes him want to laugh and cry at once!

He leans on the window ledge farthest from the bar, so he won't be drawn into the swirl of recycled jokes. He'll watch others coping. See them slap each other on the back, hit on the barmaid, shout the next round.

He lets the camaraderie wash around him.

Holy Shit! He slaps his forehead. Mary's train will be in by now.

Chapter 56
Mary and Boys

Alex meets Mary at the bus depot. "Welcome," he says. "Big changes today." He pecks her cheek.

She narrows her eyes at him. She's wondering, *Why does Alex smell so beery?*

He comes clean. "Sorry, Mare. Dropped into the pub. Time got away from me."

"Didn't pick you for a lunch-time boozer."

"Rough day." He tightens the rubber band on his ponytail. "Claire thinks she's pregnant."

"Then *she* should be drinking. Gin."

"She's crying into her artichoke soup. No test yet."

"There is no test to prove it's artichoke soup. Depends how bad she feels. Sorry. Bad joke. Let's buy a kit."

"Okay."

At Arcadia Mary hurries in, hello-ing everyone, assuming all are pleased to see her. Bypassing Cynthia, who's angling her cheek for a peck, she hurries to Claire's side. "I missed you heaps, girl," she says, embracing her friend enthusiastically. Claire manages a wan smile.

The room's quiet. Either Ma's plans have flopped flatter than the placemats, or Maureen has run out of edifying patter. Alex makes introductions. Pulls out a chair for Mary across from the CCs.

"A party!" Mary exclaims. "Only true originals have such spur of the moment parties, Cynthia."

"Thank you, dear," says Mama gratified. "When one decides to meet one's neighbours, there's no time like the present."

"Pity we didn't get the urge earlier," says Beppe. "The urge to be neighbourly, I mean," he adds, giving Cynthia a wicked leer.

Cynthia's unused to teasing of this sort; she twists her mouth into impossible grimaces until it looks like she has a serious nerve disease.

Until now the Italian stallions have been subdued, slumped in their chairs as if nothing could jolt them out of their torpor, but with the irresistible Mary, their egos inflate faster than camp mattresses.

What is it about her? Alex wonders. Is it her tartan skirts that flip wildly, unveiling shapely legs beneath red leggings? Whatever, Carlo and Cristoforo seem to cue into her mood.

Alex pours himself another wine. He studies the bottle. "Burgundy from your real actual Fraance?" he asks, to the amusement of the CCs.

"We've a well-stocked cellar," says Beppe. "We'll have you for tasting soon. Don't worry, we won't be tasting you, Cynthia, but *you'll* be drinking our wine from Umbria. Beyoudiful."

"First time I breached your boundaries was when the fence broke last week. Your cellar-opening invite must be travelling via Umbria," Alex says rudely. Cynthia glares. It's his worry about Claire, amidst this epidemic of neighbourliness that is making him act a bit unhinged.

"Don't be impertinent," says Cynthia.

So, we do need the Maccas to save our necks, Alex decides.

"This funny boy you got, Hal. Real Aussie sents of youmour!"

"He's priceless, if you mean worth no price at all," says Cynthia, tight-lipped.

"Both boys are wags," says Hal, in oil pouring mode. "Clive works at St V's with young Mary here."

"So, Mary, you are doc's fiancée," says Beppe, having earlier misunderstood Claire's role in the family.

"No, Clive is engaged to the beauteous Claire." Mary turns to Claire, who attempts a smile but her facial muscles won't cooperate and her dark rings can't be wished away.

There's a murmur of surprise at this. The stallions lean forward; they take an active interest in Mary now they know she's on the market.

Most girls would find this scrutiny awkward, Mary waves, "Hi guys! I'm available for genuine matrimonial offers from good-hearted men."

"My boys have heart of gold…"

"And gold Amex cards?" Alex asks. All titter politely.

"I'm no gold digger!" Mary squinches her eyes at Alex.

Carlo produces an American Express card and lays it on the table. "A token," he says.

Mary raises her hand, warding off evil. "No, I'm not for buying; I'm looking for a hero. Someone who's making the world a better place," says Mary. "Sorry, Carlo."

Alex wonders at her supreme confidence. To have taken over a dinner party this fast…she could be PM if she wanted. The room is full of strong women, he thinks, though Claire's not one of them today.

"So, no interview?" asks Carlo petulantly.

"Sorry. What about you, Cristoforo?"

"I'm with Fisheries and Wildlife. We conserve the beauty and diversity of Australia."

"Wow! You're only saving the whole country!" says Mary.

"With help from my workmates."

She gives him a wide-mouthed smile that shows her dimples to advantage.

"I need to check the creek later," he says, "water-weed levels. You want to come?" He raises his eyebrows, queryingly.

"You take your dates to work?" Alex asks.

"We'll all come," says Cynthia, peevishly, her luncheon having derailed.

"I can't press my suit in public, Mrs Sin."

"Sin Gin, dear. Spell it how you will. The double meanings afforded by my names are legend. But as to dating Mary on my property, I insist…"

"But what if it weren't your property?" says Chris, stilling the chatter. Cynthia's mouth hinges open but she maintains her silence.

"Which area of ecology are you in?" Alex asks, filling the shocked silence.

"I'm developing a model that takes individual floral or faunal species and excludes one at a time from the model to predict which plants and animals will thrive within various time frames, according to climatic variations. See, if all the vegetation along the Great Ocean Road died in a savage fire, after a decent season of regrowth, you could predict the make-up of the regrowth over time."

"Wow!" Alex is impressed.

"Down here, we've every right to fear fire. Some species lose ground to big bullies; they take over. A single blue gum might overgrow to billy-oh, causing loss of diversity. Certain species of flora die off altogether…to our great loss. The habitat might then become inhospitable to certain fauna."

"There's always bullies exploiting new circumstances," Cynthia agrees. "Poor Felicity. No end to the suitors queuing up since she was orphaned with a decent spread."

"Don't talk about her bottom, like that," says Alex. His mother glares.

"You mean the pretty blonde with the riding school?" asks Carlo. "I've tried being friendly, but she always gives me a dismissive wave – a push-off signal I'd say."

They laugh at Fliss' expense but it's good-natured laughter.

"Felicity mightn't like your looks," says Maureen, angling for a compliment for her sons.

It arrives on cue. Maureen seems pleased.

"Yes," says Cyn, "Fliss had a sad break-up. As she's a life-long friend of Clive, we don't go introducing her to just anyone."

Maureen recoils. "Are we not good enough for your friends?" Her offence seems genuine.

Alex tunes out while Cynthia heals her rift with the neighbours she's meant to be cosying up to; she mumbles something bland about strength in diversity and all mucking in together.

"Don't worry, Cyn," says Beppe. "Once a dago, always a dago. Never bothered me."

It's odd, Alex thinks, how much he's enjoyed the Maccas' company after years of Ma's prejudice. There's always something to learn from others. Then Alex remembers what's been niggling at him. "Excuse me, Beppe, he says. I've a question for Chris. In town today, I met a bloke; he was talking about spraying Johnson's creek flats with a dioxin-based product. Is the council spraying just now?"

"Shoot! D'you get their names?" asks Chris.

"Todd. Studying at Dookie. His folks are dairying."

"Good start. I'll get onto their student lists. Sorry, Hal and Mrs Sin. Got to go. Sorry, Mary."

"How about dusk? Meet you at the stables?" She smiles winningly.

"Okay," Chris says. "You're on!"

221

Chapter 57
Walk

"Maureen, how soon do you think I should start treating Claire respectfully?"

Maureen and Cynthia pick their careful way along the river flats, trying to keep up with Hal and Beppe but falling behind the 'boys', who seem to be getting along like a house on fire.

Cynthia's carrying a much-loathed walking stick but the ground is soggy and uneven and given her multitudinous ailments the last thing needed is a fall.

"Immediately of course," Maureen replies once she's on solid ground.

"Do you enjoy getting even?" Cynthia asks, hoping she's found a kindred soul in Maureen.

Maureen throws her head back, whoops. "Everyone enjoys seeing enemies get their come-uppance. But do befriend Claire if you're sure she's pregnant – leave it to fate to punish her. Too much humiliation grows enemies," she says, stopping in her tracks.

Cynthia is stuck behind her on the damp and narrow track. "Let me get ahead of you, Maureen, I know the way," Cyn says, moving past her guest. "I'm not vengeful, but Claire is toying with my sons!"

"Perhaps she loves them both. Are you certain she's pregnant?"

"She left her diary open for me to read. Marks her menses with asterisks! None in two months."

Cynthia gives a loud whoop. Already she feels transformed by proximity to Maureen's confidence. All this hooting and whooping is invigorating, she decides. Maureen brings out her bawdy side.

"Mind your step. The path looks solider than it is. The silly gel believes herself in love with Alex."

"Love's a powerful motivator."

"And money isn't?"

"Not so much in the young."

"At 7.00 a.m. this morning," Cyn says, "Claire hobbled into the kitchen to phone, 'Mum,' she blurted – 'it's Clive's'. If true, Clive's fatherhood will put an end to our financial woes!"

"I thought in buying the creek flats, *we*'d be shoring up your finances. So, you mayn't need to sell land, after all," Maureen says, her formerly high energy seeming to run down.

"Ah." Cyn says, needing both hands and feet for stepping over a mossy boulder. "You're our back-up."

"Back-up?" Maureen is sounding sniffy.

"If Claire aborts, then you and Beppe will be the custodians of our creek flats."

"We'd be the new owners, surely?" says Maureen.

"Of course. But if our deal falls through, Clive will put his 'inheritance' into Arcadia provided he's married with a son."

"You could've been a politician, Cyn."

Cynthia's not keen on the pejorative slant Maureen gives the word 'politician'. "No," she says, "I'm merely encouraging Clive to do what's right. Claire will be a good mother with her practical genes. Practicality was bred out of the Sins by intermarriage within the Bunyip Aristocracy."

"Must be hard being born into money!" Maureen says.

Is she teasing me? Cynthia wonders. But she's unable to twist her head around to scrutinise Maureen's face. "In earlier times the Sins needed servants to tell them the time of day. Even now the twins' cousins rarely raise a sweat, except from polo. My bourgeois bloodlines saved our boys from utter uselessness.

"A pity you're wearing such nice shoes," she says, eyeing off Maureen's snakeskin courts, "or we could've taken the track into the wattle clearing. They're blooming just now. Hal used to bring me here.

"My fears about Alex being gay were eased during the storm," Cyn says, "when my meanderings took me to the very bed he shared with Claire." She launches into the story. Clever of me, Cyn thinks, to tell Maureen in confidence what she already suspects so she's honour-bound not to blab! I could have been Machiavelli in another life.

"If Claire is pregnant Clive might disown the child," says Maureen quick as a whip.

"Every silver lining has its cloud…"

Maureen wipes an insistent glob of mud off her shoe. The plank she's standing on wobbles.

Cynthia would steady her but Hal says that the 'survival of the fittest' should work itself out unassisted by us humans. So, she's duty-bound to leave Maureen be.

"Brother Cedric's fond of Alex, but he'd prefer Clive to inherit," she continues.

"Why?" asks Maureen.

Oh, she's a sharp one, Cyn thinks. "Oh, primogeniture. Ced's fortune's not for anyone who organises their life around money."

"Then his money may remain unclaimed forever!"

"You've a satirical bent, Maureen."

"No. I meant it seriously," Cyn's new friend insists.

"No wonder Claire's infatuated, Alex is a beguiling man."

"And so is Clive…"

"But there's something about Alex…When Gwen and I saw the two together in the ute, we were reminded of our sparky youths."

"I didn't know Gwen had had a sparky youth. She's something of a 'yes' person these days."

"Gwen gives one time and space to vent freely, she's a listener," says Maureen quite perceptively, Cyn thinks.

"Yes, Gwen's a dear lady, well-educated, but she lacks your intellect, Maureen."

"You're flattering me, Cynthia. Could we go back? I'd love to dry my feet and have a cuppa."

"I should have thought to get you gum boots," Cyn says. Why hadn't she, she wonders. Did I want her at a disadvantage? Unsteady on the boards that Hal laid to access the creek flats in winter? Did I want to condescend to her? Deign to hold her up if things got difficult? For metaphorically speaking, that is what the Maccas will do for us if our deal goes ahead. "Yes, Maureen," Cyn says. "The boys don't want us tagging along."

Arriving at Arcadia, they're panting, Maureen a bit more than her Cyn thinks, though she appears fitter.

"Pop your jacket on a coat-hook and make yourself comfy. Bonnie's back from her latest emergency. She will set a fire for us," Cyn says ringing the bell and waking Bas.

Maureen removes her coat and makes a fuss of the old Basset Hound. The dog seems to like her. He's not snarling as he does with Cyn.

"Bonnie's bloody marvellous," Maureen says, licking her lips. "I've half a mind to poach her in part payment for your land."

"Never," Cyn says, but crossing towards the room bells, she wonders how it would feel to have a full-time husband. "Depends on the price," she says, feeling like a slave-trader.

Eventually, Bonnie bustles in with the tea, which she places dead centre on the Napoleonic.

She goes about her work all blank-faced determination; she's impeccable but graceless. She resents Cyn when she imposes on her good nature.

Cyn can see she's been sleeping on her left side, as a fold pressed into the skin hasn't sprung back with its normal elasticity.

No. She could never 'sell' Bonnie. She likes to watch her, knowing all that binds them while tearing them apart. 'Cleave' is a wonderfully ambiguous word! Cynthia's married to Bonnie and Hal. The bad part of Cyn wants all she stands for gone – her worse part wants to keep Bonnie around so she can watch her wanting him.

"Is that all, Ma'am?" Bonnie says, mock-curtseying, and laying it on thick.

"Yes, dear. I'll do the washing up."

She gives Cyn an incredulous glare and hobbles out in Cyn's old Cuban heels as if negotiating a carpet of up-ended penknives. The dog exits too.

"You know, Maureen," Cyn says, nibbling carefully on a biscuit. "Bonnie avenges herself on us by making the biscuits so irresistible, but so tough she'll live to see our teeth fall out."

"No!"

"Never underestimate…"

"…anyone's propensity for malice?" says Maureen, finishing Cyn's sentence.

"My hugest wish until recently was for no marriage between either son and Claire. Now, my greatest fear is that she'll stay unmarried. The thought of it turns my blood to ice. When Thelma visits she might take Claire with her. I need coaching in getting along with a woman from the lower middle classes. She'll wear 'slacks', no doubt. I'd better be at my charming egalitarian best, so Claire isn't tempted to head back to Wang and fall into an irrigation canal…or is that in Shepparton?"

Chapter 58
Stew Again

The day after the Maccas' luncheon, Cynthia reminds GwenLen they are expected for Sunday lunch as usual. "What? Parties on two consecutive days?" Hal had asked. "Are we opening a restaurant?"

"No, we're eating up the rabbit stew that Maureen and Beppe weren't keen to eat yesterday," he'd been informed.

"So," says Cynthia, carrying in the tureen. "Voila! Bonnie's *lapins aux fines herbes*. Cooked them earlier. She's gone on strike."

"Wow! Bonnie's bunnies!" Alex says. "Didn't she cook them for yesterday's lunch; the lunch our new friends were invited to?"

Cynthia sighs. "Yes, Alex our meal was interrupted."

"No wonder Bonnie's tired. It's a lot of entertaining to be doing." Gwen's curious to know more.

"Yesterday's lunch was more a business meeting. No one you'd know," Cynthia lies. "And luckily, we saved some stew."

"Hal shot these?" Gwenda asks.

"Yes," says Cyn. "Always pot the pair," she says. "Or its mate pines." She shoots Claire a look.

"Would couples rather boil together or survive alone?" asks Alex, his expression neutral.

"Hopefully, these didn't know their deaths were imminent," says Len. "I read in 'The Age'…"

"Yes," says Hal. "I read that article, too. Fear alters molecular structure; toughens muscle tissue."

"Once a microbiologist…" says Len.

"No, Len. Hal was an engineer," says Gwen.

"I obtained qualifications in both areas," says Hal. "Couldn't decide…"

"You still can't," says Cynthia, cryptically.

"Such diverse qualifications!" says Len. "No wonder your clever sons cover all bases."

"Yes, we're the 'drainage boys'," says Alex, which comment earns him a glare from his mother.

"Of course, you, Alex, are the practical one. Nothing wrong with that," Len says, as if there actually were something wrong.

"I'll give Cyn a hand with the trolley." Hal gets up to help.

"Boys of such diverse talents…" Len's words tail off.

"Without you we'd be down the drain," says Gwen referring to Alex's plumbing skills.

"Ha! Good one, love," says Len, relieved at Gwenda's tactful intervention.

"So, Len, are you moving down here permanently?" Alex always struggles with GwenLen. It's not that he dislikes them. They just don't hit it off. If only he can find a neutral topic he may yet survive this ordeal, he thinks.

Awaiting Len's response, Alex examines the pepper mill as if guessing how many peppercorns it held.

"We're moving down soon. We planned on gardening today," Gwen says. "But Cynthia called. We came."

"So, you're soliciting?" Alex makes the word sound sleazy.

"Yes!" Len beams fulsomely, unaware he's being sent up.

A rattling trolley heralds Hal's arrival with the serving dishes.

"Home is the hunter replete with his bounty," says Len.

"Bit on the scrawny side. The drought…"

"You'll fill out, Hal. Haha!"

"…but thanks to Bonnie's marinades, their flesh has been plumped up. A slow Aga does the rest," he adds.

Bertie arrives bearing tureens of vegetables. He sets them on the sideboard. Stands awkwardly, his hands behind his back.

"I can't get my oven running slow." Gwen fans her face with a napkin.

"Don't go on about the climacteric, dearie," says Len.

"Now, Len," says Cynthia warningly. "Bertie, pass the greens around, please." He obeys as if serving poison.

"So, what's Bonnie's secret?" Gwen persists.

"She stokes the Aga up to billy-oh, then starves it of fuel and lets it stew in its own juice," says Cyn. She passes a laden plate to Gwenda.

The conversation dwindles. Intermittently, Len shouts, "Compliments to the chef!"

"Splendid! Why buy lamb fillet, Gwenda, when a wittle bunny wabbit tastes so good?"

"If you want wabbit, Len, impwove your aim," says Gwenda tartly.

227

"Claire," Hal says. "Clive phoned. He'll be down soon. Not to see his old dad, I suspect."

"Oh," Claire studies her fork as if its prongs represented the choices facing her. All four tines run in parallel. Originating millimetres apart, they end right where they'd promised starting out.

It's lucky the twins aren't quadruplets or she might have wanted all four of them, she thinks, smiling a secret smile. Can one ever choose the wrong prong? Oops! Her subconscious mind's behaving badly. Surely, a fork's just a fork and not a metaphor?

Despite her anguish, Claire's mouth twitches at the lewdness she is capable of. Perhaps the tines are telling her life's forking routes only appear to offer a choice – that all roads lead home. She runs her fingers across the tines before setting down the fork.

She realises Hal's still awaiting her response. "Great," she says. Her lie turns sour in her mouth. "But Mum's visiting next week…"

"We've plenty of spare bedrooms. Enough room for Mary too. Claire's little friend is out with her love interest from next door," Cyn says. "But Claire, aren't you pleased about Clive's visit?" Cynthia, rises from the table to hand around the tureens since Bertie appears paralysed.

"I didn't sleep well. Itchy cast," Claire admits.

"Abominable," says Cynthia checking to see if she's engaged the guests' attention. GwenLen won't meet her gaze. Hal reddens. Alex glares. "Nothing worse than an itch you can't scratch, is there? The more one thinks, the itchier it gets. We'll add scratching to Alex's chores…"

"Ma!" says Alex.

Claire studies her placemat depicting Bradman hitting a six at Lords. She loathes Bradman.

"Glad the storm's blown over. We've enough wood for now," says Hal, gruffly.

"Yes," Alex raises his glass. "To our land and its fecundity." They clink. Claire sips her water.

"And to Alex, who got the fires ablaze," says Hal. "Chased our damp away. Saved us a fortune."

The Waterford crystal chimes prettily.

"Yes, and here's to dear Claire, despite her being peaky from lack of sleep," says Cynthia.

Claire's cheeks redden as though slapped. She traces a paisley swirl on the tablecloth.

"I'll fetch dessert, dear," Hal says. "Ah, here's Bonnie back on deck and with banana fritters." Bonnie isn't smiling. Hal takes the fritters, serves them up on Wedgewood plates.

Bonnie departs in silence.

"Do sit with us, Bertie. Have a fritter," says Cyn. "We'll have you moving in with us next."

Bertie looks stricken. He eases into a spare place looking like he's on Death Row.

"Didn't say grace," says Cyn. "I'll say it now. We've much to be thankful for. There's Claire, the men adore her." Heads bow while Cynthia blesses her harmonious family, the laden table.

Claire nudges Alex. Cynthia knows, she mouths. He nods wryly.

"I hate bananas," says Cyn. "Luckily, there's rhubarb for me."

Alex, wracked by a convulsion, sprays breadcrumbs on the tablecloth. "We didn't thank God for rhubarb." Alex wipes his eyes. "Sorry, I've a cold. Why do you hate bananas, Mama?"

"They're phallic symbols. They remind me of that commune, Alex." Cyn turns to her guests. "We almost lost him to a cult. All hippies, wet alpaca, and tie-dye. Ate bananas in their curry! Too indolent to cultivate root vegetables. In and out of each other's shacks all day."

"No loans, no overdrafts," says Alex.

"Here in Warrnambool, with herbaceous borders, people know where they stand."

"Have a drop of wine dear, you're getting all worked up," Hal says.

"No! Their Ugg boots stank to billy-ho. Beanbags. Psycho-babbling morons. Yogis."

"Without progress we'd best crawl into our caves and die. Agreed?" No one argues.

Cynthia glares at Alex. "I blame tie-dye for the state of the economy. Once you don't need Myer for a nice little suit for church, you don't need work, and without a job you're adrift."

"I wouldn't mind having fewer bills to pay," Hal says quietly.

Chapter 59
Meeting

Hal and Beppe are barbequing on the Maccas' expansive terrace.

Gwen whispers in her friend's ear, "I've a juicy morsel, Mau. You'll be discreet?"

Maureen nods. "Of course, Gwenda."

"Well, the other day, after lunch at the Sins…"

"But Beppe and I were at lunch with the Sins, not you," says Maureen.

"Not on Sunday, you weren't," says Gwenda, frowning.

"No, it was Saturday." Maureen says, eyeing Gwenda with suspicion.

"They didn't mention it. Anyway, on Sunday, we were shepherded into the study," says Gwen.

"Earlier, Bonnie had been resting but she volunteered to bring coffee to the study."

"'Bonnie, dear. Pour and go,' Cynthia said. But hurrying, Bonnie brushed against the urn. 'Christ!' she said. '*Ecks queues em wah, madame, je suis blesse,*' she'd cradled her arm in agony.

"'Then *I'll* pour,' Cyn said. 'I'm hardly incapacitated.'"

"What a bitch!" says Maureen.

"I know but Cynthia has a good side."

"Well, her bad side is expanding, in my mind," says Maureen.

"But you hardly know her, Mau."

"I got to know her rather well on Saturday, we'd been invited to discuss a business deal."

"She always consults Len about her deals," Gwen replies, in a whiny voice, her neck reddening.

"Just kite flying," Maureen says, playing down its significance.

But Gwen is downcast; it's one thing to criticise your friends, another to be dumped by them.

Maureen sensing her hurt, clams up. "And Bonnie?" she asks, getting them back on track.

"'I'll manage,' Bonnie said, bending to place some Blue Vein cheese on the coffee table. She rarely gets into a lather when hurried.

But I think she suspected someone was out to dud the twins – so even exhausted, she came to 'help'. Bonnie and Cyn bicker a lot, but ultimately Bonnie backs down."

"Fears for her job, I'd say."

"'Don't bob up and down, dear,' Cynthia stage-whispered. 'Gwen and Len are *democratic* people. Be good, or I'll buy you a mobcap and pinny!'

"'Yes, m'lady,' she said, bowing even more servilely. 'How do I reach that dinky coffee table without bending, me being five eight? Should get m' legs shrunk?'"

"Priceless," says Maureen.

"But Cynthia only smiled. 'You're a tease, Bonnie. Now go.'"

"Afterwards a silence fell, only broken by Hal slurping his tea and swivelling his old desk chair while the Venetians flickered and thrashed in the breeze. Cynthia rose, adjusted the blinds, then slammed the window shut. The next minute stretched forever.

"When satisfied with her theatrics, Cynthia cleared her throat. 'We've a crisis,' she said.

"I leaned forward to indicate concern. 'Anyone unwell, Cyn?' I asked."

Maureen, slaps her knee. "You're an excellent storyteller, Gwen."

"'No, dear,' Cyn replied. Her hand went up to check her pearls were centred. 'Our physical health is robust. I'll plunge in without delay.'"

"'Hallelujah!' said Hal.

"'Claire is pregnant. She wants her "Mum".'

"'You're to be grandparents. Congratulations.' said Len.

"Cynthia firmed her mouth to express contempt. 'Some shotgun weddings can tear families apart. Claire has been unfaithful, and although the child is definitely Clive's,' said Cynthia, 'the gel's "Mum" may persuade her to abort.'

"'Wish you'd told me all this earlier,'" said Hal, standing and going over to adjust the blinds.

"Cynthia glared at Hal. 'You'd have botched things up. Claire's led a sheltered life, but,' Cyn waves her wrist as if repelling flies, 'it seems she's making up for lost time. How lucky we were, Gwenda, not to have been born in such permissive times as these.'

"'Even in our day opportunities to make a fool of oneself existed if one jumped at them,' said Hal, earning himself a black look.

"'Goodness, fancy having all that choice,' I said.

"Len, thinking I was envious, glared. 'Hard for you, my *petit choux,*' he said, 'to be stuck with me.'

"He pushed off with his feet against the metal filing cabinet; the oak swivel chair wheeled away from Cynthia and me, circling through 360 degrees, stopping only when he ended up face to face with Hal, at whom he stared all comradely.

"'Lucky weren't we, Hal? Our good lady wives might have bedded myriad lords and princes had they not been forced to settle for us.'

"Hal nodded grimly.

"'Don't get huffy, dear,' I said, to placate Len. 'I'd have chosen you from hundreds anyway.'

"'Anyway? Despite my multitudinous disadvantages?' said Len. Turning back to Hal, he asked 'What does Claire want?'

"'It's a matter of what *we* want Claire to want,' said Cynthia.

"'And what might that be, Cynthia?' Hal asked.

"'We want Claire right here and doing right by Clive, of course,' said Cynthia.

"'But what if they're unhappy married?' said Hal.

"'Do we all have to be happy? We just got on with it,' said Cyn.

"'Marrying the wrong person can ruin one's life,' Hal said. At this point Cyn shot him a look of pure venom."

"What was that about?" asks Maureen.

Gwenda shrugs.

"'Claire might marry her fellow fornicator just to be awkward!' said Len wisely.

"'If she won't marry Clive, we'll…make it worth her while. We've money organised,' said Cyn."

"Though who'd lend money to the Sins?" Gwen asks Maureen.

"Who knows?" says Maureen, neutrally.

"'Anyhow, this meeting is about our sons,' Cynthia pronounced the word 'sons' forcefully.

"'Sons, plural?' I asked, gamely, so Cyn would spell it out – we'd got wind of some rivalry but…"

"Gosh! Not incest!" The unshakeable Maureen's shocked.

"'The thing is, Claire loves Alex. Thinks she does,' said Cyn.

"'A *ménage a trois*!' said Len, eyes popping. He swivelled away from Hal, back towards Cynthia and re-crossed his legs.

"'Stop it. You, silly tops!' said Cyn. 'No ménage! She fell in love with each twin, separately.'

"'We saw Claire and Alex in the ute. Like teenagers with their braces stuck,' I said.

"'Anyway, the gel's 25% in love with Clive, 35% with Alex, while leaving 40% of her capacity free to bestow on whomsoever, she chooses.'

"'Clive's not going to like it – Alex looking after her that well,' said Hal swivelling. Then he straightened up, as if Claire might fancy him if only his posture improved.

"'What a shemozzle!' Len said.

"'Remember, this shemozzle's familial links go back to the Middle Ages,' said Cyn.

"'Well, my forebears go back to Adam and Eve unless a chimp mutated into human form in 1840, when our genealogy records dwindle,' said Len.

"'Ooh! That'd explain a lot,' I said, to lighten the proceedings.

"'So, the Sins were created on day seven?' asked Len, his mouth quirking oddly.

"'No, just the concept of sin itself,' said Hal.

"'Stop making us the stuff of comedy. Clive will be hurt. And Alex. It's taken an age to bring them together since their troubles. Clive wishes he were Alex; Alex envies Clive's success.'

"Cyn sounded genuinely sad. I felt for her, Maureen. I patted her shoulder.

"'If families are meant to stick together, you can't say yours aren't sticking!' Len leant across and cut a slice of mouldy cheese, to tamp down the vein of mirth fighting its way up from his belly.

"'If Claire's developed a grand passion for Alex…grand often turns squalid. Best marry at leisure than repent in haste,' said Cyn.

"'A malapropism, dear,' said Hal.

"'The sooner Claire marries Clive, and produces our heir, the better.'

"'Why the rush?' asked Len

"'We don't pay you to be obtuse, Len.'

"'But you don't pay – except in rabbit stew. Not that it wasn't delicious…' Len said, hand raised.

"'Well, excuse me. Your bill will be my priority,' said Cynthia."

Chapter 60
Café 1

On the following Friday, Cyn phones Gwen. She's wondering how best to manage the family discussions that are looming like thunderstorms on the horizon.

Clive's arrival at The Lodge is imminent, as is Thelma's. Clive has yet to be told of Claire's 'condition', while Thelma knows only selected parts of the story.

"Unchoreographed meetings would be unproductive," Cyn tells Gwenda. "Truth needs managing."

"Yes, truth should emerge sounding as if it's truly welcome news and not the unvarnished truth," Gwen says. Cynthia wonders, *Is Gwen's tone snide? Is she less deferential than before?*

"Anyway," she says, "I'll carve the truth into bite-sized portions and keep family members apart until they know precisely what they're to make of it all. A family gathering now would be a public flaying. The family couldn't withstand so much anguish. I'll recruit Thelma to my side. A Catholic mother of six – who better?"

"None better."

"She'll be thrifty and capable, but susceptible to persuasion. For the price of a cappuccino, Thelma will fall in with my plans."

"What about Hal?" asks Gwen.

"Hal must convince Alex to keep his head down in case his brother kills him in a scene fit for Shakespeare! Bonnie will talk to Claire. Their rapport is evident thanks to social class I daresay. Gosh! Claire's having our heir, Gwen!"

"It's almost 12.00 pm! Good-luck!" carols Gwen.

Cynthia arrives at Warrnambool station. She scurries through the crush of bodies on the platform just as a redhead in a cherry red duffel coat alights. That's her, Cynthia thinks. Fancy wearing a teenagers' camping coat, and a home-dyed do!

She wears high heels. So she's no simple countrywoman. Cyn feels unnerved. She'd pictured her in Hush Puppies? *Tout le monde* knows they're for traveling. Nothing in Thelma's attire says, fashion plate. Cyn allows herself a covert smile. She has Thel's measure.

Locals alighting from the train advertise their status – 'conservative farmer's wife' – via gabardine trench coats from Fletcher Jones.

Thelma's dowdiness heartens Cynthia. But if she lacks fashion sense, she mayn't notice Cyn's 'monied' look. Can she discriminate between wool and cashmere?

Thelma's home-dyed hair shows she cheats on mileage albeit ineffectually. Holding herself tall and proud she's not unprepossessing. Cyn squares her shoulders, prepares for battle.

Challenges buck her up. She removes her Hermes scarf tied peasant-style for anonymity. She hurries towards Thelma, her right arm wavering like a divining rod – a cunning trope. Denoting warmth without intimacy, it precludes the pressing of the flesh.

"Welcome, Wilma."

"No that's 'The Flintstones'. I'm Thel. You're Cyn, I presume."

If there's a way of pronouncing Cyn as Sin, she's done it.

Thelma thrusts her right hand within shaking range of Cyn, who draws hers back, and slips it into the pocket of her cashmere coat and lets her eyes glaze. Thelma's smile freezes in place.

Offended? Too bad. Best leave scope for warming up later, Cyn decides. Heartiness is hard to retract. "I'll call you Thelma," Cyn says. "Christian names deserve their full due. I was fortunate with Cynthia, although I abhor Cyn."

"Me too," Thelma says. Now that makes Cyn's head snap back. She studies Thelma's face for signs of irony. Cyn hopes she won't prove one of those quick-witted sharp-tongued women that that background occasionally throws up. Golly! Thelma has her rattled already, and yet they've hardly exchanged a dozen words. "You're Catholic," Cynthia says, "and that's fine with me."

"Is it?" Thelma replies, listlessly.

That went well, thinks Cyn. "Later on," she says, "we'll broach the issue of mixed marriages but not yet." Cyn shepherds Thelma down the railway ramp her arm as close as possible to Thel's elbow crook without actually touching it.

"I'm worried at Claire's refusal to name the father!"

"Of course I'd planned to approach the topic obliquely," Cyn says. "We'll need a coffee for that."

"Yes," says Thelma. "But first, I must see Claire."

"She's at a specialist's appointment so we can get acquainted."

"Claire promised to be *here!*" says Thelma becoming het-up. "I won't enjoy a cuppa until I see her. How's she coping?"

"The situation's hardly ideal but young and in love…"

"Imagining oneself in love at 19 is bad enough but *with whom* is she in love?"

"Don't worry, dear, do relax on that score. The paternity issue has been settled satisfactorily. We drink cappuccinos, not cuppas these days."

"We have short blacks if we're feeling daring," says Thelma, meting out parry for thrust.

"I've never had a short black."

The ghost of a smile plays on Thelma's face. "Wangaratta has a cosmopolitan population these days. Perhaps here?" Thelma indicates a smart Victorian façade.

"No, dear." Cyn steers Thel towards a hippie café where she won't be recognised by Ganesh or any Indian god festooned on its muraled walls. "Such colours perk me up," Cyn says.

Thelma puts her hand to her brow and peers in through the window. "Oh, gosh," she says, drawing back as if stung. "Hectic!"

"Yes. Acid yellow's stimulating!" Cynthia agrees.

"To our bile ducts," says Thelma, quietly.

Cynthia yanks the door open, pretending she hasn't heard her. She holds it wide for Thel, who waits, unsure of etiquette. Sensing her hesitation, Cyn barges in first.

Satisfied that proper protocols have been established, Cynthia smiles tentatively. Eschew enthusiasm. That's the problem with GwenLen, they assume themselves to be on a level pegging because they've got on by working hard. They don't get it. Class isn't about economic achievements or usefulness, it's about accidents of birth. But Hal needed someone to shoot his blessed clay pigeons with. Professional men come in handy but their wives believe their superior buying power elevates them stratospherically. Still, Gwenda's a dear.

Thelma is from a 'mixed' farm in Wangaratta. Mixed! The term brings on an involuntary shudder in Cyn. That farming should be a bit of this, and a bit of that! Amateurs degrade life on the land; they're like kids in a lolly shop buying one of everything, she thinks. She's wrenched from her reverie by Thelma tapping her on the shoulder and mouthing at her like a fish underwater.

"I said, will this table do, Cynthia?"

"Yes, it's perfect, Thelma." Cyn puts her handbag down and takes a view of the doorway. "You can order at the counter, dear."

Thelma hesitates. She shoots Cyn a shrewd look then draws her mouth into the rictus of a smile. "You want me to order for you?"

"Since you're up and I'm down. I'll have a pot of Earl Grey. And a chooks pastry please."

Thelma's look says, 'so it's the guest who's doing the buying then!' She smiles wryly. "*Choux,* I think you mean."

"Chew? I suppose so." Cyn runs her tongue around the teeth she can't afford to have seen to if provisional tax is to be found and last year's fine.

"No, I said, *'choux',*" Thelma persists.

"Oh, 'shoe'! Of course," Cyn says. Smart of her to guess these Danish pastries resemble shoe leather.

Thelma approaches the counter with its glass display cases and its mounds of pastries, looking like they'd made the trip from Denmark by outrigger canoe, so mucky is their glazing, so gluey and marooned their glacé peaches! Their *mille feuilles* are clumped in sodden blocks, as ruined as are her hopes of seeing dear Claire married into a welcoming family and not this snobbish lot.

The acid yellow walls press on her brain. She's heard that colours have a 'frequency', that each colour affects us differently. Shouldn't yellow create a sense of warmth, of joy, and not hysteria?

She sighs. Is Cynthia capable of subverting everything that's fine and good? You'd think she chose this café on purpose, decreed that it be painted acid yellow, on hearing of Thel's imminent arrival.

God help me, Thel berates herself. I'm going barmy! Not even Cynthia!!! She pays the cashier, tells herself to get a grip.

Chapter 61
Café 2

"Where would we be without a cuppa?" Cynthia rhapsodises, as a waitress sets the cups down.

Thelma studies Cynthia, who evades her gaze, considers her pastry. With great effort, Cyn stills her hands. She has a tendency to fiddle nervously with cake; she's apt to reduce it to confetti when stressed. It's a 'tell', according to Hal.

"So who is the child's father, Cynthia?"

"Goodness, you're direct, my dear. Let's be mindful of the 'now', like Buddhists."

"The pastries are more Zen than now," retorts Thelma.

"You've a zany sense of humour, Thelma. We'll get on like hotcakes."

"How will Claire and Clive get on?"

"Those two!" Cyn flaps her hand, camping it up. "Meant for each other," she gushes, hoping Thel will let the cliché pass. Resting her elbow on the table, she anoints Thelma with her 100-kilowatt smile, including bridgework. "The quintessential thing is," she says, seconds before realising she has no idea what argument her theatrics were meant to promote. "Um…"

Crumbs! Cyn thinks. Where was that sentence headed? As a decoy she drops her spoon onto the Laminex, grabs a napkin, fans her face. "The climacteric!" she says, buying time to convert vague clamorous feelings into a sentence with a destination.

"They fell in love in Collins Street – he was walking, she was falling. He picked her up and ticked her off for wearing silly shoes. She was slim, pretty. He rescued her."

"So, her prettiness qualified her to be knocked up by a stranger in Collins Street?" says Thelma. "Why do men fall for a dress size?"

Cynthia shrugs. "Anyway, Clive phoned me that night. 'Ma,' he said, 'I've met a healthy country nurse. Unspoiled.'"

"Now she's bruised produce."

"They became inseparable. Clive will stand by Claire."

"Does she want him to?"

"He's her fiancé." Cyn drops her fork with a clang. "A wedding date will shut the gossips up."

"Gossips?"

"Claire and Alex have been seen out driving together. They're great mates! Some may question Clive's paternity. Claire formed an attachment to Alex after Clive left but a child needs its biological father."

"Would a child know or care?"

Cynthia waves her sugar snake towards Thelma, in an appeasing way, but doesn't see she's weakening its sachet until it spills over the tabletop. Thelma reaches across and they corral sugar grains, salvaging whatever they can. Clearly, both abhor waste. They smile wryly at each other.

"So Alex is the alternative father?" Thelma asks.

"Shh!" Cyn checks the adjoining booths. "Only theoretically," she hisses.

"No!" Thelma recoils. "Did they have a theoretical fuck?"

Cynthia wrings her hands, mortified.

"You said they went driving!"

"Yes. Claire must marry Clive." Cyn abandons her pastry mess, pushes the plate away. She orders more coffee. "Clive is the father. I heard her telling young Mary: it's Clive's child fifty to one."

"How lucky we sent Claire to a good school, so she can calculate the relative paternity claims of her rivals!" says Thelma with a crooked grin.

"It's almost undoubtedly Clive's."

"'Almost undoubtedly' is an oxymoron! Doesn't Clive know what causes pregnancy?"

"He'll have been careless, I suppose, just a normal red-blooded male. No one's pinned him down until now."

"Well, I hope he's feeling duly pinned," says Thelma, exasperated. "He spills his seed carelessly."

"Is it my fault young men are as they are? When we met Claire, we were charmed. Then she fell from *Beau Fils*. Clive had to leave. Claire saw a lot of Alex…"

"In terms of surface area?"

Cynthia ploughs on. "Alex wheeled her to the bathroom…"

"You forced her into intimacy with Alex?"

"Don't be touchy, Thelma. Nothing happened in the lavatory – it was the drawing room."

"That's so much better…"

"Recently there was a Biblical storm. Claire needed comforting."

"Alex cosied up to Claire when she was vulnerable?"

"The attraction was mutual."

A waitress in a long cheesecloth frock brings coffee. They order grilled cheese sandwiches. "With extra butter," calls Cynthia, as she departs. "We need our nutrients, Thel. Claire must be persuaded to marry. Gels want good providers like Clive. My brother Ced's estate goes to the first nephew to bear him a grandnephew. Ced is dying. With the bequest Claire could be a stay-home mum."

"That's patently a bribe," says Thelma.

"An inducement. I rented a flat in town for them," Cynthia lies, wishing she had. The weight of a home address would be harder to argue with than the vague designation father. "Hal and I intend signing over Arcadia to Clive and Claire, as our sole heirs, provided they undertake its upkeep and we can remain there in perpetuity. If Clive reneges, then Alex will step up."

"So, Claire will become the property of the most responsible son. You don't care who the child's father is or which son Claire truly loves."

"As long as Claire is the mother of the heir."

"What's Alex like, as a person?"

"Good; perhaps better than Clive. He's a plumber, envious of Clive. If something untoward happened, he'll have seduced Claire."

"Claire would never be seduced against her will."

"Good then. No St John could ever seduce Claire on the way to the lav." Cyn settles back on the bench seat and runs her tongue across her teeth. What a terrier is Thel! They might become friends.

Cyn leans towards Thel. "Claire was probably testing her feelings for Clive."

"Claire mustn't marry the wrong man. I'll see to that." Thel squares her shoulders. "She might be a few days pregnant to Alex," she muses.

Cynthia drums her fingers on the table. "Then it wouldn't show in a test!" she says, as sandwiches oozing butter arrive.

Thelma eyes them with relish. Cyn pushes the plate her way. "Go on," she says. Thel takes a sandwich and chews it meditatively. "You let this go on under your own roof?"

"I can't be everywhere, dear." Cynthia takes a bite of her sandwich, then sets it on the plate. To Thelma it looks like she's sculpted the Great Australian Bite from the middle of her sandwich.

"Will Claire keep the child?"

"Keep?" Cynthia's voice quivers!

"She could have an abortion. She's six months into her diploma. To be left with no career, no marriage and a child to support…"

"Which marriage are you referring to?"

"Precisely!"

"Marriages in this family endure however bad they get. Wouldn't you love to be a grandmother?"

"No, Cynthia, it's a decade since my youngest was in nappies. I'd never wish my children away, but I remember all that scraping by with hand-me-downs, bottled preserves, and wringing the neck of my best layer because butchers' meat's too dear. And all that plucking! Pluck! Pluck! Pluck!"

With Thelma repeating 'pluck' in a near-hysterical voice, Cyn fears someone may mis-hear her!

"How I'd adore a hobby like bottling!" she announces.

"It's not a bloody hobby! I'm worn out. Look at my hands!" Thelma holds them out.

Cyn knows the look of chicken skin. If pinched, they'd take an age to revert to normal.

"I'm old before my time," Thelma says, tearing up.

Cynthia pats Thelma's hand.

Chapter 62
Hal and Claire

"Hal, tell me something true about yourself," Claire calls from the backseat of the car.

"True?"

"Yes, Hal. I'm always with Cynthia. She's improving me. You're always disappearing. I want a proper pow-wow. How did you meet Cyn?"

Hal speaks in his soft low voice, "I wanted things light and bland between us, Claire. Feared you'd tire of us."

"No, Hal. Never."

"Thank you, dear. As for Cynthia, she says, 'your problem is that you're too dependent on science. You need empirical evidence to decide whether it's raining or not.'"

Hal's using Cyn-speak – adopting the portentous tone she affects. Claire relaxes. Listens keenly.

"'It's the bane of my life, Hal,' she'll say, 'that your career went nowhere.'

"But I'd retired at her insistence. She was jealous of my job in research, I was no slouch, yet Cyn told me, 'Hal, up polo sticks, leave that lot. Embrace your birthright, become a gentleman farmer.'

"I love being on the land but I'm not of it. Graziers count livestock by the score. I notice the state of Pearlie's hooves. One lives the life one lives. To argue with destiny is…He lifts his hand from the wheel and lets it fall back listlessly. Fate's not what you deserve, Claire; it's what happens. Cynthia happened to me."

"Go on."

"I admire her. Truly. Cynthia's a force of nature! Friends were puzzled. No one thought we'd last, Cynthia's charms were…unorthodox. There's a difference between falling *in* love, falling *for* someone, and falling *over* someone, which was what happened to me. It's like I got stuck in molten lava from Vesuvius. Love her, in my way."

"Mm."

"Vesuvius documentaries chill me to the bone; the victims' horror as magma engulfs them moves me beyond reason. Cynthia's determination to have me left me breathless. I was in love with someone else. My fiancée was away – Cynthia saw her opportunity and leapt. Still, I can't regret a union that produced such wonderful boys."

"No," says Claire.

"I tried laughing her off, fighting her off, but confirmation of her pregnancy sealed my fate. I was a man thirsting for spring water who'd fallen into a brackish lake.

"Her take on science irritates me no end. She needles me with her ignorance! *'Why is DNA structured "helically", Hal?'* she'll say. *'DNA's only a corkscrew viewed through a microscope.'*

"'And as for dining tables being fluid collections of molecules? Tables stop Wedgewood falling through 'putative' holes between 'putative' atoms. Here's your proof that a table's hard enough,' she'll say, thumping my hand onto the ancient elm. How could one not feel something for her?"

"You'd have felt hurt by her!" Claire says, with a giggle. Hal joins in.

They're on the Western Highway. Claire's experiencing *rien vu*. This can't be the road she travelled along five weeks ago.

Arcadia had been magical; a decadent neo-gothic pile, its silken day beds frayed and grubby, its chandeliers too dust encrusted to reflect the light, its general clamminess too clammy for words.

Smithfield rolls itself up behind her like a magic carpet sneering at her. Piss off imposter townie!

Have last months' joys and tumults been obliterated? This has been the best and worst time of her life. She'd rather live the extremes than live a smooth life with all the knotty bits untangled.

Claire rearranges her cushion. Wishes she could start again from the tramway's safety zone, remove her shoes, stand flat-soled upon the bumpy asphalt, knees bent, feet apart for stability! But would it help? What then would her life boil down to? Sensible shoes? And no Alex?

Scrubby trees lining the verges blur like photos do when taken by an arty camerawoman.

There's an adage: one can't sleep in the same bed twice. Nor in beds belonging to twin brothers…

Claire goes quiet.

"Is it your leg hurting, Claire?"

"My heart hurts," Claire says.

Hal studies her in the mirror. "I'll stop. We're early," he says.

"No thanks, Hal."

Returning from outpatients, she's a snail learning to live without its shell. The surgeon certified her leg good to go. He failed to tell her where to go. They approach the turn-off to the tourist road, the one taken just four weeks ago. Its image is branded on her synapses.

Tears turn the scenery into an impressionistic blur. Claire covers her face with her trackie hood.

Hal checks the rear vision mirror. He brakes and makes a U-turn towards the beach.

A bank of cloud leans like a masonry balcony over the sand. Hardy sea-gulls wheel and caw in the charged air currents.

"The clouds!" Claire says, regaining control. "I came here with Alex. It was windy. But bright and clear. It's his beach," she says.

"It was mine first," Hal says. "I used to bring the love of my life down here."

"Cynthia?"

"No. Look, a storm is brewing," says Hal. He pulls into a parking bay and winds the window down.

"Wow! It's as if the air here's thinner, like it donated molecules to thicken that cloud," she says.

"Storm fronts don't last. That's the point of them. They blow over. You're the one holding all the aces, Claire."

"Am I? Then I want a happy ending for everyone."

"Impossible, or we'd die laughing in our sleep. A child is the sum of two souls added up and divided by two. Your child will be unique."

"But I don't know which two souls were added up. Oughtn't she be brought up by her dad?"

"Whoever brings her up with love is her father."

"Mm. Clive would worry if she made mud-pies. Alex would worry if she didn't."

"Clive would lavish gifts on her. Teach her to read at three," says Hal.

Claire smiles at this. "Yes! Alex would watch her write her name in the sand and wait until a wave washed it out. That storm was exhilarating. But I'm sorry for the cedars," Claire says.

"They'd had a good life – the boys made cubbies in the branches. We lopped them only when desperate. We're bankrupt, Claire."

"I'd guessed as much. Cyn's elbows are out of her dressing gown. The light bulbs are 30-watt."

"Yes. I wish I could help with your difficulties, Claire…"

"It's enough that you're here, Hal. Clive was my prince for five minutes."

"Mm."

"When I met Clive, I thought, Wow. Handsome, well bred, smart; he loves me, me, specifically! But it was his night for falling in love. He'd had an epiphany buying ice-cream." Claire gives a snorting laugh. "I'm in an interesting condition because he couldn't buy a curvy pistachio parfait. I was his vanilla tub with sprinkles. He bought me because there was nothing else left. I melted into his life. He wanted my youth and compliance. I wanted his impulsive, devil-may-care attitude!

"Now our conversation is all budgets, mortgages, financial goals. But Alex observes the world closely, he theorises, he has a beautiful spirit." She wipes her eyes, all watery from the wind.

"If you married Alex, Clive would bounce back soon enough."

"I wish he'd marry Fliss…"

"Thought you disliked her?"

"Girls are taught to hate their rivals. But she looks at him with such longing. I'd leave here happier, knowing he'd be loved. But the child is Clive's. Should I be a single mum?"

"I don't know. But I'll support you if it's Alex you want."

"No, Alex wants us to run away. But I'm facing things."

"Listen, Claire. I shouldn't tell you this but if Clive has a child pronto, he inherits an estate in NSW. Cyn tried to keep it from me and I'm cross."

"I know about the bequest. So, if I marry Clive, I'll have enriched Alex's brother; he'll be poor. If I marry no one, then everyone hates me equally. Shit!"

"Cynthia will use the inheritance. She's counting on Clive helping us out once he's rich. He'll inherit Arcadia, so making repairs will be in his interest."

"And Alex wouldn't help?"

"Alex would bequeath the property to 'Friends of the Earth', Wave us off to a villa unit. Marry Clive, and you'll own Arcadia one day."

"Why does everything hinge on me? I didn't know any of you eight weeks ago. Now I'm responsible for all of you."

Chapter 63
Claire and Thelma

The paternity of Claire's unborn child has become a matter for universal speculation in the hamlet of Smithfield. Is the outrage caused by this pregnancy justified? Can't a young woman have sexual encounters with two young men over the course of two months? Didn't the sexual liberation movement of the '60s sanction at least that amount of sexual activity?

Apparently not, for this topic's been shanghaied by every man and his sheep dog, becoming fodder for opinions, sought and unsought.

Everyone has an angle. Hal fears its potential for conflict. Cynthia thinks the pregnancy fortuitous – this baby will not only graft the family tree onto sturdier bloodlines, but it will restructure family debt. Alex, the idealistic boy/ sage, thinks Claire's pregnancy wonderful, provided he's the designated father.

Hal slows at the turning circle, but seeing Clive's Porsche parked under the portico, he continues around behind Arcadia and parks under skeletal twigs of wisteria twined sketchily over a pergola, like old ladies' hair over rollers.

He turns to Claire. "Well, my dear, does Thelma drive?"

"She has a licence but she rarely drives."

"Never mind, she'll rise to the occasion. Take the Rover. Tower Hill's the ticket. There are blankets in the boot. Come back only when good and ready to deal with Clive, Alex et al."

"Okay."

"Everyone will be importuning you," said Hal.

"Pardon?"

"Sorry. I'm in the habit of long words from Scrabble tournaments," said Hal. "Don't be ambushed."

"Thanks, Dada, for everything. Would you please find Mum for me?"

"Oh, Claire, thank goodness!" Thelma leans through the car door and clasps Claire to her in an embrace that's necessarily clumsy. She

246

gestures towards the gloomy imposing house, "I thought their minions had locked you in the dungeon."

Claire giggles. "They're not so bad when you get to know them."

"Your poor leg!" Mum touches Claire's thin leg.

"That's easily healed. Though not the other stuff…"

"Being pregnant isn't stuff, Claire. You should have told me of the complications, not her!"

"Sorry, Mum. I've given up my beliefs," Claire says irrelevantly; "I'm a heathen."

"It's beliefs that give you up. Why's your hair different?"

"A French plait." Claire says, tucking in a stray wisp.

"Time-wasting!" Thelma adopts a sing-song voice; she angles the rear-view mirror to examine her own face; she massages it in an upward motion. "There's a beautician in Wang these days. Her treatments bring the bloom back. Ha! But you! Fiddling with plaits! You're fleeing womanhood!"

"Forthright as ever, Mum."

"You're not ready for motherhood, Claire."

"Motherhood's ready for me. I don't regret Clive. Without him I'd never have met Alex. And I really do love him."

"So, Hal will let me drive his Rover?"

"Sure. Just pretend it's a brand-new ute."

Thelma backs out slowly but picks up speed as her confidence grows.

They drive in silence. Thel stops dead at the first intersection. She peers at the road sign, unable to decide what next. Claire elbows her gently. "We can't stop here, Mum. Turn left."

"Good Lord, Claire, there's a dog in the back."

"It's Hal's Basset Hound. Hal takes him on short trips. Cynthia's always trying to prise them apart. Bas takes the bribe but follows Hal."

"Dogs know."

They follow the sign to Tower Hill, an extinct volcano: a rare high point in the landscape; at the viewing platform, they park. Claire opens the door and struggles out.

Thelma fossicks in the boot, gives Claire a crotchet blanket and Hal's polo cap.

Claire lets the dog out on the leash. "He's wracked with arthritis," says Thelma. "Poor old thing. Good boy, Bas." The dog looks up at her through filmy retinas.

Claire grips the metal edge of the viewing platform. "Mum, I hate my life. Its possibilities have shrunken so in the last 48 hours. I'll be a…other…ow…ever." Her words are atomised by blustering gusts.

"Yep. A lifer. That's…otherhood. A rat…rap."

"I wanted to…ravel, play tennis."

"You'll ravel all right. Forget tennis, love. We all have disappointments. We write ourselves new lists of smaller things to do. Look at that remnant of a once fearsome volcano. It once spewed fire, shed molten lava, now it's cold black soil, but fertile! It has another, different life. Can I speak my mind, love?"

"You will anyway, Mum."

"Cynthia is a toxic snob! Is this the family you want?"

"I'm not marrying her. Cynthia's not too bad…You get to know people; see reasons for their faults, Mum."

"You're very tolerant. You'd want a family that's not too bad?"

"I'd be marrying Clive, not the whole family. I really thought I loved him for five minutes. Now he wants someone different once a week. We simmered for a while and then went off the boil," Claire giggles and then starts to cry. "I can still be myself with you Mum. At Arcadia, I'm always acting." Her shoulders shake from emotion and cold.

Thelma hugs Claire to her. "Growing up is hard, love. Those with an easy ride towards maturity don't always get there."

Claire gives her mum a long hard look. "That first night with Clive, it was such a hoot dancing the tango – I thought 'this is bliss!'"

"Until bliss turned to blip," says Thelma.

"The feeling lasted all night long. Next morning, he went AWOL. During our first month as a couple, he volunteered for emergency shifts! It was hard finding time together! That made the time we had seem extra precious! But it was Alex who brought me herbal tea in bed in the mornings. Already, I loved talking to him but I pushed my feelings away. Clive wanted me to cure his phobia about queuing. Poor Clive! I couldn't help him, so he drinks."

"Queuing! Phooey! He's an alcoholic. Needs help. Look at that magpie, shooing the mynah away from the wattle. Magpies are aggressive little shits; they don't queue either."

"You've decided about Clive."

"So have you, it seems."

"I want to be with Alex. I don't deserve him. I've broken all the rules. So Clive's my fate."

"For an atheist, that sounds like divine retribution. If you make a mistake, you rectify it."

"How? By abortion? No. I could only be happy with Alex; therefore, I must give him up."

"Oh, Claire. You're turning Presbyterian. They're only happy unhappy."

"No, Mum. But I couldn't be happy if I were – subjunctive – making someone else unhappy. Cyn insists on good grammar. Let's get out of this wind." They return to the car, help Bas into the back seat. Thelma flicks on the ignition and leaves the car park with a dash.

"Clive will want me more than ever now – a pile of money is at stake. The first to have a son inherits…" Claire's words tail off. Fluid leaks down Claire's cheeks; belatedly, she realises she's crying.

"They're using you as a cash cow." Thelma notices Claire's distress. "Sorry," she says and pulls into the nearest lay-by and cuts the engine.

"Clive doesn't know about the inheritance yet. Ma's on the balcony telling him now. He'll want the baby and the money, who wouldn't? Marrying's better than depriving a child of its father."

"So, you'll fit in with the norm or is it the mean?"

"Or what? Have an abortion?"

"Maybe it's the lesser evil. Would Suzy take you back?"

"She and Alex had a fling. He phones her sometimes. I'd be gutted if…" Claire drums her fingers on the cast.

Thelma reaches over and stills her hand. "Stop it, dear. You're getting on my nerves."

"I'm worrying about everyone I'll hurt. But a baby should be wanted for herself, and not to save a property. If the Sins are forced to live in a unit in Warrnambool, *tant pis,* as Cynthia would say. I'll abort. Get my life back. Enrol in medicine, cure cancer."

"Now you're talking, love. Now you've got a life-plan that's worth failing at. Better than one that isn't worth succeeding in. We'll support you if you marry either of these donkeys, but it'll end in tears."

Chapter 64
Cynthia and Clive

Cynthia phones Clive, demanding that he absent himself from work to attend an urgent family meeting. "Ma, I'm saving lives," he protests.

"Yours will need saving if you don't come quick," she said.

Gees, Clive thinks. It's serious if Mama's dropping her adverbial suffixes.

"Be here," she said. "Much is at stake."

"Ma," her favourite boy wheedles, "I've patients."

"Let them die. If you love Arcadia, come! Foot flat to the boards, relish your ridiculous Porsche, let it whisk you along the highway like a comet through the heavens. You'll never experience such freedom again."

"Ma...aa! You've gone all poetic." The phone dies. Ma's tart communiqué bodes trouble.

Clive makes good time to Camperdown; he stops at a Golden Fleece. The revulsion brought on by a rubbery ham roll with its vacuum-sealed-in staleness reminds him of childhood car trips. Eating it, he feels cheated of satiety.

Money, sex, death: which of this trio of calamities threatens his peace of mind? *Can family fortunes have fallen since last week,* he wonders. *What's with Mama?* The cancer of fear gnaws at his gut, with nothing substantial to feed on. Clive whips into the fast lane, drives belligerently. Dicing with death's a sure-fire mood enhancer.

He hopes Claire's okay. She's seemed low recently but he'd glossed over it, fearing if that he showed concern, she'd come back to Melbourne when loving her from afar suited him better. It's lucky Alex is with her. Despite his aimless intensity, he's loyal. He'll thank him today.

Entering the property, he notices the battered cedars lining the drive from the storm they'd mentioned. Branches lie in draggled heaps. Bloody Alex, he thinks, disavowing all former gushy sentiments. The tall, skinny drink of water might have tidied up at least.

The front door of Arcadia creaks open. Bonnie's wiry frame emerges. "Hullo, me darlin'," she greets him, slipping into fake Irish brogue.

"An' if it ain't grand ter see yer," he replies, kissing her cheek resoundingly. "What's new?"

Bonnie's face clouds over. "It's not all bad news. Go up, Cynthia awaits you in the tower."

"I'm for the chop? She's on that dodgy balcony, I suppose?"

"She won't listen to reason, Clive. She's up there every day – when she's not organising luncheon parties. Takes the dog with her when she has something to bribe him with. Gets all dolled up in her candlewick gown an' with blankets swaddling her knees it's like she's practising being dead."

"Jesus!" Clive hurries through the portico.

He mounts the steps determined. He'll coax his mother down from her eyrie. "Mama," he calls from the door.

"Come," she replies listlessly.

"It's blowing a gale. Why are you here?"

"Why is anyone here?"

"Excellent question." Clive scrambles through the lower half of the sash window, tiptoes over to Cyn, stepping carefully on nail rows denoting a connection, however tenuous, to joists. She's seated on a retro butterfly chair that's charming for muscular young bodies flitting in and out of pools in summer, but…

He kisses the brittle hair on her crown. Noticing that her home dye has grown out, his eyes tear up. "Ma, do take better care of yourself. That old chair's full of rust."

"Me too. My joints need oiling."

"Get dressed before 4.00 pm. Go to a day spa. Your hair's all wiry like Miss Haversham's."

"*Tant pis*. My life is over."

"How do you get out of the chair?"

"I strike the gong," Cynthia indicates the Chinese paraphernalia. Hal rigged up this pneumatic lift thingy. She points to a metal contraption the chair's back legs rest on. "Foot pumps. Two pumps and one goes flying up like James Bond. Then one swings one leg across to the side to get leverage on the butterfly wings. Between Hal and Bonnie, they manage me. Clever, your father. He might have gone somewhere."

"He did."

"He did what?"

251

"He did go somewhere. He came to Arcadia with you. And you'll go somewhere too – like flying off the balcony. We wouldn't be the Sins without you Ma."

"Don't suck up, Clive. Things are dire."

"'Things is crook in Tullarook!' What's the latest calamity?"

"Everything. Claire's mother is down for a few days. Nice enough woman. Too clever. She's the least of what's bothering me." Cynthia pats her chest. "Words can't do justice to such a tale of lust and betrayal," she says, as if she's been practising before the mirror.

"'*Greener pastures*: a family saga of trusts lusts and cruel betrayals'."

"Shut up!" Cyn snaps. "Claire is in an interesting state."

"'Victoria: The Garden State'?"

"She's pregnant, you fool!"

"Wow! Pregnant, that's great! But why isn't she telling me?"

"She's seeing about her cast."

"Let's break out vintage champagne."

"Have a soda." Cyn gestures to the jug, whose contents have lemon slices floating on top.

It's Cynthia's home-made lemonade that Clive's always loved. All sugar and lemon zest.

"'Oranges and lemons, the bells of St Clements'. So, who's for the chop, Ma?" Clive pours himself a beaker of lemonade. Sips. "Shit! Cold Duck's been added. You are a cheap lush. Oh well, it'll bring on a coma as fast as expensive stuff. 'Oh, for a beaker full of the deep South, with beaded bubbles winking at the brim and fairy casements open…something…foam…'"

"Don't garble Keats. As I said, Claire's pregnant."

"I won't forget that, Ma."

"If only we knew who the father was."

"Whom! Good Lord! Are you serious?"

"God's not involved in this annunciation, Clive!"

"So?" Clive sucks on a lemon quarter, spits it out. "Bugger! No, it's my child. We'll bring him up as ours. Still, I'm disappointed in Claire. Poor thing! Bet she's worried she'll lose me."

"She won't care. I know the gel better than you. I'm your silly besotted mother who indulged you. I know how you use girls. This is worse than you imagine," Cynthia makes demented movements with her hands as if gesturing might help propel her awkward lumps of words through the wind gusts. "It's she who must get over the man," says Cynthia.

"What? Some yokel got her pregnant down here? With her bad leg and all! Ridiculous. Wasn't Alex keeping an eye on her?"

"Yes." Cynthia makes a noise like an animal in pain. Clive pats her knee. She looks up, her eyes wide with horror. "He looked after her too blooming well…he… It was Alex."

"What the…! My little brother, lover of camp poets, climbed into the sack with Claire? Holy crap! It'd be hilarious if it wasn't so unlikely."

"Yes," says Cynthia, glaring at the ancient vines. "But do stop swearing," she says half-heartedly. Even she cannot summon any indignation over Clive's language.

"Alex and Claire! I'm off the hook…if I want to be. Did he start wooing her the night of the ice-cream?" Clive drops to the balcony floor. He shakes his head, as if dislodging a stubborn nightmare.

"No, down here. He took her to the loo at night."

"Then, the child's mine. Hang on. Did Alex bathe Claire? I assumed Bonnie…"

"No. You assume we're managing down here. We can't pay Bonnie; she's been on leave mostly. You left your fiancée with another man. He felt what he felt."

"Thanks, Mama, for your profound sympathy."

"I'm being fair."

"Why now?"

"At last I see you as you are. Alex isn't bad. You always acted superior. He'd have felt it."

"You're certain Claire's pregnant?"

"A pharmacy test, I believe. Clive, do you still intend marrying this fickle girl?"

"Ah, I get it. You're putting me off her, Ma. Gees! No way am I falling for your scheme. It's my baby. And I'll forgive her."

Cynthia smiles a private smile for the benefit of the stunted olive grove that never really 'fruited'. Good, she thinks, he's taken the bait.

"Ma, you knew that fatherhood was on my list of things to do this decade. Claire's perfect. Great teeth. Thick, glossy hair. Good figure. I shouldn't have neglected her. I'll forgive her after an interval of sulking." Clive coughs, though possibly it's a strangled sob that's broken out. "We haven't talked much lately. Been falling into bed exhausted."

"Claire knows you've been falling into bed with friends in tow. Someone was always giggling in the background. I heard it too, on the extension."

"You're worse than ASIO, Ma."

"My listening paid off, Clive. Now I don't care who marries Claire. Your uncle's will…"

"Uncle Ced's not dead."

"His cancer is inoperable. You didn't visit. His will stipulates that his estate goes to whomever marries and sires a child toot sweet." Cynthia crosses her fingers saying this.

"Really?" Clive scrambles up, dusts down his trousers and frantically works Cynthia's foot-pump.

Chapter 65
Claire and Clive

Clive sees the Rover leave the turning circle and head towards the parking area behind Arcadia. He lets Cynthia sink back into the butterfly chair.

"There's Claire now, Ma," he says.

"Send Hal up to free me from this contraption. I won't be left out of things," she says, pettishly. Basil the Basset Hound nuzzles Clive's hand; he whines to be let out through the sash window. Clive lifts him over the sill. He slobbers all over Clive's hands.

Hastily, Clive wipes them on his jeans, glad to be unobserved by Claire.

Once in the car park, Clive claims Thelma's attention by tapping on her window.

Leave the car, I'll park, he mouths.

Thelma turns off the ignition; winds the window down. "Clive S'n J'n, I presume?"

"Delighted, Thelma, might I use your Christian name?"

"Whose might you use instead?"

"Thelma," he says commandeering her hand. "How can I play the charming fiancé if you're cleverer than me? Hi, Claire," he calls across to her in the passenger seat. "Sensational news. It's all good."

As she struggles from the car, Clive lets go of Thelma's hand and rushes to Claire's aid.

But Claire applies her crutches like a pro.

"Oh Claire." Eventually, he blocks her way and bends to kiss her mouth. He gets her cheek.

"Darling! You're blooming!"

"Blooming vomitous!" she says, heading for Ma's winter roses.

"Don't throw up until I help your mother out…" Claire vomits anyway, and the doughty Thelma extracts herself from the Rover alone. "Oh, Thelma. Do hop back in again and play the helpless ma-in-law," says Clive.

"Will that help you feel better about yourself?" asks Thelma.

"Stop stage managing everything, Clive," says Claire, wiping her mouth with her sleeve.

"You got me pregnant through carelessness. Now you want me to vomit on cue? Who, I mean, how are you?"

"Who am I?" Clive's aghast.

Settled on the garden seat at last, he's exhausted. "Thelma," he asks, tactfully, "which is your room?"

"Oh, yes," Thelma says, "I'll make myself scarce. You'll want…Claire."

Clive beams winningly. "Such fabulous news! But yes, we must de-brief."

"Buzz off Mum, I'll be all right," says Claire, uncertainly.

"Lovely woman," he says, neutrally, when she's gone. "Good stock!"

"You sound like a chef."

He ignores Claire's remark. "Let's go into the library." He smiles benignly.

Seeing her former lover acting like a used car salesman yet to meet his monthly quota disorients Claire. The balance of power between them has shifted her way. Such a reversal might be gratifying if she entertained even a shred of respect for him. She doesn't need what he's selling. In the library, settled into a wing-backed armchair, Claire expels a breath she hadn't realised she'd been holding in. She surveys the stacks of books on the antique shelving, admires the gallery that encircles the room at first floor level. It's accessed by a ladder of elm wood. She loves this room – her sanctuary from Cynthia's chores.

Here knowledge seems palpable; as if it's been weighed on old-fashioned shop-scales, gift wrapped and sold with a guarantee that it will enrich lives by a given percentage. *Can one marry into erudition,* she wonders. *Does proximity to others' learning rub off on one?*

"So, Claire?"

"I'd forgotten the shape of your face, Clive."

He looks slapped. "Sorry, Claire. Ma would drive anyone to…" He doesn't say: 'fuck my brother', but the words hang in the air.

"Listen, Claire. All's forgiven and forgotten."

"No, it's not. I love your brother."

"He's a lovely guy in his way."

"No. He's lovely, full stop."

"But we're pregnant. We're the viable couple."

"I'm pregnant."

"You're the perfect mother."

"You'd know. You've searched high and low, auditioning women."

"Oh, Claire…" Clive can't meet her gaze. "I'm sorry," he says. "The laddishness stops now."

"Laddish? There's a word for what you are? I thought it was a 'shit'!"

"I'll change. Be what you want me to be."

"You can't even be what *you* want you to be! Let alone what I want. Start by being honest."

"I'll be an honest philandering shit if you want. Okay. I was with girls some Saturdays. Because I missed your…"

"'Good teeth'," Claire suggests.

"That was shallow of me. I value so much more in you. Please marry me."

"You used to be smug. Now…you'll be *what I want!*"

"You think I'm influenced by Ced's bequest."

"Yes."

"The olds need…"

"The olds. Phooey!"

"Marry me, Claire?"

"No. I'd spend my life collecting shoes."

"Sensible shoes for running after kids. I've heard on the grapevine that you want to write. I'll support you. We'll get a nanny, a cook."

"No!"

Clive gets up. He wanders over to the tall window, looking onto the garden, where he sees Bonnie on her knees weeding herbs. She looks up. He waves. He turns back to Claire. "You'd impoverish Bonnie, who depends on us?"

"Don't bring Bonnie into this!"

"You'd deprive me of access to my child?"

"Never!"

"Hang on a tick." Clive climbs the set of wonky library steps giving access to the domed second level. "There's a history of the St John Smiths somewhere here," he says. "The family name goes back to the Norman Conquest. There's baronets, earls, wrong side of the blanket royals…" He ascends rapidly but at the top he stands awhile, blinking as his eyes adjust to the light; his footsteps raise a powdering of dust motes. "Phfft!" he says, waving his hands in front of his face as if they were ghastly pathogens. He shrugs. "Can't find what I was looking for in all this dust." He shrugs. "If only you were a snob!"

"Get off that creaky ladder. Too many bits of this building are held together by sticky tape. Move your parents out of Arcadia and rebuild."

"A fine sentiment coming from she who could help – but chooses not to."

"I'm not your restoration fund."

"It offends you – all this privilege."

"I'm not ready for marriage."

"A child is coming, ready or not. Why punish the olds?"

"I won't ruin my life to repair your family finances."

"How will you live?"

She shrugs. "I'll work. You could help with child support."

"The kid mightn't be mine."

"I won't fight you for support, Clive. We Kellys don't have Gothic piles or debts."

"Okay." Clive draws his shoulders together and spreads his hands as if tamping down unpleasant information. "You won't be budged. I get it. I don't grovel. If you want 24 hours to think about it, fine. If not, leave soon please. I'll drive you into Warnambool to a motel. Ma's planning a drinks party to welcome Thelma. It'd be a fiasco. I'm disappointed you're no gold digger. Does Alex know of your decision?"

"Not yet," Claire says.

"If you fall for Alex's sweet talk after refusing me, I'll…" Clive makes a wringing gesture with his hands.

Chapter 66
Fliss Pregnant?

Claire heads for the kitchen, seeking Bonnie, the powerhouse of the Sins' empire; she'll know where Alex is.

"Bonnie!"

"Yes, love?"

"Alex?"

"He's in the pantry plaiting garlic into ropes waiting for you!"

"Bonnie. Tell me what to do…"

"No, dear. You must decide. Talk to the lad." She indicates the pantry door. "He's in a state."

Claire checks her appearance in a hand mirror. Straggles of hair escape her plait. She looks a fright.

"You didn't care that Clive saw you looking dishevelled. And Alex won't care."

"I'll care."

Bonnie wipes her hands on her apron, undoes Claire's plait.

Claire bends from the waist and rakes her fingers through her curls to untangle them.

Raising her head, she asks. "Honestly, Bonnie, how do I look?"

"Like a wild woman. Natural 'n beautiful. He loves you."

"I know. Bonnie, do me a favour?"

"Yes, darlin'?"

"Invite Felicity to come early to cheer Clive up. He wants me gone. But I'm not ready."

"Sure. Now go in, love, or he'll…"

Claire opens the pantry door. Alex is re-arranging tomato relish on the shelves. He doesn't acknowledge Claire…

"Alex," she whispers.

He turns to face her but in the semi-dark she can't read his expression. "I wondered when it'd be my turn," he says. "You've talked to everyone else."

"Not Cynthia."

"You're marrying Clive, then?"

"No."

"You'll marry me?"

"I…" Claire starts to cry softly.

"Abort?" He circles his long arms around her.

Claire shrugs and wipes her nose on Alex's shoulder.

"Do you regret the last eight weeks?"

"Not the hours and minutes, with you in them. I'll have a go at living alone."

"Brave. In Wang?"

"It's all I can afford."

"You'd always be welcome in Carlton."

"I couldn't sleep chastely under your roof."

"You wouldn't have to."

"There'd be the ghost of Clive hanging over us. The child will remind me of him every day."

"I guess. Now, Claire, I've news I couldn't mention in case you hopped into bed with Clive and his huge bequest."

Claire giggles nervously. "What?"

"In the pharmacy earlier, I saw Fliss lurking near the pregnancy kits."

"Well, that's nice. Her tutor boyfriend?"

"I said, 'Hi Fliss, anything doing?'

"She said, 'Alex, I'm in an interesting state.'"

"I'd have said I was buying the kit for a friend," admits Claire.

"Maybe she wanted me to know. I said, 'But you haven't used it yet.'

"Poor Fliss fell apart. 'I've tried every bloody brand. It never comes out right,' she sobbed.

"I put my arm around her. 'By "right" you mean un-pregnant?'

"'Yes,' she sighed.

"'The father's against fatherhood?' I asked.

"'He's with someone else. Why am I telling you this?'

"'How pregnant are you?'

"'Five weeks,' she said. No hesitation.

"'A one-night stand,' I said. 'Is that how you can be so precise?'

"She nodded. 'You don't want to know.'

"'Maybe I know already,' is what I said. Now Claire, listen, I do happen to know when and where she had her one night stand."

"No. Surely it wasn't you, Alex?" said Claire.

"Of course not. I was an unwilling witness to some shenanigans with Clive."

"How come?" Claire says, puzzled.

"What happened exactly five weeks ago, Claire?"

"I broke my leg."

"And what else?"

"I met Cyn and Hal."

"And?"

"There was a Bachelor and Spinsters' do."

"And?"

"Lobster sandwiches. Clive and I told everyone we were engaged."

"Were the olds pleased?"

"Cynthia scurried off to phone Fliss. She wanted Clive to see the English rose beside the wild Irish redhead. She plotted to pair Clive with Fliss at the ball. I was totally manipulated."

"Yes!" agrees Alex.

"I wanted to prove something to myself. I went with Dada. Hal wasn't complaining."

"The old roué."

"I wore silk tied…"

"…like a Greek goddess. And?"

"Clive and Fliss danced loose-limbed like brother and sister."

"I saw something unbrotherly that night, Claire. If you knew, it would mean no one would have to marry anyone they didn't fancy."

"Don't tell me Clive is the father of Fliss' child. He had the perfect alibi – 70 LCP members. He and Fliss were on a different supper sitting from us but…"

"Swear you don't love Clive, and I'll tell you what I saw."

"I don't even like Clive, actually," Claire says, and shocks herself. "I doubt I ever did."

"Okay. That night I drank too much…went outside; flopped on a hay bale. I was joined by a couple intent on…well, coupling. The bloke started 'calling the race', the voice, it was Clive; he and Fliss were having a – sorry, Claire – tumble in the hay, but they remained upright."

"Bastard. Thanks for the details!"

"When Fliss went indoors, I hung Clive out to dry. It was the most honest conversation we've had."

Claire's gone quiet now, figuring out the implications.

"What's up?" Alex asks.

"Wow! The bastard had foresight," she says.

"Yes," Alex says. "He'll marry her for the bequest. It's a way out of all our problems! You could have your child or not. Decide at leisure."

"Mm," Claire says. "He'd love having Fliss' child as the official heir."

"Fantastic," says Alex, kissing Claire.

"But I'm still having a baby I don't actually want."

"Would you abort?"

"I don't know."

"At least Clive will give up all paternity claims on your child. To father children on different mothers at the same time would be tacky. The decision is up to you."

"Oh, Alex!" Claire screams shrilly and hugs him. "It's the best news ever. A fortnight ago I'd have been humiliated. It's about context, isn't it? Already, I've asked Bonnie to get Fliss to come here early tonight for Clive's sake."

"You're an angel, Claire, thinking of others at such a time. An heir and five million will cheer Clive. He might cough up for smoked salmon."

"Hardly," Claire says.

"Let Fliss tell Clive. Lock them in the pantry until she's wised him up," Claire says.

"I'll call her now," Alex says.

Chapter 67
Alex and Fliss Plot

Alex checks that the hallway's quiet so he can phone. "Hello, Fliss. Alex here. Can we talk?"

"Sure, I'm just making parsnip and dandelion soup."

"Is that even a soup?"

"It's edible and lately, I'm so poor…"

Fliss is making heavy work of breathing. "Listen, Fliss, will you be honest with me?"

"Ye-es, I guess…"

"The child you're expecting; it's Clive's."

"No-o."

"Fibber! Night of the ball I went for a lie down in the potting shed."

"Oh God! You weren't spying?"

"Thankfully, it was too dark. I was a cad. I shut up and let it happen, despite my anger over Clive betraying Claire. Some instinct stopped me…kept me quiet…"

"Instinct? Ha! Sounds weird from Mr Rationality."

"It was something inexplicable. You know I'm never tactful."

"And you're so logical, Alex. The idea of you acting on instinct – well, it's a bit spooky."

"I know, I admit it. Maybe Shakespeare was right after all: 'There are more things in heaven and earth than are dreamed of in your philosophy, Horatio.'"

"You really love Claire, don't you?"

"Of course! That night I kept schtum! Though I gave Clive a right bollocking after you left."

Fliss is quiet at the other end. He imagines her stirring parsnip soup on the Aga in her grim, draughty kitchen, licking the spoon from nervousness and drawing a shawl about her shoulders. Alex goes quiet too. How does he deliver this news to Fliss so that she'll see it – as it is – a chance to change several lives for the better. "I'm glad I shut up that night, Fliss," Alex says. "If I hadn't done…I wouldn't be making this call."

"Why are you calling. To humiliate me?"

"I need you to know that some good came out of what happened that night."

"You mean I'm up the duff and I wish I wasn't?"

"No, I mean I know who the father is."

"Yeah, well, under the circumstances it hardly makes you a genius."

"Listen, if Claire had known what a love rat Clive was, she'd have left the next morning, instead of falling off a horse. If she hadn't fallen, I'd never have looked after her…"

"'Look after'. Great euphemism."

"Touché!" Alex says, "I was keen to help."

"Keen all right. Does Claire think her broken leg's a lucky break?" Fliss asks, sarcastically.

"You're in good form, Fliss. But every event has an immediate effect plus long-term effects and countless mid-range outcomes; some harmless-seeming events reverberate throughout our lives like ripples."

"Ripples get smaller over time, don't they?"

"You're killing me, Fliss. Yes! But what if a small wave pushed our ship of life off course and away from an iceberg? It'd be the Titanic in reverse!"

"So, tell me if I've got it. If you'd made a fuss that night, then Claire would still be pregnant but not me! And you'd be desperately sad at her marrying awful Clive; alternatively, if you hadn't been drunk and hadn't witnessed anything untoward…then…Da de da de da! I'd still be preggers but you wouldn't know who the father is!"

"You get the drift, Fliss. This could be the lucky break we all need."

"Me pregnant to a man I can't marry. What a happy turn of events!"

"Maybe you are fated to marry Clive after all."

"Whoo! Is fate your new religion? Does fate name every sparrow that farts or is it God?"

"Give me a hard time, why don't you?"

"Shit, Alex…Who am I to talk? I'm the dumb blonde. So, because you decided not blab about the shed, Claire went on thinking she loved Clive longer than otherwise, and if you hadn't known Clive was such a fickle bastard, you'd never have jumped Claire?"

"You're quick, Fliss." Alex sighs, and rubs his eyes wearily. "Exactly."

"Clive's infidelity let you make a move on Claire, which now gives me a chance with him?"

"Yep. True happiness, with Cliiiiive!"

"Don't make fun of me."

"How do you know I made a move on Claire?"

"You're the one on about instinct. I only have to glimpse Clive and my hormones riot…but I'm ashamed…"

"You behaved opportunistically in the shed. It's not a crime. Opportunism fuels evolution. I love Claire. We took our chance. She loves me. But she's scared of changing her mind again."

"Did she ever love Clive?"

"She felt responsible for a while." There's a silence. "You still there?" Alex says.

"Mm. How extraordinary," Fliss says, at last. "Not to love Clive."

"She was infatuated, I guess."

"So why marry him?"

"She isn't going to."

"He'll be devastated, poor chap."

"Devastated? No. Disappointed at losing a bequest."

"Clive's more ambitious career-wise than greedy. And he's always been a resilient chap," Fliss insists.

"Or he never really wanted Claire. He's not a 'chap', he's a bloke. He saw his life going nowhere…"

"But to marry on a whim…"

"Listen, Fliss, would a pregnancy test show up positive in five weeks?"

"Who the heck would want to know that?"

"I would. Claire and I have known each other for five weeks. It's conceivable, word play intended, she may be pregnant with my child, not Clive's."

"Golly. It is possible. That'd be beaut! We could be best friends. Will Claire stay friends with Suz and Mary? They were nice and there's no one to be friends with down here."

"Settle down, Fliss. This isn't Oklahoma."

"Even some atheists I know believe in fate and happy endings," she says pointedly.

"Once Clive knows your baby news, he'll snaffle you up. Would have then but you left."

"Do you really think so?"

"If she knew Clive was happy, Claire might move in with me – she so hates making anyone unhappy. She'd be especially keen if she thought there was a chance I might be the father of her child," he says.

"Oh, how super! We could have dinner parties and be the bestest of friends," says Fliss, doubtless picturing endless happy days stretching out ahead of her. "Our boys could run under the hose in summer…"

"I guess," Alex says, doubtfully. "Fliss, hardly anyone is perfectly happy. Still we live in hope. You know that Clive drinks too much."

"He didn't drink when we lived together…"

"Listen, Clive needs to know your news within the hour. Did you keep the test kits?"

"Yes."

"Good. Then go to Bonnie, she's organised a private place for you to meet before Thelma's drinks. Tell Clive the bare facts. Don't pressure him."

"I'm not a complete dill!"

"Would you live in Melbourne, Fliss? That's where he's made his life."

"Yep. I'd go to the back of Bourke for Clive."

"Then go to it, girl. Good luck!"

Chapter 68
Claire and Cyn

Cynthia's in the study totting up the accounts. Hal won't do his share. He always says, 'Have to see a man about a dog, and you've an eye for detail, love,' avoiding his duties without an atom of shame. And yet he is no better with the broad-brush aspect of their lives than Cynthia.

It's down to me, like it or not, she thinks. Darned Bible! One should *always* hide one's light under a bushel or one'll find oneself thoroughly used up.

Should debts be allowed to accrue while hypothetical propositions are discussed socially? Cynthia wonders.

Len often waxes fulsome, discussing matters legal. Leaning forward in his chair, flush faced, he leads his audience down obscure legal paths, expounding on abstruse points of law. Surely, his hosts deserve some recompense for making Len feel good about himself? Len's dozen or so bills land on the bottom of the pile.

GwenLen rarely mention the matter of payment, provided Hal comes up with vintages both rare and excellent and rescued from the back of some truck connected to the polo club. Then there are unavoidable bills like electricity and the butcher. Cyn's ill disposed to freeze to death while living on watercress sandwiches. She robs Peter but is reluctant to pay Paul.

Her few sacrifices, include retiring to bed of a night wearing a flea-bitten mink, her feet warmed by a hottie from the electric jug in her dressing room, the one Hal tells her not to use, its cord being frayed. Meanwhile, she raises her body temperature with a mediocre sherry.

Bonnie has so much on the Sins, they're stuck with her as part of the family. Still, they may have to send her away on sabbatical until one of the twins fornicates fruitfully; otherwise, Cedric's bounty will be frittered away in legal bills.

Bonnie is their bulwark against accusations of snobbery. She's cost-effective, not needing overtime, now she's counted as one of them. Sacked, God help them, she might claim indexed back pay! Or holiday loading for keeping the laird happy Friday nights.

Bertie has billed them for pruning! Officially, he's farm manager but with so few stock to manage, he is mostly paid in kind. He has the tack room to bunk down in. Cynthia thinks Bertie handsome, despite him being a small, nuggety man. Such men must be her type, she muses. He uses the jacuzzi prolifically. Cynthia believes she has caught him gazing at her speculatively.

Claire could not be happier to learn Fliss is pregnant to her ('her' is applicable to either subject of this sentence) former fiancé. She feels blissed out about Fliss. Assonance intended.

She's been deputed to share the happy news with Cynthia. What she'd dreaded earlier is a now a gentle walk through horse pastures. Who'd shoot a messenger – even one with horse dung on her boots – who is bearing such happy news? Especially a messenger on the way to the story's happy ending?

Does 'dungaree' have anything to do with dung? Claire wonders.

At the study door, she observes Cynthia at work. Her estimation of Cyn has altered. She's been promoted from social dinosaur to flawed family-centred soul. Claire knows Cyn cannot envisage what real hardship is. Can her lack of compassion be Cynthia's fault if she wasn't blessed with such a quality at birth? Empathy is unlikely to burgeon later in life along with chronic health deficits. Nevertheless, Claire wonders at the mildness of her judgement; has she been drawn so far into the Sins' lives that she's letting them off the hook?

After Cynthia has moved documents from the top of the pile to the bottom twice, Claire coughs. Clearly, Cynthia had heard her clumping approach, given the flagstones and Claire's inflexible prophylactic boot. She knocks loudly. Cynthia turns. "What the dickens? Oh, Claire. I was expecting you."

Claire waits on the threshold, her smile pasted on. She thanks Alex's pantheon of rationalists her own mother doesn't play games.

"Make yourself at home. It might have been yours." Cyn cannot let a jibe pass by unsaid.

Claire perches on an oak swivel desk chair. "So, Clive told you…"

"Yes," says Cynthia. "Sorry, I was so mean to you at lunch with GwenLen the other day."

"Oh."

"I was feeling vindictive and someone had to suffer. It was you. Were you hurt?"

"A bit. But I'm over it."

"And I was aiming for harsh and punitive!" Cynthia jokes. "We got off on the wrong foot. You, arriving in the flower of youth, you seemed to be the enemy, the usurper of Clive's affections."

"Cynthia, you love him in a way that's unhealthy in a mother and son. Blinds you to faults."

"That's quite insightful, Claire."

Claire waves away the compliment. "I was naughty caricaturing you in my diary. But you *spied!"*

"I wouldn't go that far," says Cynthia.

"I would," says Claire. "And I have to tell you I'm in love with Alex."

"Is there a chance that *he's* the father of your child?" A shrewd gleam flashes in Cyn's eyes.

"Oh, the inheritance? Yes, there's a minuscule chance."

"So theoretically he could have fathered a child on you?"

"Yes. Theoretically."

"Well, that's something to think about. Those who say money doesn't matter either have none or too much. To walk away from a fortune takes character, Claire."

"Cynthia…"

"Yairs. I know. You're leaving all this decadence behind. Bad news travels fast."

"But I have some very good news for you."

"Mm?" Cynthia looks sceptical. "Go on," she says.

"Felicity is also pregnant, pregnant with Clive's child."

"Impossible!"

"No."

"But how is she pregnant…?"

"In the usual way."

"How far gone?"

"A month."

"Oh. Good Lord! One minute one has no heirs, then at the mention of an inheritance there are pairs of heirs to spare."

"That's pure poetry, Cynthia."

Cyn smiles a sweet coy smile. "Get on with your story! I no longer fish for compliments. My Toastmasters maiden speech went well enough. It's not as if I'm aching for praise."

Although you fished for praise just now, Claire thinks. "I'd love to hear your speech. Perhaps at the party tonight."

"We'll see."

"It must seem odd – two of us pregnant to Clive, but it's a fact verifiable by numerous pregnancy tests."

"Spare me the details. One heir will satisfy the terms of Ced's will. Are you certain Clive will marry Fliss?"

"I hope so. Fliss is hoping to tell him before the party. He's not about just now."

"…he's on an errand."

"Errand?"

"I sent him to Warrnambool for the biggest diamond he could find."

"To buy me off?"

"You. Or now, Felicity, perhaps."

"Cynthia, your kind words meant nothing. You'd buy me off with a cold hard piece of coal. I loathe diamonds. And Fliss will have Clive without a bribe."

"I thought it worth a try."

"Alex had better go after him. I'll call him." Claire hurries to the door. "Alex! Oh God, you're spying. Stop grinning, smug bugger! Go on. Go after Clive! But leave the talk to Fliss."

"When *did* this conception occur?" asks Cyn.

"At the ball, Ma," says Alex.

"So, I did right in asking Clive to partner Fliss?"

"You did the wrong thing that fortuitously turned out well. It might have been disastrous. Claire might have bolted. Fliss' reputation could have been destroyed."

"It's easy to love the bearer of good news," says Cynthia. She throws her unpaid bills into the file all higgledy-piggledy. She wipes her hands on her navy woollen frock as if they'd been dirtied by commerce. "The bills can wait another day." She holds out her arms to Claire, smiling so warmly her skin falls into brackets at the corners of her mouth. "Dear girl," she says. Claire goes to her, submits to an embrace, but she's imagining her own dear mother lying stiffly on an ill-sprung bed upstairs.

Alex grins, bends, winks at her, gives her a hasty kiss; one that lands badly. He leaves.

He's behaving like a clumsy puppy today, Claire thinks, smiling.

"By the way, Cynthia, I know about Bonnie."

"You know what about Bonnie?" She's stern again. Her eyes have lost their twinkle.

"I won't spell it out."

"Who told you?"

"I notice things. I'd never talk. Alex would love to know if ever you…Anyway, I think you three manage the situation rather well – except for the shoes."

"They're expensive shoes, my dear. She pays me back ten-fold in those horrid rock cakes. They've ruined my teeth."

"The shoes are abominable. It's cruel to make Bonnie wear them."

"How could I force Bonnie to do something she doesn't want to?"

"You give her a choice of Cubans or Hush Puppies. No woman wants to seem an absolute hick. And there's something else. My baby might be Alex's. It depends whether she's a blonde angel or a swarthy gypsy. I'll love her whoever the father is."

"Good Lord, girlie!" she says, when Claire shrugs. "What a soap opera."

"Or a moral tale. I haven't yet fathomed the moral of this story," Claire says.

"Don't fall for the first man you fall for, perhaps?"

"But if I hadn't fallen for Clive first, I couldn't have fallen for Alex second."

"True."

"Or maybe it's this: if you always wear sensible shoes, then no astonishing, thrilling, awesome disaster will ever befall you."